ReFocus: The Films of Lawrence Kasdan

T0379420

ReFocus: The American Directors Series

Series Editors: Robert Singer, Gary D. Rhodes and Frances Smith

Editorial board: Kelly Basilio, Donna Campbell, Claire Perkins, Christopher Sharrett, and Yannis Tzioumakis

ReFocus is a series of contemporary methodological and theoretical approaches to the interdisciplinary analyses and interpretations of neglected American directors, from the once-famous to the ignored, in direct relationship to American culture—its myths, values, and historical precepts.

Titles in the series include:

edinburghuniversitypress.com/series/refoc

ReFocus:
The Films of Lawrence Kasdan

Brett Davies

EDINBURGH
University Press

Edinburgh University Press is one of the leading university presses in the UK. We publish academic books and journals in our selected subject areas across the humanities and social sciences, combining cutting-edge scholarship with high editorial and production values to produce academic works of lasting importance. For more information visit our website: edinburghuniversitypress.com

Grateful acknowledgement is made to the sources listed in the List of Illustrations for permission to reproduce material previously published elsewhere. Every effort has been made to trace the copyright holders, but if any have been inadvertently overlooked, the publisher will be pleased to make the necessary arrangements at the first opportunity.

Edinburgh University Press Ltd
The Tun – Holyrood Road
12(2f) Jackson's Entry
Edinburgh EH8 8PJ

Typeset in 11/13 Ehrhardt MT by
IDSUK (DataConnection) Ltd, and
printed and bound by CPI Group (UK) Ltd,
Croydon, CR0 4YY

A CIP record for this book is available from the British Library

ISBN 978 1 3995 2407 0 (hardback)
ISBN 978 1 3995 2409 4 (webready PDF)
ISBN 978 1 3995 2410 0 (epub)

Contents

Illustrations

TABLE

Acknowledgments

I am very grateful to the editors of the ReFocus series—Gary Rhodes, Robert Singer, and Frances Smith—for their support and advice in writing this book, as well as to Gillian Leslie and Sam Johnson at Edinburgh University Press for their enthusiasm and encouragement. The origin of this project was my doctorate research at De Montfort University, and I could not have done it without James Russell, who was so knowledgeable and kind in guiding me over five years; a more dedicated and insightful mentor would be impossible to find. Thank you, also, to Jason Lee, Justin Smith, Pier Ecole, Tracy Harwood, and Matthew Jones, and to Yannis Tzioumakis for recommending that I develop the work for publication.

I am indebted to Rachel Parsons at Kasdan Pictures for her patience and professionalism in facilitating my interview with Lawrence Kasdan; as well as to Mr. Kasdan himself, who was extremely generous with his time, and who was so open, warm, and erudite in discussing his work.

Finally, my family have shared my love of cinema and writing through the years. They have been my constant companions through countless viewings of Lawrence Kasdan's films, and through the highs and lows of bringing this book to life. To paraphrase Steve "Spaz" Williams in *Light & Magic*, they made the way that I thought okay, and I am forever thankful.

Introduction

On April 20, 1999, Lawrence Kasdan returned to his alma mater, the University of Michigan, to deliver the annual Hopwood Lecture. In a frank and self-effacing speech on the craft of screenwriting, he describes a scene from one of his favorite movies, *Lawrence of Arabia* (1962): T.E. Lawrence, played by Peter O'Toole, has trekked across the Sinai Desert, exhausted, covered in dirt, barely alive. On reaching a derelict, bombed-out building, Lawrence just stares into space, almost catatonic after the ordeal that had cost the life of one member of his party. The surviving servant, Farraj (Michel Rey), throws water on Lawrence's face to revive him, revealing sunburned European skin under the heavy mask of dust. The only sound is the creak of a loose door swinging back and forth in the desert wind. Then, incongruously, the blast of a foghorn breaks the silence. Lawrence looks up to see a great steamship cutting through the sand. It is a bizarre juxtaposition of the eponymous character's two worlds: his place of birth and his adopted home.

Lawrence and Farraj step forward gingerly, peering over the dunes. The Suez Canal reveals itself, but Lawrence remains stony faced, as if trying to process what he is seeing: the vast blue water after endless desert, the monument to modern progress slicing through a landscape that has barely changed in millennia. On the opposite side of the canal, an army motorcyclist stops and calls out, his accent unmistakably British: "Who . . . are . . . you?"

Kasdan continues his commentary:

> Finally, only now, do we cut to a close shot of Lawrence's face. And once again, over his face, do we hear the shouted question which has been at the center of this epic film since its first frame. A question which Lawrence does not know how to answer. "Who . . . are . . . you?"[1]

In signposting this moment as an exemplar of great screenwriting, we learn much about Lawrence Kasdan: his focus is upon character rather than spectacle, even in a film of epic scale; he favors concision over verbal grandstanding; and he is drawn toward ambiguity. Do T.E. Lawrence's eyes glisten with relief at meeting his goal, or sadness at returning to his old life of steamers and motorcycles? Or perhaps they have simply been stung by the sand.

The moment is pertinent to much of Lawrence Kasdan's own work, too, in which questions of identity are so often at the center: the quarter-life crisis facing the group of friends in *The Big Chill* (1983), the search for self in a changing world in *The Accidental Tourist* (1988) and *Grand Canyon* (1991), and the literal renaming of characters in *Mumford* (1999), *The Force Awakens* (2015), and *Solo: A Star Wars Story* (2018). The same question resonates again and again: *Who are you?*

The words also speak to Lawrence Kasdan as a filmmaker, seemingly a collection of paradoxes and contradictions. He is a director renowned for "promiscuous genre-hopping"[2] who made some of the least generic mainstream dramas of the 1980s and '90s; he is the writer of four Star Wars[3] scripts who calls Hollywood's sequel culture "discouraging;"[4] and he is a socially progressive filmmaker whose pictures have been accused of espousing Reaganite values.[5] And, even as Kasdan appears to perceive himself as a director first and foremost, likening the role of writer to that of a co-pilot,[6] he is perhaps better known for his screenplays than his direction.

With so many conflicting perceptions, and a marked lack of existing analysis, this volume will explore the same question that was asked of his namesake: *Who are you?*

A child of America's post-war baby-boom, Lawrence Kasdan was born in Miami Beach, Florida, in 1949, to Clarence, an electronics retail store manager, and Sylvia, an employment counsellor. As a young child, his family moved to Pittsburgh, briefly, then to Wheeling, West Virginia, where, Kasdan says, "I had a small-town American upbringing. We could ride our bikes; we owned the town with our bikes. You could go downtown, you could go anywhere."[7] However, Kasdan's childhood was far from perfect. His family returned to Miami during his early teens, which Kasdan describes as a culture shock: "Many of the kids I went to school with were very wealthy, they were getting driver's licenses early. [. . .] They were sexually way far advanced of anything I had even heard of in West Virginia."[8] Two years after the move, his parents, "who had been fighting for almost twenty years," divorced.[9] His father stayed in Miami, while Lawrence moved back to West Virginia with his mother and two sisters (his elder brother was already studying at Harvard). Soon afterward, Clarence Kasdan passed away.

After a brief return to Wheeling, Lawrence Kasdan completed high school in nearby Morgantown, where he says that he felt settled after so many years of movement and uncertainty, "where you don't believe anything's going to be solid or that you're gonna be here long."[10] It was during those final years of adolescence that Kasdan began writing in earnest. He says that he "grew up in a house where writing was seen as a legitimate undertaking,"[11] and in the 1950s, his mother had sold some stories to magazines. Perhaps more importantly, "she believed in writing and she preached the religion."[12] In Morgantown, Kasdan began providing humorous columns for the school newspaper, receiving instant positive feedback from his peers: "everyone would come up to me and say, 'That was funny. That's pretty cool. That was nice.' And that reinforcement probably set me on my path forever."[13]

Kasdan always loved cinema, visiting his local theater regularly as a child. "I would see [films] once, twice, three times. It was just a place I was very happy in the darkness."[14] *The Magnificent Seven* (1960) was a major influence, as Kasdan explains: "It represented so many paradigms of heroism and manhood and the pull between darkness and light and courage and fear. [. . .] I knew that's where I wanted to be: in that world."[15] But it was in 1962 when he discovered just how powerful an impact a film could have. His elder brother and future collaborator, Mark, took him to see the aforementioned *Lawrence of Arabia*, and, Kasdan says, "it changed my life."[16] From then on, "I knew that I had to make movies. But I had no idea how to go about it. The idea that movies were written had never been considered in the town where we lived."[17]

After high school, Kasdan was accepted on the University of Michigan's English Literature program. A major reason behind his choice of college was his interest in the Hopwood Awards, a prestigious writing contest that counted Arthur Miller among its previous recipients. At university, Kasdan says, "I was writing all the time. All the time, that is, when I wasn't going to the movies."[18] In and around the Ann Arbor campus, Kasdan was exposed to a far wider variety of films than he had seen in West Virginia. "When I was in Michigan, not only did I see American movies, I was seeing all the foreign movies, so I was seeing all of Kurosawa and all of Truffaut and all of Bergman."[19] He began writing his own screenplays at this time, in addition to winning the Hopwood Awards for both drama and fiction, gaining recognition that would influence his career profoundly:

> You get this award that says someone thinks you're for real. And that's all you need to hear. Even though I had many discouraging years after that, there was never a day after I received that letter that I doubted I would be able to make my way as a writer.[20]

After briefly attending film school at UCLA, where, he says, he felt intimidated by the city of Los Angeles, Kasdan returned to Ann Arbor and studied for a master's degree in education. He admits that he did this not because of any desire to teach, but as a means of avoiding the draft to fight in Vietnam,[21] a choice that would foreshadow a narrative strand in *The Big Chill* over a decade later. On graduating from college, and with no high school English teaching jobs available, Kasdan accepted an offer from a family friend of his future wife Meg, and he entered the advertising business in Detroit. He continued to work on scripts in his free time, and three years later, with no screenwriting success forthcoming, he and his young family moved to Los Angeles in order to be nearer the film industry. For two more years, Kasdan continued his day job in advertising while writing in the evenings and lunch breaks, until finally making his first script sale, for *The Bodyguard* in 1977, a film that would eventually be released in 1992. Within weeks, Steven Spielberg acquired Kasdan's screenplay for *Continental Divide* (released in 1981), which subsequently led to his being hired to write *Raiders of the Lost Ark* (1981) for Spielberg to direct with George Lucas as executive producer. Lucas then asked Kasdan to rewrite the second episode in his Star Wars saga, *The Empire Strikes Back* (1980), offering him the job on the very day that he submitted the first draft of the *Raiders* script, after the death of the original *Empire* writer, Leigh Brackett. The rise from unproduced novice to screenwriter on the sequel to the highest-grossing film of all time was remarkable, and it began a writing and directing career that has remained active for more than forty years.

In spite of Lawrence Kasdan's success and career longevity, however, there has been little critical discourse on his films. In fact, until now, there is no book devoted entirely to Kasdan, and only a solitary academic article that attempts to examine his work beyond a single movie, written by Marina Heung in 1985, after Kasdan had directed just three pictures.[22] This lack of scholarly engagement with Lawrence Kasdan's canon may be due partly to the difficulty in categorizing his *oeuvre*. The notion of a "Kasdan film" appears to vary quite widely depending on which critic's review one reads. He has been discussed at various times as a social commentator, a genre revivalist, and as a creator of intimate dramas, ensemble comedies, and sci-fi adventures. There is not, then, an obvious school of filmmaking in which to place Kasdan when examining his career as a whole. In fact, he has said that "when you don't get to make many pictures, maybe each one should be different."[23] This is perhaps the main reason why he does not fit neatly into any single category of filmmaker. It also partially explains why his filmography is rarely examined as a complete body of work: the characteristics of a Kasdan film are less clearly defined than those of his peers. So, while there are entire books devoted to, say, Robert Zemeckis, John Sayles, Barry Levinson, and Nancy Meyers[24]—all contemporaries with whom he shares some similarities— there has been no retrospective publication on the work of Lawrence Kasdan, despite many of his films receiving critical acclaim and box-office success.

The lack of wider scholarly analysis means that there is no agreed "canon" of Kasdan films in academia, although I posit that his pictures released in the 1980s and early 1990s are those that are most often viewed as "Kasdanite,"[25] both in his writing for Lucasfilm and through his movies as writer-director that have had lasting cultural resonance, such as *Body Heat* (1981), *The Big Chill*, *The Accidental Tourist*, and *Grand Canyon*. This volume will examine these films in especial detail, but I shall also endeavor to explore Kasdan's lesser-known works, as it is perhaps this very versatility that defines his career. Through such a longitudinal and inclusive approach, too, it may be possible to gain a more global appreciation of Kasdan's filmography and the concerns that consistently underpin his creative works, even as they are so varied in style and setting.

The first section of the book, Part I, will examine what attributes Kasdan's screenwriting possessed that made him so central to the development of *Raiders of the Lost Ark*. This assignment would lead directly to his work on the Star Wars sequels, yet these big-budget Lucasfilm productions appeared at odds with the kinds of films that he wished to make himself.[26] Specifically, I will employ discourse analysis to interrogate the extent of Kasdan's involvement in the story conference for *Raiders*, his very first paid assignment. The transcript of this conference is a unique document for a major Hollywood film and one that has never been analyzed before within cinema studies; therefore, the investigative method is necessarily unconventional, with the empirical analysis of speech, borrowed from the field of linguistics, measuring Kasdan's contribution to the initial story and plot design. Then, by analyzing his screenplay drafts as texts, the next chapter will establish the extent of Kasdan's authorship in a motion picture that altered audience expectations of blockbuster movies.

Part II will begin to interrogate Kasdan as a director, attempting to establish just what his directing style is, and how it complements or contradicts his apparent preference for classical literary structure in his scripts. I will apply historical poetics to analyze Kasdan's earliest two films as writer-director, *Body Heat* and *The Big Chill*. The aim will be to demonstrate the visual styles that he employed in order to serve the respective narratives and begin to create a "Kasdan style" of directing, even as he adopted very different approaches to the respective works.

Part III asks why Kasdan's movies have become so emblematic of the baby-boom generation. Taking a socio-historical approach, it will examine how and why Kasdan is sometimes discussed as a "spokesman" for the largest demographic in US history,[27] the generation that shaped American society in the second half of the twentieth century and beyond. It will interrogate the themes and perspectives that he has favored while reporting on his cohort's concerns over nearly half a century, as the boomers moved from 1960s radicalism toward the Trumpism of the 2010s.

Like many of his generation, Lawrence Kasdan is a student of cinema, inclined to pay homage to movies and moviemakers of the past. He is also a writer-director who displays remarkable humility in crediting his influences and collaborations, a believer in the notion of the "auteur," yet someone who works repeatedly with the same creative partners. Part IV will begin by exploring Kasdan's major influences from the past; in particular, the work of Akira

Kurosawa, of whom Kasdan says, "he did everything, and he did it better than anybody."[28] Do these allusions enhance or detract from Kasdan's own worth as a filmmaker; and how do they conform to or reject the postmodern proclivity for pastiche? The first chapter in the section will describe an intertextual analysis of Kasdan's work against that of Kurosawa. It will show how he has been able to borrow from existing works in order to address contemporary issues, simultaneously exemplifying the trend for homage among his cohort. The second chapter will examine how Kasdan's work has been inflected by his collaborations with behind-the-camera talent, as well as the repertory of performers with whom he repeatedly works. He has been called "an actor's director,"[29] and he told me in our interview that "I admire them like athletes. I don't understand how they do it." The chapter will examine how their performances have contributed to Kasdan's films, both in creating archetypes that exemplify his chief concerns, and by working as disruptors when playing roles at odds with audience expectations.

Finally, Kasdan's return to Star Wars, with *The Force Awakens* and *Solo: A Star Wars Story*, frames his filmography neatly, coming over thirty years after his screenplays for *The Empire Strikes Back* and *Return of the Jedi* (1983) began his career. This enables scholars to measure his importance as a co-creator of arguably the most influential film series of all time, both in its formative years and in its recent incarnation under the stewardship of Disney. What elements did Kasdan bring to the movies and to what extent did his writing affect the direction of the saga as a whole? Part V will investigate Kasdan's contributions and examine how he was able to impart his own worldview through his screenplays. Additionally, it will demonstrate how his reputation within Lucasfilm—and the Hollywood industry—has changed over his four-decade involvement with the saga, in terms of his role in production as well as the way that his work is perceived by audiences and critics.

By adopting a holistic, multi-disciplinary approach, then, this volume will attempt to contextualize and analyze Kasdan's output for the very first time, while suggesting avenues for further investigation in the future. In doing so, it will redress the current lack of academic criticism of his work. More importantly, it will establish the extent of Lawrence Kasdan's contribution to modern American cinema, as the screenwriter of some of its most popular movies, and as the writer-director of films that defined a generation, and had deep and lasting cultural resonance.

NOTES

1. Lawrence Kasdan, "POV," *Michigan Quarterly Review* 38, no. 4 (1999): 568.
2. Kim Newman, "*The Big Chill*," *Monthly Film Bulletin* 51, no. 600 (1984): 42.
3. For clarity, throughout the book I will use italics only when referring to the original film in the Star Wars series, but when discussing the entire franchise, I will not; so, for example: "*Star Wars* (1977) was the first instalment in the Star Wars saga."

4. Kasdan, interviewed by John August and Craig Mazin, "Episode 247: The One with Lawrence Kasdan," *Scriptnotes*, audio podcast, April 26, 2016, http://johnaugust.com/2016/the-one-with-lawrence-kasdan (accessed June 29, 2023).

5. See, for example, Michael Ryan and Douglas Kellner, *Camera Politica: The Politics and Ideology of Contemporary Hollywood Film* (Bloomington & Indianapolis: Indiana University Press, 1988): 277–9.

6. Kasdan, "POV,": 571.

7. Kasdan, quoted in an unpublished interview with James Russell (2013).

8. Ibid.

9. Kasdan, quoted in Jim Hemphill, "Lawrence Kasdan," *Academy of Motion Picture Arts and Sciences: Oral History Collection* (Los Angeles: AMPAS, 2022), transcript, 6.

10. Ibid.

11. Kasdan, "POV," 565.

12. Ibid., 566.

13. Kasdan, quoted in Hemphill, "Lawrence Kasdan," 7.

14. Kasdan, quoted in Russell, unpublished.

15. Kasdan, quoted in James Russell and Jim Whalley, *Hollywood and the Baby Boom: A Social History* (London: Bloomsbury, 2018), 61.

16. Kasdan, interviewed by August and Mazin, "Episode 247."

17. Kasdan, "POV," 568.

18. Ibid.

19. Kasdan, quoted in Russell and Whalley, *Hollywood and Baby Boom*, 94.

20. Kasdan, "POV," 568–9.

21. Kasdan, quoted in Hemphill, "Lawrence Kasdan," 9.

22. Marina Heung, "The Big Score: Work and Survival in the Films of Lawrence Kasdan," *Michigan Quarterly Review* 24, no. 4 (1985), https://quod.lib.umich.edu/m/mqrarchive/act2080.0024.004/49:3?page=root;rgn=full+text;size=100;view=image (accessed June 29, 2023).

23. Elaine Dutka, "Lawrence Kasdan's Grand Balancing Act," *The Los Angeles Times*, December 24, 1991, http://articles.latimes.com/1991-12-24/entertainment/ca-947_1_grand-canyon/3 (accessed June 29, 2023).

24. Norman Kagan, *The Cinema of Robert Zemeckis* (Lanham, MD: Taylor, 2003); David R. Shumway, *John Sayles* (Chicago: University of Illinois Press, 2012); David Thompson, *Levinson on Levinson* (London: Faber & Faber, 1993); Deborah Jermyn, *Nancy Meyers* (London: Bloomsbury, 2017).

25. A term coined by Harlan Jacobsen, "Surviving," *Film Comment* 19, no. 5 (1983): 21.

26. See Prince, *New Pot of Gold*, 253.

27. Heung, "The Big Score," 548.

28. I spoke to Lawrence Kasdan over Zoom in February 2023. Any unattributed quotations in the text are from that interview. For further excerpts, see Part VI at the end of this volume: An Interview with Lawrence Kasdan.

29. Prince, *New Pot of Gold*, 254.

"I'm making this up as I go": Lawrence Kasdan and *Raiders of the Lost Ark*

CHAPTER I

Smith and Jones: Discourse Analysis of the *Raiders of the Lost Ark* Story Conference

In 1977, just a few weeks after his very first script deal, with Warner Bros. optioning *The Bodyguard* for thirteen thousand dollars,[1] Lawrence Kasdan sold the screenplay of *Continental Divide* to Steven Spielberg's Amblin Entertainment. The same year, George Lucas pitched a movie idea to Spielberg: an action-adventure about a globetrotting archaeologist. Lucas had already conceived a basic outline for "The Adventures of Indiana Smith" with Philip Kaufman. However, Kaufman, who would later share a "Story by" credit with Lucas, had moved on to direct other films, so the project had stalled until Spielberg mentioned to Lucas that he was interested in directing a James Bond picture. Lucas told him, "I've got something better than that," and Spielberg committed to the movie immediately.[2] Lucas and Kaufman's outline was only partially complete, so Spielberg suggested Lawrence Kasdan as the writer to develop the script. According to the official Lucasfilm history of the franchise, Lucas and Spielberg were attracted to the "1930s and '40s sensibility" evident in Kasdan's screenplay for *Continental Divide*.[3] Kasdan concurs, saying that Lucas and Spielberg wanted "someone who could write *Raiders* in the same way that [Howard] Hawks would have someone write a movie for him—a strong woman character, a certain kind of hero. So that's what got me the job."[4]

Before Kasdan began writing the screenplay, he joined Spielberg and Lucas for a series of story conferences between January 23 and 28, 1978,[5] in which they developed the main characters and story. In recent years, the transcript has appeared intermittently and unofficially online, and it provides an invaluable insight into the creative process.[6] Its study affords us the opportunity to discover how much of the story had already been established by Lucas (and Philip Kaufman), which of the conference participants contributed which ideas, and how much was left for Kasdan to devise independently in his subsequent screenplay.

By examining these points, and by comparing the story conference transcript to various drafts of Kasdan's script as well as the final movie, it becomes possible to establish the screenwriter's authorial presence in the production of

Raiders of the Lost Ark, a film marketed as coming "from the creators of *Jaws* and *Star Wars*."[7] As the only available document of its kind for a major Hollywood movie, the conference transcript is a unique and important document, yet it has never been formally analyzed before. Therefore, I hope that its study will have wider value, too, in providing a fresh insight into the creative process behind a large-scale studio release, and this may have significant repercussions regarding established notions of authorship in popular American cinema.

QUANTITATIVE DISCOURSE ANALYSIS OF THE STORY CONFERENCE

While the transcript of the *Raiders of the Lost Ark* story conference is indisputably of interest to film scholars and enthusiasts, this chapter will strive to avoid an overly simplistic "he said" summary of the 115-page document. Instead, the investigation will appropriate methods of discourse analysis from the field of linguistics, as this will allow an objective overview of the meeting and will be the most effective means for discovering the extent of each participant's contribution.

Discourse analysis examines language "beyond the sentence" and is commonly used to study larger chunks of text, particularly between two or more participants.[8] While less forensic than some areas of linguistics that focus on the micro level (for example, phonetics, phonemes and morphology), discourse analysis allows for an eclectic, interdisciplinary approach that can be both quantitative and qualitative, providing a broader perspective of a text.[9] By examining various aspects of discourse, such as speech acts (the type of utterance; for example, hypothetical questions versus informational questions), turn-taking (how an exchange is "shared" between speakers), or frame analysis (examining the context of a speech act in order to interpret any wider meaning), then it may be possible to measure the relative contributions of speakers in an exchange. So, in applying aspects of discourse analysis to the *Raiders of the Lost Ark* story conference transcript, we can begin to understand the ways in which George Lucas, Steven Spielberg, and Lawrence Kasdan each shaped the plot and characters. Of particular use will be Grice's notions of pragmatics, which establish the ways that the participants negotiate toward agreement.[10] This will be complemented by aspects of conversation analysis outlined by Schiffrin, demonstrating how the speakers structure their individual utterances as well as the discussion as a whole.[11]

The latter section will take a qualitative approach, examining what ideas were devised by whom during the conference; but this first section will employ quantitative analysis of the transcript, in order to establish empirically just how frequently and for how long each participant spoke in the meeting, and what kind of speech acts they performed. By doing so it may give a clearer picture of the respective roles in the meeting, allowing an insight into who deserves credit for building various aspects of the story during the early development process.

At the most macro level, there were 1164 distinct utterances in the transcript, 543 by George Lucas, 346 by Steven Spielberg, and 275 by Lawrence Kasdan, with five utterances unattributed (part of page thirty-nine is illegible), as shown in Figure 1.1. Immediately, this gives a clear sense of the roles within the story conference: Lucas is the story writer and executive producer; the prospective movie is being developed by his company, Lucasfilm, and he is the most vocal; conversely, Kasdan, by far the most inexperienced participant, speaks the least of the three.

The discrepancies in output are even greater when we measure the number of words spoken by each participant. Excluding speech that is "garbled" or unclear to the transcriber, the document contains 49,572 spoken words. Lucas uttered 36,202 of these, Spielberg 8324, and Kasdan 4987, with fifty-nine words unattributed (Figure 1.2).

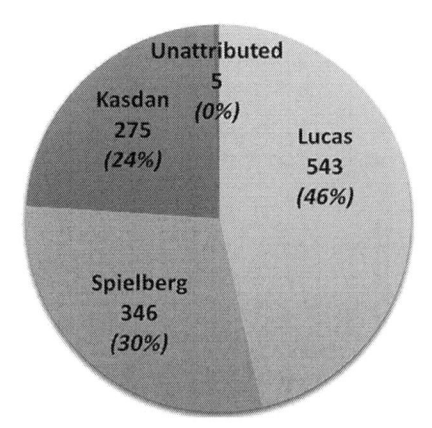

Figure 1.1 *Raiders* Story Conference Transcript: Number of distinct utterances (per cent of total)

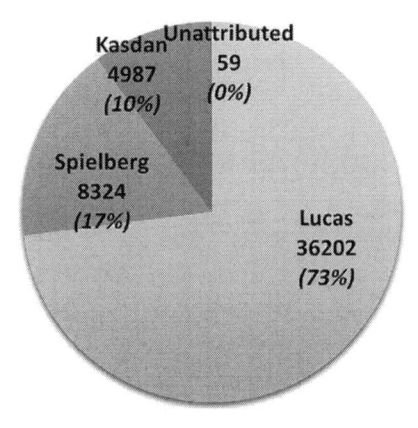

Figure 1.2 *Raiders* Story Conference Transcript: Number of recorded words spoken (per cent of total)

Table 1.1: *Raiders* Story Conference Transcript: Average number of words per utterance

Participant	Total utterances	Total words	Number of words per utterance (mean)
George Lucas	543	36,202	67
Steven Spielberg	346	8324	24
Lawrence Kasdan	275	4987	18
Unattributed	5	59	12
TOTAL	1169	49,572	42

Lucas, then, generated nearly three-fourths of the output in the meeting, while Kasdan produced just one-tenth of the total words.

If we then compare the number of utterances to the number of spoken words, we can see that the average lengths of each participant's unique contributions were quite disparate too, as shown in Table 1.1.

These figures show that, on average, Lucas held the floor in each of his utterances for sixty-seven words on average, 2.79 times as long as Spielberg (twenty-four words per utterance) and 3.72 times as long as Kasdan (eighteen words), suggesting a dominance by Lucas over the group in the meeting. This might be expected considering the "film" existed only in Lucas's mind at this juncture, and his main role was to impart his prior ideas and knowledge of the Ark of the Covenant, the story's "McGuffin."

This transactional dynamic—Lucas as the provider of information, and Kasdan and Spielberg as gatherers—is confirmed by the number of genuine questions asked by each participant. By "genuine," I mean questions that are seeking some new information, so this excludes questions asked in quotations to tell the story (for example, on page seventy-nine, Lucas describes a scene in which "some Germans go 'Why aren't you at the digging?'"), as well as suggestion ("What if. . .?"), clarification ("You mean. . .?") and rhetorical questions. Lastly, I excluded questions about other movies used to help describe a character (for instance, Lucas asks on page two: "Did you see 'The Good, the Bad And the Ugly?' The Eli Wallich [*sic*] character is a goofy character"). The remainder are unequivocally informational questions, and there are 137 of these, of which Spielberg asks forty-eight, and Kasdan asks seventy-one, over half of the total questions in the meeting, as shown in Figure 1.3.

These data confirm Spielberg's, and particularly Kasdan's, roles as collectors of information, especially considering their fewer contributions relative to Lucas's. Kasdan's seventy-one questions come in 275 utterances (averaging one question every 3.87 utterances), Spielberg asks forty-eight questions in 346 utterances (one every 19.22 utterances), while Lucas asks eighteen questions in 543 utterances (one every 30.16 utterances).

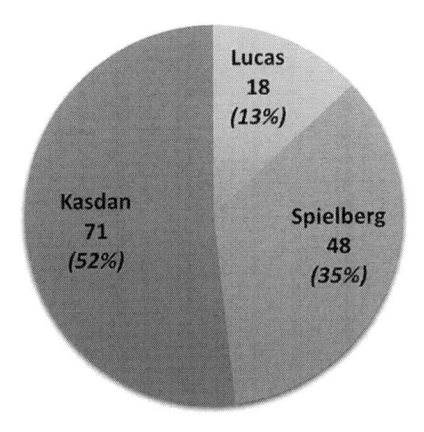

Figure 1.3 *Raiders* Story Conference Transcript: Number of informational questions (per cent of total)

In many instances, Kasdan appears simply to be trying to keep up with Lucas's detailed plot outline. For example, early in the meeting, when Lucas is discussing the point in the story when army intelligence experts explain the history of the Ark to Indiana Jones, Kasdan asks, "What does he know about it so far?" Other questions are concerned with logistics and the way in which they might impact on the story, then followed up with a suggestion based on this information. For instance:

Lucas:	an underground submarine base.
Kasdan:	How big is this base?
Lucas:	Small. One sub.
	[. . .]
Kasdan:	He can watch them unload the Ark, and see where they're going.

This exchange shows that, even in his position as questioner, Kasdan was not necessarily playing a passive role; questions were often followed by a suggestion. In fact, one of his questions features the first recorded occurrence of the protagonist's nickname. Until this point, nearly forty per cent into the entire transcript, no name was given for the central character, with all three participants referring to him as the "guy" (thirty-eight times), "hero" (twenty times), or by the pronoun "he." But then, the following exchange occurs:

Kasdan:	Do you have a name for this person?
Lucas:	I do for our leader.
Spielberg:	I hate this, but go ahead.
Lucas:	Indiana Smith. It has to be unique. It's a character. Very Americana square. He was born in Indiana.

> *Kasdan:*   What does she call him, Indy?
> *Lucas:*   That's what I was thinking. Or Jones. Then people can call him Jones.

Despite Lucas's claim of "[t]hat's what I was thinking," this exchange suggests that Kasdan was responsible for the moniker most commonly used throughout the whole franchise: "Indy." After never being mentioned, it was picked up by all three participants in the conference and subsequently used in the transcript on forty-three occasions (thirty-one times by Lucas, ten times by Kasdan, and two times by Spielberg). Conversely, "Indiana" was employed just seven more times (four times by Kasdan, three times by Spielberg). Neither "Smith" nor "Jones" were used again during the conference, but the exchange, instigated by Kasdan, appeared to consolidate the character's first name and nickname in the creative team's minds.

Of course, the dynamics of the conference, especially in the early stages, can be explained by the gap in knowledge about the project between the participants. Lucas had already spent time developing his idea with Philip Kaufman ("a couple of weeks" in the latter part of 1974, according to Kaufman[12]), and he had pitched it successfully to Spielberg, persuading him to direct. Nevertheless, Spielberg's knowledge still seems scant, as shown by his question: "What's he afraid of? He's got to be afraid of something." Then, early in the meeting, he asks: "His main adversaries will be the Germans?" Furthermore, Spielberg seems pleasantly surprised by many of Lucas's ideas, again pointing to a lack of familiarity; for example:

> *Lucas:*   [. . .] I just thought it would be amusing if people could call him a doctor.
> *Spielberg:*   I like that. The doctor with the bullwhip.

Conversely, there are indications that Lucas and Spielberg had discussed some elements of the film before this meeting, as illustrated by the way that they seem to finish each other's thoughts at times, especially when discussing the overall concept. For example, at the very start:

> *Lucas:*   One of the main ideas was to have, depending on whether it would be every ten minutes or every twenty minutes, a sort of a cliffhanger situation that we get our hero into. If it's every ten minutes we do it twelve times. I think that may be a little much. Six times is plenty.
> *Spielberg:*   And each cliffhanger is better than the one before.
> *Lucas:*   That is the progression we have to do.

Prior dialogue between Lucas and Spielberg is also evidenced more directly soon afterward when Lucas suggests some models for the character, including John Wayne, Clint Eastwood, Sean Connery, and Humphrey Bogart in *The Treasure of the Sierra Madre* (1948). Spielberg interjects: "Or even the Clark Gable thing we talked about." Lucas agrees and adds, "Now, several aspects that we've discussed before. . ."

Furthermore, when Lucas begins describing the opening scene in a South American jungle, he references an earlier conversation with Spielberg:

Lucas:	There's a . . . We actually talked about it a little different from this, but you can correct me if I have gone off what we had talked about the last time. I'm going back, I think, to the original.
Spielberg:	Where he goes into the cave?
Lucas:	This is where he goes into the cave. We had it where there's a couple native bearers, whatever, and sort of a couple of Mexican, well not Mexican . . . Let's put it . . .
Spielberg:	They're like Mayan.

Kasdan, in contrast, seems to have no prior information, as his question about the protagonist's name testifies. The conference really did appear to be his introduction to the entire concept. For this reason, his lack of input, particularly early in the meeting, is understandable, and Kasdan's first contribution is near the bottom of page three, after 1226 words in seventeen utterances exchanged between Lucas (1071 words in nine utterances) and Spielberg (155 words in eight utterances). Clearly, Lucas was using the opening exchanges to provide as much information as possible about the overall concept, the main character, and the basic story outline. In fact, his first utterance in the transcript explicitly states: "We'll just talk general ideas, what the concept of it was. Then I'll get down to going specifically through the story. Then we will actually get to where we can start talking down scenes." Spielberg has both the confidence and knowledge to provide some comments, but these are mostly confined to character traits and ideas for set-pieces rather than plot. For example: "As long as he has brains. He should be able to talk his way out of things;" and "[t]he guy should be a great gambler, too." For Kasdan, however, we can presume that in the early exchanges he is simply trying to process the vast amount of new information. Furthermore, his early silence is perhaps symptomatic of his nervousness as a newcomer to the film industry. He later said: "It was my first job writing for someone else. [. . .] I was daunted maybe for the first hour—you know, *Oh my God, I can't believe I'm in this room with these two guys.*"[13]

There is a clear change in the group dynamic as the meeting progresses, and even a cursory glance at almost any page from the latter part of the transcript shows a more even balance between the participants' contributions compared to any earlier segment. For example, the first four pages of the document show twenty-one speaking turns (eleven by Lucas, nine by Spielberg, and one by Kasdan); in contrast, pages 112 to 115 (the last four available full pages) show sixty turns (twenty-six by Lucas, seventeen by Spielberg, and seventeen by Kasdan).

Some of these changes in the dynamic are borne out more clearly if we divide the transcript into two halves (based on total number of audible words recorded), as shown in Figure 1.4.

This graph shows that the second half of the conference generated a far greater total number of utterances, with 729, compared to 435 in the first half (a sixty-eight per cent increase), evidence of more frequent turn-taking, and indicating a faster exchange of ideas and less obvious dominance by a single member of the group. In the early pages of the transcript, as noted earlier, George Lucas is primarily outlining all that he has devised previously, often in long, unbroken monologues. For example, on pages four to six, he speaks for 893 words uninterrupted about the main character's role as an archaeologist who hunts down artifacts for museums. His longest single utterance is on pages twenty-one to twenty-three, when he talks continuously for 1231 words about the action in Cairo, most of which would make it into the final cut of *Raiders of the Lost Ark*: the Germans digging in the wrong place in the desert, Indy disguising himself as a local worker then getting thrown back into the underground chamber from where he had just excavated the Ark, followed by a chase on horseback to retrieve the Ark from a German army truck.

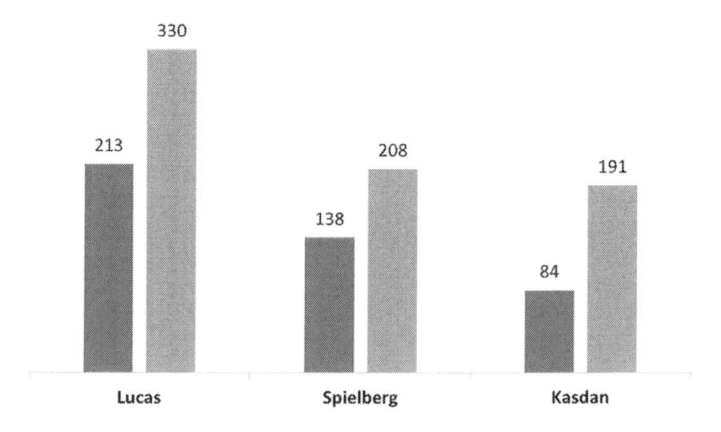

Figure 1.4 *Raiders* Story Conference Transcript: Number of utterances—*FIRST HALF vs SECOND HALF*

In the second half of the meeting, though, the speaker changes much more frequently, and within this overall increase in the number of utterances, Kasdan's output rises the highest proportionately, a 127 per cent increase in speaking turns, compared to Lucas's fifty-five per cent increase and Spielberg's fifty-one per cent. These figures support Kasdan's observation that, after feeling overawed at the beginning of the conference, "It's a real democracy as soon as there's the problem of creating something. All the intimidation goes away very quickly."[14]

However, Lucas still provides by far the highest number of utterances in both halves of the conference. Furthermore, despite Kasdan and Spielberg's increased output in the latter stages, Lucas still dominates the total number of words spoken in both halves of the conference, which suggests that he is still the driving force throughout the meeting, providing the majority of ideas (Figure 1.5).

The extent of Lucas's dominance is markedly less in the second half of the transcript. Certainly, there is a more free-flowing exchange of ideas and far fewer long monologues compared to earlier, and the average length of each utterance is thirty-four words in the second half, down from the fifty-seven-word average in the first half, with Lucas's average utterance length down from ninety-one to fifty-one words, a forty-four per cent drop.

Another notable aspect of the second half of the transcript is Lucas's less confident grasp on the latter parts of the story, as expressed by his increased use of the qualifier "maybe": thirty-eight times in the first half, but fifty-one times in the second, despite producing thirteen per cent fewer words. For example, on page ninety: "And maybe in the next temple it's like a tomb. There's all this embalmed stuff. A little spook house stuff, not a lot, five or six shots. Maybe

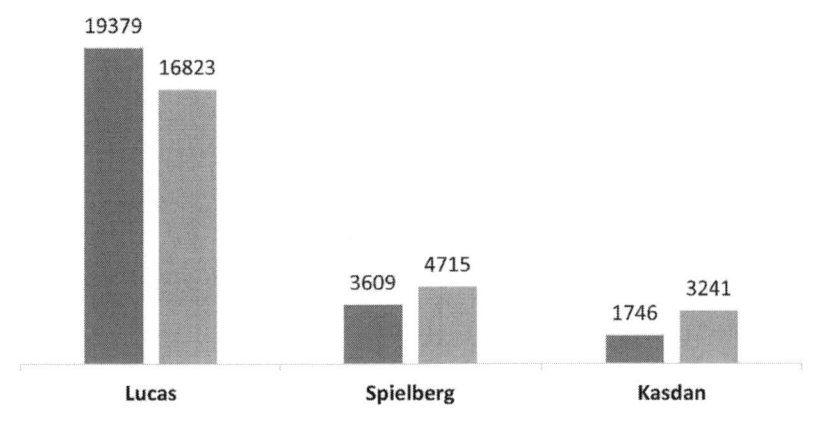

Figure 1.5 *Raiders* Story Conference Transcript: Number of words spoken—*FIRST HALF vs SECOND HALF*

like a one minute sequence where he goes through all this stuff." However, even this increase in the use of "maybe" does not necessarily prevent him from devising some ideas that not only would make the final film, but also become some of its best-known moments:

> *Spielberg:* It would be funny if, somewhere early in the movie he some-
> how implied that he was not afraid of snakes. Later you real-
> ize that that is one of his big fears.
> *Lucas:* Maybe it's better if you see early, maybe in the beginning
> that he's afraid, "Oh God, I hate those snakes." It should
> be slightly amusing that he hates snakes, and then he opens
> this up, "I can't go down in there. Why did there have to be
> snakes. Anything but snakes."

However, Lucas's less assured hold on the latter parts of the story provides more opportunity for Kasdan and Spielberg to contribute, and there is considerable back-and-forth as the participants build on one another's ideas, sometimes making it difficult to accurately state who was responsible for a particular suggestion. For example, after Lucas talks about the "spook house stuff" when Indy and "the girl" are stuck in the hole where the Ark had been kept:

> *Spielberg:* Maybe little tiny mice climbing around on the corpses.
> *Lucas:* Rats.
> *Kasdan:* Can we use the bat in the first scene, since we've taken away
> the snakes?
> *Lucas:* Okay.
> *Kasdan:* There can't be too much light, because they've been dig-
> ging in the middle of sand dunes.
> *Spielberg:* All the light would come from above. Is there anything he
> could light, rags or something?
> *Lucas:* He has torches there. It would be a matter of relighting them.
> *Spielberg:* Walking through these catacombs, you don't see the dead
> people until the light hits them.
> *Kasdan:* If he reaches into his pocket and lights the torch again, that
> hurts it for me. He always had that capability.
> *Lucas:* Or we just don't let the last torch go out. He jumps down
> with the torch.
> *Kasdan:* I think it would be good if it were almost gone, and he
> brings it back to life. He's blowing on it and he gets a burst
> of light. . .
> *Spielberg:* He's in the catacombs and the bodies are piled like cord wood.
> *Lucas:* Bodies and skulls and things.

Clearly, Spielberg and Kasdan were more confident in their grasp on the story at this stage of the conference, and Lucas was more open to his collaborators' suggestions. The above sample also shows remarkable concordance between the participants, with very few explicitly positive or negative phrases utilized; instead, the group would add details or offer alternative suggestions in order to tacitly accept or reject the others' ideas.

This quantitative discourse analysis has established George Lucas as the dominant partner in the *Raiders* story conference. He started the meeting as the imparter of knowledge and remained the most vocal throughout, even if he allowed the others to contribute more as the meeting progressed. Conversely, Lawrence Kasdan and Steven Spielberg began primarily as gatherers of information (especially Kasdan, as his high number of questions testifies), who contributed new ideas more frequently in the latter stages. However, even in the few short excerpts reproduced above, the story conference transcript reveals that all three participants provided ideas both for the plot and the main characters. The next section will examine these contributions in more qualitative terms.

QUALITATIVE DISCOURSE ANALYSIS OF THE STORY CONFERENCE

Any qualitative analysis, by its nature, requires some interpretation; and when working from a transcript rather than an audio or video recording, important cues are lost, such as tone, gestures, or visual demonstrations. Additionally, as the exchanges in the previous section illustrate, the three participants would question and build on each other's ideas in a way that makes it difficult to establish precisely who was responsible for some contributions. There may be more subtle connections linking one person's ideas to another's, too. For example, one of the major plot points in the final movie is when the Gestapo agent Toht has the marks from Marion's pendant seared into his hand after picking it up from a fire; then, from this impression, the Nazis discover the approximate location of the buried Ark. The idea was proposed by Lucas, with Kasdan saying "I love it." However, earlier in the conference, Kasdan had pitched: "The actual piece [showing the Ark's burial site] is no longer there. But it's been sitting on felt or in glass, and there's an impression of it." Kasdan's suggestion, then, of the impression of an item revealing vital information, may have inadvertently led to Lucas's later idea that would appear in Kasdan's screenplay and the film.

But, while allowing that no analysis can be definitive, I will attempt to summarize George Lucas's, Steven Spielberg's, and particularly Lawrence Kasdan's contributions to the story conference, in order to gain a clearer sense of each participant's authorial presence in the finished picture.

The *Raiders of the Lost Ark* story conference begins with Lucas outlining the overall concept for the film. He cites the Republic serials of the 1930s then says that "it's James Bond and it takes place in the thirties," and over the first seven pages he focuses on describing the main character, one recognizable to viewers of the movie: a college professor who is also "a grave robber, for hire" and "quasi-ethical." His costume and weapons are all clearly established in these opening moments of the conference too: khaki pants, leather jacket, and felt hat; a pistol, and his "trade mark" bullwhip. Lucas calls Indy a "playboy," an element that would become less overt through Kasdan's screenplay drafts.

Lucas spends most of pages ten to twenty-seven outlining the basic plot, and it is remarkably close to what we would eventually see on screen, particularly the opening scenes in a Peruvian temple. Interestingly, Lucas appears less sure of the entire section in Cairo, which would occupy fifty-seven minutes of the 115-minute film. He spends only about three transcript pages covering this, half as many as he took to explain the South America "teaser" sequence, and discusses this middle passage only in broad strokes. However, most details in Lucas's nearly unbroken monologue would eventually appear on screen, right up until the end of the movie, when Indy is completely helpless as the Nazis open the Ark of the Covenant and are annihilated by its supernatural power. The story ends with the Ark back in the United States, where, Lucas says: "They crate it up [and] put it in an army warehouse somewhere. [. . .] The bureaucracy is the big winner in the film."

These eighteen pages of the transcript confirm Kasdan's summation that "George already had all the elements," as well as Lucas's own opinion that Kasdan and Spielberg "personalized a lot, but essentially the concept remained the same."[5] However, as established in the quantitative analysis, Lucas's grasp of the story becomes less assured as the conference progresses. His uncertainty, though, also reveals his willingness to allow his partners to contribute. Lucas rarely rejects suggestions completely, and he repeatedly encourages Spielberg and Kasdan to expand on ideas. For example, Spielberg concocts a sequence in which Indy is asleep on a plane when his fellow passengers jump out with parachutes. Lucas says: "That's great. Then what happens? One sentence further and it's a great idea." All three participants then develop the premise into a sequence that, while not making it into *Raiders*, would become a major setpiece in the sequel, *Indiana Jones and the Temple of Doom* (1984).

Even when building on others' suggestions, Lucas often has ideas that would eventually appear on screen; for example, when Spielberg proposes that the Ark's burial chamber is filled with snakes, Lucas suggests that they should establish first that the character is terrified of them. In fact, it is notable throughout the conference just how much audiences of *Raiders of the Lost Ark* would recognize in Lucas's contributions to the story conference. His initial concept that the movie pay homage to 1930s serials is evident, with six "cliffhanger situation[s]." (The film has six separate action sequences, plus the final spectacle of the Ark's opening.) Indy's personality and appearance are clearly established, then Lucas's plot outline on pages eight to twenty-six of the transcript covers many of the same beats that would feature in the movie. In addition, Lucas provides new contributions during the later exchanges, such as the one noted earlier, when the Germans discover the Ark's probable location due to an impression left on a Nazi agent's burned hand.

Lucas appears to have most difficulty in establishing exactly who "the girl" in the picture might be. During the conference, Lucas, Kasdan, and Spielberg develop a character that begins to resemble Marion in the final film, but Lucas still uses the word "problem" five more times when referring to her. Kasdan confirms the difficulty of fitting Marion into the story in his later assertion that he had been brought onto the project "[b]ecause I wrote a certain kind of thing. [. . .] There was no Marion when I came on, but that's what I wrote."[16] However, it is clear that Lucas already had a strong sense of the story and plot of *Raiders of the Lost Ark*, much of which would remain intact through the conference, Kasdan's later scripts, and the film itself.

In the early stages of the meeting, director Steven Spielberg is limited primarily to adding visual additions to existing ideas. For example, when Lucas mentions that the protagonist carries a bullwhip, Spielberg immediately offers two gags utilizing it in unusual ways. Then, as Lucas discusses the opening sequence in which Indy enters a booby-trapped tomb, Spielberg proposes that tarantulas crawl on the hero; and after Lucas describes spring-loaded spikes coming out of the wall, Spielberg adds that there should be skeletons impaled upon them. Spielberg also concocts the idea of a Gestapo agent assembling some sort of metal contraption that appears to be a torture device, before it is revealed as a coat hanger, a darkly comic moment that would not appear in any of Kasdan's script drafts but would make it into the movie. Spielberg's contributions, in most cases, are sight gags or subtle embellishments to existing plot points, but that does not detract from their impact on the final picture. For example, Lucas is describing Indy's escape from the tomb, when Spielberg cuts in: "There is a sixty-five foot boulder that's form-fitted to only roll down the corridor coming right at him. And it's a race." It is an improvised, offhand comment, given without deep introspection, yet it would lead to one of the most memorable stunts in *Raiders*, and, indeed, an enduring moment in the history of Hollywood cinema. Another flourish provided by Spielberg comes when the conference participants are discussing what is in the Ark's burial chamber, and he suggests: "What about snakes? All these snakes come out." He immediately follows this with the notion that Indy uses the snakes' entry point to guide him to the weakest wall in the temple, and therefore a way out of his entombment. As one would expect from a director—albeit one who has occasionally written too[17]—Spielberg's ideas tend to begin with images first, but they still contribute to forwarding the plot in meaningful ways.

A major point of contention in the story conference is Spielberg's insistence that Indy blow up the Greek island at the end of the film. In order to accommodate the idea, he proposes a subplot involving a hidden Nazi base, which turns out to be on the same island as where the Ark is opened. Lucas appears unsure, complaining that "we wind up the way every Bond movie has ended" with an exploding island. Spielberg counters: "Every Bond movie has made money, too." In the story conference, Lucas and Kasdan develop this idea, and it would remain in the first four (of five) script drafts before Kasdan excised it in the final screenplay.

In terms of story, Spielberg appears to invest the most thought in discussing the actions and motivations of the female lead. Soon after Lucas's initial outline, when "the girl" is not clearly defined, Spielberg stresses that "if she weren't in this picture, a lot of this stuff wouldn't have taken place. [. . .] She's not just somebody to be around for comic relief or romantic relief." Later, talking about when Marion helps Indy hijack a German plane and steal back the Ark, Spielberg says: "She becomes the driving force. She's so tired of being tied up and pushed around. She becomes a real active part of the story now." These comments suggest that Spielberg wished to make the female lead a stronger, rounded character, much more in keeping with what would be seen in the final movie.

So, if Lucas provided the initial concept and plot, and Spielberg injected the piece with visual panache and a request for a stronger female co-protagonist, the final question is what Lawrence Kasdan, the youngest and least experienced of the three, contributed to the story conference. As stated previously, Kasdan admitted to feeling nervous early in the story conference for *Raiders of the Lost Ark*. George Lucas had already written and directed three movies, including *Star Wars*, released just eight months prior and on its way to becoming the highest-grossing film of all time; Steven Spielberg had also directed three motion pictures, including the previous biggest money-earner in history, *Jaws* (1975). Kasdan, in contrast, had no screen credits at all, having only sold his first scripts the previous year. Additionally, he clearly had very little knowledge of the film's concept before this conference, and his early contributions reflect his disadvantage. It is near the bottom of page three of the transcript before Kasdan is recorded as speaking, and his first four utterances are single sentences. However, each of these ideas is greeted positively by Lucas, either tacitly or directly. For example, on page six:

> *Lucas:*   [. . .] When he confronts his antiquities and stuff, half the time he's dealing with hoaxes. [. . .]
>
> *Kasdan:*   Some of the hoaxes may have been set up by the natives.

Lucas:	Yeah. They may be an original native thing, or it might be some shyster in town [. . .] It also makes him somewhat of a ghost chaser in his own way. [. . .]
Kasdan:	He's bound to run into those kind of things.
Lucas:	Yes.

Each of these are either minor additions to Lucas's ideas, or simply confirmation of understanding. However, Kasdan's fifth utterance is notable in that it is the first time any of the participants suggest the main character might have a weakness. Up to this point, Lucas had described Indy as "a real professional. He's really good. And that is the key to the whole thing," someone who "not only is not afraid to stand up against any man, but he's also not afraid to stand up against the unknown." But Kasdan says: "It seems like it would be nice if, once stripped of his bullwhip, [it] left him weak, if we had to worry. Just a little worried about him being too . . ." The notion is picked up immediately by his collaborators, Lucas agreeing: "If we don't make him vulnerable, he's got no problems." This vulnerability would be referenced repeatedly throughout the conference (for example, his fear of snakes) and would become one of the traits that make Indiana Jones such an engaging protagonist. Similarly, when Spielberg suggests a mentor for the hero, Kasdan questions the idea: "Is it necessary that he really be trained?" Clearly, Kasdan prefers a less polished lead, and while we cannot give him all the credit for this aspect (Lucas had already described Indy as "scruffy"), at this early stage it is Kasdan who argues most strongly for the kind of imperfect character that Harrison Ford would eventually portray.

Kasdan's next significant contribution is when Lucas is explaining the major exposition scene in which army intelligence agents first approach Indy to discuss the Nazis' search for the Ark of the Covenant. Initially, Lucas has it that Indy "doesn't know anything about it," but he quickly adjusts his position: "We can play it where he's sort of explaining some of it to the Army officer or something." Kasdan agrees, then adds an element that would transform the scene from a standard "This is your mission" scene (as Lucas puts it) into something more nuanced: "Maybe the fact that he knows more about it than they do is the turning point of the scene. He sort of talks himself into the job." This is how the scene would play out in the final picture, the two government representatives exchanging impressed glances as Indy interrupts, explaining to them exactly what the Ark is and why Hitler may want it, even after they had initiated the meeting.

The next idea of Kasdan's that would impact the story significantly is on page thirty-three of the conference transcript, when he suggests that "the girl" has inherited part of the map from her father, who was also Indy's mentor many years before. "That's why he's going to Nepal, to get it from her. That's why they know each other. That's why she's reluctant to part with it." This is the point at which Lucas abandons the existing notion of the female lead being a German singer-spy, and instead makes her an American bar owner in Nepal. Kasdan is quick to add that "I don't want to soften her. I like the fact that it's greed [motivating her]. I like all the hard stuff, but you're going to love her." Then he suggests that Indy's rivals may have reached her first, asking about the tablet in her possession: "When [Indy] comes to her, 'That's funny, I've had this ten years since my father died. Now in this week two people want it.'" Kasdan then decides that the German agents are "a half hour behind" Indy. When they come to get the map, "She is in immediate jeopardy and he represents some security to her," just as happens in the final film.

Another major contribution Kasdan makes here is in describing the piece that Indy is searching for—previously referred to as a "map" or "tablet"—as something that Marion could wear as jewelry: "The thing hasn't been worth anything up until now, so she wears it around her neck, or it's on the mantle. It's like a joke." This suggestion would enable the plot to move forward differently than if, for example, it was a stone tablet; and it also personalizes the piece for Marion, giving it added resonance in establishing the central relationship.

Regarding the motivations of characters, Kasdan seems to prefer ambiguity, having Indy try to steal the pendant during the night after Marion refuses to give it to him. But when he goes to take the piece, she is already being pressured by the Germans to give it to them, and "he winds up rescuing her. He stumbles into the heroic role. She could doubt his motivation from then on." Equally significantly, in response to Lucas's assertion that the male and female leads be "cemented into a very strong relationship" quickly, Kasdan suggests that not only was Marion the daughter of Indy's mentor, but that they had once had a romantic relationship: "Then you don't have to build it."

Later, the meeting participants are again discussing Marion's introduction in the Nepalese bar, and Lucas suggests that "you cut to [Indy] walking in the bar, and he sort of walks up and sits down and she comes up and says . . ." But Kasdan interrupts: "I don't want to throw away their first sight of each other." Then he develops the idea with something that would make it to the final cut: "What if we lose him, see her dealing with the rowdies[?] She clears the place out and then sees him sitting there." Kasdan physicalizes her emotions on finally seeing him again: "I wonder if her first reaction isn't just to hit him. Something unusual, not just a slap. First sight, register who it is, wham." Again, this is very similar to how their meeting would play out on screen and it adds to the element of surprise as we learn more about the characters' past relationship.

Not all of Kasdan's ideas regarding this scene would make it into the film. His next suggestion is that Indy and Marion eventually kiss in the bar, and this is when Indy notices that Marion is wearing the piece he is looking for as a pendant. But Kasdan quickly changes tack, again preferring ambiguity. Following Lucas's suggestion that "it would be interesting if she were putting on an act" regarding whether she has the piece or not, Kasdan says: "He doesn't have to tell her exactly what he wants. [. . .] You can play it either way, she's holding out on him or she doesn't know what he's talking about. We know she has it, but he doesn't."

Kasdan urges further uncertainty between the leads when they return to his idea of Indy trying to steal the pendant from Marion. Lucas and Spielberg seem agreed that there needs to be ambiguity; but, while Spielberg says that Indy is "plotting how he's going to take it off her," Lucas seems concerned that this makes him "a real rat." Kasdan takes a more nuanced middle ground: "That's all right. He never does it. What he does is just the opposite, save her life." When Lucas remains concerned about Indy being too unscrupulous, Kasdan says, "I'm a little confused about Indy at this point. I thought he'd do anything for this pendant." Lucas insists on Indy being "a person we can look up to," and Kasdan provides a more equivocal solution in which, after they part ways, they are both contemplating their next actions and "it's clear that she's going to give it to him. Then he saves her and she doubts his motivation, was he coming to steal it? Or was he coming to rekindle the romance?" He summarizes by saying, "It doesn't have to be crystal clear to her."

Kasdan continues to petition for a less cleanly-defined hero when he proposes that Indy burn down Marion's bar, "her only stake in the world." It is not clear whether Kasdan intends this act to be deliberate or accidental, but he does suggest that "[t]he pendant might lead him to the fire. He uses the fire." Spielberg and Lucas appear enthusiastic about this idea and immediately develop it, although Lucas differs from Kasdan's intent by having the Germans cause the fire instead. However, Lucas reminds his colleagues that "[h]e's the one who brought the Nazis there, so it's all his fault anyway. [. . .] He feels sort of obligated to bring her along, since he does feel sort of guilty."

Kasdan's next major contribution follows Lucas's suggestion that Marion is kidnapped by the Nazis after she and Indy reach Cairo. The notion stems from Spielberg's complaint that "I don't know what we do with her" in Egypt. But her abduction leads to a new problem whereby Indy's continued quest to find the Ark rather than rescue Marion feels, to Lucas, "pretty mundane." At this point, Kasdan asks, "Is there some way to really convince him she has died? [. . .] And then he could feel bad about it until he sees her again." The suggestion solves the problem of the female lead simply "tagging along for conversation," as Spielberg puts it. Simultaneously, it keeps her directly involved with the story, while removing her from the middle act in a way that allows Indy to hunt for the McGuffin without appearing callous.

After Lucas suggests a monkey be poisoned as a way to inject tension into an exposition scene about the pendant and staff, Kasdan posits the idea of "a villain monkey" who has been trained to help his master steal information from the protagonists. He takes the idea further, suggesting that in the earlier street fight scene, "the girl jumps into a basket to hide and the monkey leads the Arabs to the girl. That's how they get her." Additionally, Kasdan says that the monkey "charms his way into their confidence," rather than sneaking around, and is willingly carried along by the lead characters. The creature even consoles Indy after Marion is apparently killed, the hero unaware that the monkey is an enemy agent. All of this would make it into the final picture, showing that Kasdan has a flair for the kind of visual gag that Spielberg appears to enjoy, and not only for developing relationships and characters.

Kasdan is an active participant in the discussion about exactly how the pendant and staff can show the Ark's hiding place in the Map Room, then the to-and-fro regarding what peril Indy faces in the burial chamber, finally agreeing upon Spielberg's idea of "hundreds of thousands of snakes." However, Kasdan's next significant contribution is when he suggests that Marion become "involved" with the villain Belloq during her imprisonment, "For her own purposes. [. . .] A tough woman of the world, which would appeal to him." Kasdan wants to see Indy left in the underground temple alone, Marion still with the antagonists as they seal off the chamber. He says: "As the thing slams shut you see her mixed emotions, but she's siding with the rival," Lucas and Spielberg do not appear enamored with the idea, and when Lucas suggests that they throw Marion in the hole with him, Kasdan does not protest. However, the idea of Belloq's attraction to the female lead resurfaces seven pages later in the transcript, with Kasdan's next major suggestion. By this point they are talking about the Nazis boarding the pirate ship that is taking Indy, Marion, and the Ark to England. For plot purposes, Indy needs to be alone as he would later board the enemy U-boat and pretend to be a German soldier, but Lucas is not sure how to structure this: "We have to figure out a reason for them to take the girl at this point." Kasdan responds: "Maybe here is where we can have the other thing. The Frenchman wants her, even though she's not receptive to it." Lucas agrees then incorporates Kasdan's earlier idea of an attraction when Marion was Belloq's prisoner in Egypt, and this ambiguity would be present in Kasdan's screenplay and the movie itself.

Regarding the climax, the most contentious aspect of the plot in the transcript, Kasdan would later claim that he was averse to Spielberg's wish for Indy to blow up the island where the Germans take the Ark.[18] During the story conference, Lucas is vocal in his preference for a less bombastic finale, one that does not resemble a James Bond movie. Kasdan, too, seems to favor alternatives to Indy deliberately destroying the island base; for example: "[The Ark] threatens the ammo stock. Now he does have a time problem. [. . .] That would be an improvement on the Bond thing." The argument remains unresolved by the end of the transcript; and it would be one of the aspects changed most radically in various drafts of the screenplay.

Throughout the story conference, Kasdan is more active when discussing characters and their motivations. His contributions are generally longer and more frequent when establishing Indiana Jones's persona, in particular his possible weaknesses, at odds with Lucas's description of a "Super Samurai Warrior" at the start of the conference. But Kasdan appears most engaged when discussing the female lead, establishing the fact that she is the daughter of Indy's old mentor, as well as an ex-lover. To accentuate this nuanced relationship, Kasdan personalizes the film's first McGuffin, making it a pendant that Marion inherited from her deceased father, so justifying her reticence in giving it to anyone else. This contributes to Kasdan's preference for uncertainty in the central relationship, with Marion punching Indy soon after their reunion, then kissing him, before "holding out on him" when he wants the medallion. Equally, Kasdan petitions for Indy to be someone who would "do anything for this pendant," even as Lucas asks for "a role model for little kids."

Kasdan is also especially vocal when discussing the film's two most exposition-heavy scenes: the intelligence agents outlining the mission to Indy, and the old college friend (who would be replaced by a local imam in the movie) explaining how the pendant would reveal the Ark's hiding place in the Map Room. Interestingly, Kasdan, who generally seems to prefer character development over action set-pieces, injects each of these scenes with more visual appeal and dynamism than initially suggested by his creative partners. Certainly, his contributions are not limited to the spoken word as one might expect, given his later reputation as a writer of dialogue-heavy scripts.

Even though he produced fewer words and utterances than his colleagues, this analysis demonstrates that Lawrence Kasdan contributed significantly to the *Raiders of the Lost Ark* story development, and the transcript gives us a strong understanding of the starting point from where he would develop the screenplay over the following months. In our interview, he said that, despite feeling intimidated at the beginning of the conference, "within a day I felt like oh, I get where I fit in here. I can do this part they can't do; and them setting it up, and us working out the story together." Steven Spielberg was satisfied with the process, too, stating later that "George, Larry, and I sat in a room and contrived a very structured story that is eighty per cent of what the script turned out to be."[19] Kasdan would now have the task of turning the plethora of ideas into a workable screenplay, as he told me with dry understatement: "All they were asking me to do is, 'Can you make this work great?'"

NOTES

1. Aljean Harmetz, "How He Became Hollywood's Hot Writer," *The New York Times*, November 1, 1981, http://www.nytimes.com/1981/11/01/movies/how-he-became-hollywood-s-hot-writer.html?pagewanted=all (accessed June 29, 2023).

2. Jim Windolf, "Q&A: Steven Spielberg," *Vanity Fair*, January 2, 2008, https://www.vanityfair.com/news/2008/02/spielberg_qanda200802?currentPage=4 (accessed June 29, 2023).

3. J. W. Rinzler, *The Complete Making of Indiana Jones* (London: Ebury, 2008), 21–2.

4. Lawrence Kasdan, quoted in Joseph McBride, *Steven Spielberg: A Biography*, 2nd ed. (Jackson: University Press of Mississippi, 2010), 314.

5. According to Rinzler, *Making Indiana Jones*, 22.

6. The 115-page document (the pages numbered 1 to 117, with pages 101 and 116 missing) was only tacitly acknowledged by any of the participants, until Kasdan referenced it directly in an interview. Jim Hemphill, "Lawrence Kasdan," *Academy of Motion Picture Arts and Sciences: Oral History Collection* (Los Angeles: AMPAS, 2022), transcript, 17: "That recording found its way eventually onto the internet, which was not an internet at that time but years later. And everybody who loves that movie and everybody who wanted to be a screenwriter or director has listened to this recording." While Kasdan refers to the "recording," it has only been available in transcript form. At the time of writing, the PDF is unavailable online, but an accurate transcription (without page numbers) is available at Indie Film Hustle (https://indiefilmhustle.com/tag/raiders-of-the-lost-ark-story-conference-transcript/).

7. For the *Raiders* publicity poster, see *Film/Art Gallery*, https://filmartgallery.com/collections/raiders-of-the-lost-ark-posters (accessed June 29, 2023).

8. Deborah Tannen, "Discourse Analysis—What Speakers do in Conversations," *Linguistic Society of America*, 2019, https://www.linguisticsociety.org/resource/discourse-analysis-what-speakers-do-conversation (accessed June 29, 2023).

9. For a concise but comprehensive explanation of discourse analysis, see Ruth Wodak, *Aspects of Critical Discourse Analysis* (London: Sage, 2009).

10. H. Paul Grice, "Logic and Conversation," in Peter Cole and Jerry L. Morgan (eds.), *Syntax and Semantics*, Vol. 3 (New York: Academic Press, 1975).

11. Deborah Schiffrin, *Approaches to Discourse* (Oxford: Blackwell, 1994), 232.

12. Philip Kaufman, quoted in Rinzler, *Making Indiana Jones*, 17–18.

13. Kasdan, quoted in Rinzler, *Making Indiana Jones*, 22. Original emphasis.

14. Ibid.

15. Rinzler, *Making Indiana Jones*, 22.

16. Kasdan, quoted in Adam Rogers, "Star Wars' greatest screenwriter wrote all your other favorite movies too," *Wired*, November 18, 2015, https://www.wired.com/2015/11/lawrence-kasdan-qa/ (accessed June 30, 2023).

17. Spielberg is a credited screenwriter on *Close Encounters of the Third Kind* (1977), *Poltergeist* (1982), *A.I. Artificial Intelligence* (2001), and *The Fabelmans* (2022).

18. Kasdan, quoted in Rinzler, *Making Indiana Jones*, 49.

19. Steven Spielberg, quoted in Rinzler, *Making Indiana Jones*, 22.

CHAPTER 2

Visual Language in the *Raiders of the Lost Ark* Screenplay

G iven his lack of experience and the likely cost of an action-adventure film set on five continents, it is remarkable that, after the story conference, Lawrence Kasdan was allowed almost total autonomy in writing the screenplay to *Raiders of the Lost Ark*. He says: "During the six months that I was writing *Raiders*, I never met with George Lucas or Steven Spielberg, except for occasionally checking in with them to say that my script was coming along. [. . .] They left me totally alone."[1]

This chapter will establish which ideas from the story conference remained in the screenplay. In doing this, it may be possible to understand what new elements Kasdan added with regards to character, dialogue, and plot, as well as those more visual elements that are not always associated with the screenwriter. Primarily, I will analyze the first draft, in order to examine the script before Kasdan received feedback from Lucas and Spielberg.[2] It will also be useful to compare it to the revised fifth draft (officially the "final" draft, including some later revisions made during production) to see exactly what document the cast and crew worked from on set.[3] Additionally, I will utilize the third draft, to help gauge when major changes may have occurred.[4] The close reading will provide fresh insight into Lawrence Kasdan's contribution to *Raiders of the Lost Ark*, not only regarding dialogue and character, but also in terms of the visual style of the effects- and stunts-heavy picture, even before shooting began.[5]

MAKING CHOICES

Following the story conference, it took Lawrence Kasdan five months to deliver the first draft of his screenplay. Superficially, the most noticeable aspect is its length, coming in at 144 pages, much longer than the 120 pages that George Lucas had anticipated during the story conference. Another instantly recognizable point is the density of scene description; for example, the first page is dominated by scene text, with only two lines of dialogue and very little white space.[6] Although the opening scene follows very closely what was discussed in the conference, Kasdan adds detail that rounds out the minor characters. The men whom Lucas described as the "local sleazos" in the story conference become "Satipo (the fox)" and "Barranca (the rat)," Spanish-Peruvians "armed with guns and machetes." While some later scene text, particularly in action sequences, will be more functional, the opening page reflects much of the style found throughout the draft: a fluid prose style, dense chunks of text, and descriptions that are unlikely to be relevant to the eventual audience of the film. For example, the very first words in the script read:

```
FADE IN:

EXT. PERU - HIGH JUNGLE - DAY

The dense, lush rainforests on the eastern slopes
of the Andes, the place known as "The Eyebrow of
the Jungle". Ragged, jutting canyon walls are
half-hidden by the thick mists.
```

The phrase "The Eyebrow of the Jungle" is certainly evocative but will be superfluous to the viewer of the final movie, so the question is why Kasdan would include it. In this case, the specificity of the term, as well as much of the detail in this opening scene, serves three functions. First, it provides the reader with a clear image of the environment in a more expressive way than a simple "There is" description. In practical terms, this will be of use to the many department heads who will eventually utilize the screenplay to guide their choices of location, costume, props, sound design, and camera set-up. Second, the employment of such details tells the reader that, even though we will soon understand that this is an action-adventure with a fantastic tone, the writer has researched the subject and is approaching the script seriously. At the beginning of the pre-production process, in particular, this may be helpful in attracting talent and finance. Third, the "literary" style is entertaining, lending credence to film theorist Claudia Sternberg's claim that the screenplay is a text in its own right.[7] Perhaps more pertinently, it also has practical value in keeping the reader engaged. We can presume that the more enjoyable the script, the more likely potential collaborators will be motivated to continue reading, increasing the chances of them joining the project. Kasdan's approach appears to contradict Osip Brik's assertion that a screenplay is merely "the outline of a future film set out in words," and indicates that it has far greater practical and literary worth.[8]

The first eighteen pages of Kasdan's first-draft screenplay are very similar to what would appear on screen. This is perhaps a result of how fully formed many of the ideas already were even at the beginning of the story conference when, of the sixteen pages of barely interrupted monologue that George Lucas spent outlining his existing ideas for the plot, he devoted seven pages to the opening sequence alone. The only significant differences between the first draft and the fifth were Satipo being killed slightly later (originally, by the spear of an indigenous warrior, after exiting the temple; rather than being impaled upon booby-trapped spikes), and the absence of Belloq in the jungle, meaning that Indy manages to escape with the golden idol he had just taken. Even in the very first draft, the sequence demonstrates the same rugged verve that would become so familiar in the film itself. For example, as Indy and Satipo are fleeing the temple:

```
The rumbling is very loud now and we see why:
right behind the two men a huge boulder comes
roaring around a corner of the passage, perfectly
form-fitted to the passage-way. It obliterates
everything before it, sending the stalactites
shooting ahead like missiles.

Indy and Satipo dash for the light of the exit.
Indy's hat flies off his head. Almost immediately
it is crushed by the boulder. [...]

The boulder slams to a perfect fit at the entrance,
sealing the Temple.
```

The "stalactites shooting ahead like missiles" were missing from the movie, of course, as was the loss of Indy's hat (with its almost magnetic attachment to him becoming a running gag throughout the franchise), but their inclusion here and in the final draft conveys the raw, breathless energy that was so unique to *Raiders* at the time, and that would go on to inflect the entire genre. In the first draft, this moment is immediately followed by Satipo pointing a gun at Indy in order to take the golden idol for himself. But Satipo is felled by the spear of a Hovitos warrior, allowing Indy to flee. He scrambles onto a waiting amphibian plane where he finds the pilot's pet snake "Reggie." It is an apparently frivolous comic moment, but it artfully introduces the protagonist's "Achilles' heel" that will become more consequential later in the narrative, while also helping to humanize him.

As in the movie, the next scene has Indy meeting his university colleague Brody back in the US, before being introduced to the army intelligence agents who reveal that Hitler is searching for the Ark of the Covenant. In the first draft of the screenplay, Kasdan then has Indy take the men to see a friend at the museum who gives further exposition about the Ark. The extra scene adds five and a half pages to the script (after four and a half pages of exposition in a conference room) and is followed by another three and a half pages in a Washington hotel room, in which the intelligence officers insist that Indy helps them by going to Cairo. They also mention, for the first time, Indy's French nemesis, Lovar (the name changed to Belloq by the third draft). There is a danger when analyzing an early draft of a screenplay that any scene not making it into the final movie, by very virtue of being excised, feels super-fluous. However, the length of these three exposition scenes is particu-larly marked compared to the final picture in which the entire scene with army intelligence—in which the Ark's power, location, and significance to Hitler is revealed, as well as the involvement of Indy's old mentor, Abner Ravenwood—lasts exactly five minutes. Conversely, this first draft expends fourteen pages on the same exposition, which, if we follow the rough guide that one page equals one minute of screen time, is a significant difference. However, during this sequence, Kasdan clearly establishes the process required to locate the Ark of the Covenant, most of which had been discussed in less specific terms in the conference. While fourteen pages appears very long for exposition alone, it is perhaps understandable that the complex set-up would initially require these many pages, before Kasdan was able to distil the infor-mation into approximately seven pages of script in the final draft. Harrison Ford's rapid-fire delivery and Steven Spielberg's economical direction were then able to reduce this to five minutes of screen time.

Another element that was eventually excised from the final movie was the "playboy" aspect of the lead character, with Indy mistaking a late-night knock on his hotel door in Washington for a woman ("Sheila?"). Variations on the theme continued through to the fifth draft, wherein Indy is shown in bed with a student whose name he can barely remember. Again, this was something ini-tially discussed in the story conference, although it is interesting that Spiel-berg, presumably, chose not to use this in the final film, replacing it with a more playful flirtation from a student ("I love you" written on her eyelids), which flusters the professor in front of the class, making him less predatory and, I argue, more relatable.

As agreed in the story conference, there then follows a sequence with Indy going to Shanghai to steal one part of the headpiece (another detail confirmed in this first draft; not strictly a tablet nor a medallion, as originally described in the story conference) from a Chinese warlord's museum. While these scenes would be cut by the fifth draft, they remained in the third, suggesting their omission was relatively late in the process. Kasdan is often perceived as a writer who focuses on dialogue, yet what is striking in this script is the pace, clarity, and dynamism of his action scenes.[9] Sternberg's scene text "modes" are all present: description (of people and locations), report (of action), and comment (technical and para-technical instructions to the filmmakers, as well as literary comment).[10] The page is not broken into taut, one-line paragraphs or punctuated by ellipses and dashes, as is customary during many screenplay action sequences. Instead, Kasdan appears comfortable relying on the language to keep the reader both informed of every physical element and engaged in the narrative. By making the prose entertaining, while simultaneously informing the reader of characters' actions, props, and locations, Kasdan is serving the dual functions of keeping readers interested and creating a "blueprint"—that common but imperfect analogy for the screenplay's function—that production heads can use to carry out their roles most effectively.[11]

Indiana Jones then heads for Nepal, escaping from the plane on a life raft after the pilots and crew deliberately evacuate.[12] Marion Ravenwood, the female lead, is finally revealed on page fifty-two, more than one-third of the way through the script, in the Himalayan tavern that she owns. First, Kasdan establishes Marion independently, describing her as "beautiful, but a bit hard-looking. At the moment, however, that look does not hurt" as she breaks up a fight, chastizes her customers ("Nepalese natives, fierce Sherpa mountain guides, sleazy international smugglers, fugitives, and, of course, mountain climbers from every corner of the earth"), then kicks them out of her bar.

By the fifth and final draft, the introduction to Marion is even more surprising: before sending the unruly mob of mostly male characters home, she beats a burly Australian climber in a drinking contest, a scene that would make it into the movie. Like the initial heroic impressions of Indy that would soon be flipped when we see him terrified by a snake, the assumption that Marion is in total control of her surroundings would be contradicted by revelations later in the scene as we learn more of her and Indy's past. In the first draft, the audience watches Marion berating the customers, from the perspective of "one remaining Patron huddled over a glass at the end of the bar," his face unseen to her or the audience, until the mysterious figure looks up and smiles. We then take Marion's point of view as she stares, shocked, when she realizes that the man is Indy, before punching him in the face. By taking the viewpoint of each character in turn, their first view of one another receives added emotional weight, and it alerts the reader to a complicated history between them, without the need for excessive dialogue. The use of a subjective point of view is commonly employed in films when introducing a major character, of course. *Seven Samurai* (1954), for example, which Kasdan has professed to watching thirty times, uses long lenses and low angles to distance the new character from the off-screen observer with whom the audience is already aligned. However, it is rare to use this technique on two sides of an exchange, and it serves to elevate both the connection between the characters and the obvious antagonism. It also subtly foreshadows the return of Indy to the bar after he argues with Marion and she tells him, "Come back tomorrow." She is still undecided whether to give him the part of the headpiece he desires (in all drafts, as well as in the finished film). We then see Indy leave, only to return a few minutes later and rescue Marion from the gang of Nazis and Sherpas that arrives shortly afterward. Film academic Warren Buckland attributes Indy's return to his being there all along, stating that, in the film, "his backward glance and a second pause suggest that perhaps he does not intend to go anywhere."[13] Additionally, Buckland argues that two unattributed point-of-view shots indicate Indy being an off-screen presence, possibly hiding behind a pillar throughout the scene. Buckland credits Steven Spielberg with the employment of an off-screen presence, associating it with more prominent examples in his other films, such as *Jaws* (1975), *Close Encounters of the Third Kind* (1977) and *Hook* (1991). However, by examining these screenplay drafts, we can see that the use of an off-screen presence had already been posited by Kasdan, even though in his script he then explicitly shows Indy driving away from the bar and the Nazis watching him leave before they enter. While this suggests that Indy is not hidden in the bar throughout the scene, as Buckland suggests, it allows the possibility that he drives away as a ruse before swiftly doubling back. Additionally, the fact that the scene of him driving away was cut from the movie might suggest that Spielberg decided to keep him physically closer, lending credence to Buckland's claim that Indy may be in the room throughout.

Before Indy's apparent departure and return, however, there is a chance for Kasdan to employ the rat-a-tat dialogue present in his script for *Continental Divide*, as the two leads bicker acrimoniously. Kasdan does this with apparent enthusiasm, their dialogue lasting nine pages in the first draft, pared down to seven pages by the fifth. The argument is full of 1930s-romantic-comedy barbs, and it reveals some less salubrious aspects of their pasts; for example, that Indy and Marion had been in a romantic relationship before, with Marion saying that she was a child at the time: "It was wrong, you knew it." Additionally, Marion hints that she had to prostitute herself after her father died, a surprisingly downbeat backstory that would be excised in the movie but that presumably informed actor Karen Allen's performance.

The scene in Marion's bar, when Nazi agents and local strongmen come to take the medallion, remains nearly unchanged throughout the drafts, as does the fight when Indy returns and rescues her. This would be one of the most memorable set-pieces in the picture, with Indy and Marion sometimes working in tandem and sometimes separate within the chaos of a blazing fire, with machine guns blasting, bottles breaking, and countless punches thrown. George Lucas has spoken of Steven Spielberg's aptitude for keeping track of disparate elements even within a busy action scene,[14] and this sequence is a prime example, the audience never allowed to lose track of who is doing what. However, Lawrence Kasdan deserves credit too, with the sequence taking up three pages of script, almost every beat of which would appear on screen. In the story conference, Indiana Jones was described more as a classic matinee hero, competent and commanding. It is in sequences such as this, though, that Kasdan showcases the improvised quality of Indy's actions, making him a less composed hero than the "super-man" archetypes that Lucas mentioned in the conference, such as a Toshiro Mifune samurai or Clint Eastwood's Man with No Name. The more visceral quality of the visual language of *Raiders*, then, first appears in Kasdan's script, which Spielberg would follow closely when realizing the scenes. Kasdan gives the central character a more rough-round-the-edges quality, and this informs the entire film. Whether deliberately or not, Kasdan's writing matched with Spielberg's pledge to Lucas that he would complete the complex international production on-time and on-budget, after overages on *Jaws*, *Close Encounters of the Third Kind*, and *1941* (1979). In order to keep his promise, Spielberg said that on *Raiders*, "I learned to like instead of love. If I liked a scene after I shot it, I printed it. I didn't shoot it again seventeen times until I got the one that I loved."[15] The rag-tag sensibility of Kasdan's screenplay and its central character was perfectly suited to such an approach.

Now that she has lost her bar, Marion joins Indy as his partner as he heads to Cairo to locate the Ark of the Covenant itself. In the first draft, this middle passage begins with a brief dialogue-free scene of an American agent, Stanton, conversing with Indy and Marion. The moment is representative of an aspect that becomes less prevalent in later iterations: the suggestion that Indy is part of a larger government network, with Stanton in Cairo and another US agent in Shanghai assisting him in his quest. Of course, in all drafts Indy is acting on the government's behalf, but there becomes a stronger sense in Kasdan's later versions that he is on his own against far more powerful enemies, relying on his wits rather than on any grander institution. This, I argue, became one of the features that endeared the character to filmgoers and distinguished him from Lucas's initial James Bond archetype.

In the first draft, the agent Stanton would soon be murdered ("not one, but three Arabian daggers" in his back) before a fight with local thugs in the marketplace. As in the film, Marion is kidnapped and thrown into the back of a German truck; then, as requested by Spielberg in the story conference, Indy gives chase on a camel. He shoots at the vehicle, causing it to crash, apparently killing Marion. By the third draft, the camel chase has been excised in preference for something very similar to the final movie, with Indy chasing on foot then the truck exploding. The only major difference between the third draft and the finished picture is the inclusion of the Arab henchman showing off his impressive swordsmanship before Indy shoots him dead with one shot. Kasdan did not approve of the gag, which was improvised on location, calling it "brutal in a way the rest of the movie wasn't."[16] It is difficult to reconcile this stance with much of the violence that occurs frequently in Kasdan's screenplay, including deaths by fire, blade, and strangulation. It may be that he responded negatively to the audience reaction rather than the scene itself (he noted that it was "very popular" with viewers), but it is entirely in keeping with much of the cartoonish violence inflicted upon various Egyptians, Asians, and Germans in Kasdan's script, as well as upon the American agent.

Many of the following sequences remain similar throughout all drafts: Indy and Sallah finding the map room and calculating the Ark's resting place, then digging for the Ark itself, before Indy and Marion are entombed as the Nazis take their prize. Something that remains consistent throughout is the sense of Indiana Jones as capable but imperfect. For example, all of Kasdan's screenplay drafts describe him opening the Well of the Souls, the resting place of the Ark, after an all-night dig. He looks inside and notices what seems to be "a strange, dark carpet" on the floor. The scene text encapsulates Indy's fallibility in a few words: "He breaks off, realizing exactly what that carpet is. He blanches. Indiana Jones blanches." Then the dialogue text confirms it, calling back to that comic moment with "Reggie" the boa constrictor in the opening sequence: "Why snakes? Why did it have to be snakes?"

Indiana Jones is constantly stumbling, uncertain, lacking the supreme confidence of a Bond or a Superman. A prime example is Indy's utterance that Kasdan calls "my favorite line I ever got to write."[7] It appears completely unchanged in all available drafts plus the finished film. When Indy and Marion finally escape from the Well of the Souls, Indy says he is going to chase the German trucks transporting the Ark out of the country:

```
Marion looks at him like he's nuts. Indy jumps
up, looks around desperately.

                 MARION
          How are you going to get that
          truck?

                  INDY
             (still searching)
          I don't know. I'm making this
          up as I go.
```

In the first draft, this is followed by Indy giving chase on a stolen motorcycle, but by draft three it has become "a magnificent white stallion" as per the final movie, and an even more striking cinematic image. Besides this change of initial transport, the truck chase barely alters from draft one to five and is described in remarkable detail while remaining an entertaining read. For example, in all drafts, Kasdan writes that Indy "tears along a parallel ridge, like an Indian shadowing a wagon train." As in the fight scene in the Nepalese tavern, as well as the deleted scenes in Shanghai, there is a clear sense of geography within the hectic sequence, both in terms of the wider location and in explaining exactly where each player is in the two cars and two trucks that make up the convoy. The approach reveals a more visual storytelling style than Kasdan often receives credit for, with his work described as "irretrievably *written*."[18] In fact, Kasdan has said that what interests him most about writing movies is

Figure 2.1 Indy chases after the Ark

"the power of the images and the way you can do [things] that has nothing to do with dialogue."[19] These action scenes, largely unchanged throughout the rewrites, and followed quite faithfully by Spielberg, illustrate that point.

After retrieving the Ark, Indy and Marion board the pirate ship bound for Britain and there is an opportunity for Kasdan to write the kind of scene for which he was brought onto the project. The two leads are forced to share a cabin, and the scene, which remains unchanged from draft one to three, ends with this exchange, after Indy apologizes for burning down her bar and Marion apologizes for blowing up the plane they had hoped to escape on:

```
                    INDY
          Seem things have worked
          out kind of even.

She turns so their lips are very close.

                  MARION
          That's the way I like them.

                    INDY
          Maybe we should consider all
          past accounts closed.

Marion thinks about this for a long time.

                  MARION
          No. Not yet.
```

```
                        INDY
          What else?

    She looks into his eyes. A smile jumps from her
    lips to his. He kisses her and they sink slowly
    to the cot.
```

The final draft, however, includes a revision dated June 11, 1980 (during production) on pages eighty-three and eighty-four, in which Marion inspects Indy's numerous injuries, causing him to wince, until she asks "Where doesn't it hurt?" As Indy points to various parts of his body in turn, she kisses them, ending with a lingering kiss on his mouth. Kasdan did indeed write something like this scene, but in his script for *Continental Divide*, not *Raiders of the Lost Ark*. Soon afterward, Kasdan clarified this point in a *New York Times* interview in which he is described as "mildly amused and mildly annoyed" about claims of self-plagiarism. He confirms that Steven Spielberg took the idea from the former script (owned by Spielberg's production company) and placed it in *Raiders*, without Kasdan's approval.[20]

There are few changes between drafts one and five regarding the ensuing scenes: the Germans boarding the ship, stealing the Ark back, and taking it to a remote Mediterranean island, with Indy strapping himself to the U-boat in order to follow them. Until the third draft, the screenplay follows the sequence as outlined in the story conference: Indy and Marion escaping with the Ark on a mine car after the supernatural light causes the oil and munitions to explode. This is replaced in the fifth draft by the more pseudo-religious finale seen in the movie, something that Kasdan was glad to do because "I always hated [the island blowing up]."[21]

Again, the text in these climactic action scenes is dense, but clear and evocative. For example, when Lovar/Belloq opens the Ark:

```
    Two aspects of this ghastly, beautiful display
    are somehow communicated in the chaos, although
    the communication is subliminal. First, that
    Lovar, in the instant of his destruction, has
    experienced some kind of sublime, transcenden-
    tal knowledge. If a death's-head can smile and
    look satisfied, that is how Lovar's incandescent
    face would be described. Secondly, this event
    is accompanied by a sound like no other. A sound
    so intense and so odd and so haunting that the
    suggestible among us might imagine it were the
    whisper of God.
```

Aside from the name change, this description would remain through all five drafts, and it contributes to a fluid, absorbing read, as well as acting as a practical tool that conveys invaluable information to the performer, cinematographer, sound designer, and effects department. More importantly, while parts of the passage are somewhat abstract, the prose is so rich and expressive that the reader would have little difficulty imagining how it would play in the movie, an iconic audiovisual moment that feels as vivid on the page as it would eventually appear on the screen.

CO-CREATOR OF *RAIDERS OF THE LOST ARK*

In writing the screenplay for *Raiders of the Lost Ark*, Lawrence Kasdan was allowed remarkable freedom by his more experienced creative partners, and this analysis suggests that he was able to influence numerous elements that would be present in the film. In the story conference, George Lucas had said that the picture must be "totally believable," yet Steven Spielberg tended toward a more cartoonish tone, calling the opening sequence "a real horror ride, like a Disneyland ride." Kasdan's script manages to reconcile these two approaches, creating sufficient verisimilitude to keep the stakes high, while injecting humor that feels congruous within the heightened story world. Lucas's original models for *Raiders* were James Bond, the Spaghetti Westerns, and, most directly, the Republic adventure serials of the 1930s. Kasdan employs aspects of each, but rather than simply imitate, he pays homage while creating something completely original, a big-budget action picture that is at once slick and ramshackle. The archetypal protagonists and antagonists are given credibility through their interactions, following Kasdan's maxim that people can only be "illuminated by contrast,"[22] and the far-fetched plot is made plausible through exposition scenes that convey the necessary information, even as they build tension and reveal aspects of character.

I argue, too, that the screenplay for *Raiders of the Lost Ark* possesses literary value in its own right; but rather than detracting from its practical worth, the dense, engaging prose would aid Kasdan's collaborators in creating the final picture. There is a seat-of-the-pants physicality in the language that clearly affects the dynamism of the film, eventually influencing the action-adventure genre as other filmmakers attempted to emulate the pace and wit of *Raiders*. Lawrence Kasdan's screenplay, then, contributed significantly to shaping one of the most beloved American films of the twentieth century, and twenty-five years later it would be voted one of the Writers Guild of America's "101 Greatest Screenplays."[23] Furthermore, it foreshadowed Lawrence Kasdan's subsequent career transition, in which his aptitude for stylistic, visually driven storytelling would play a major part in his debut as writer-director.

NOTES

1. Lawrence Kasdan, quoted in J.W. Rinzler, *The Complete Making of Indiana Jones* (London: Ebury, 2008), 25.
2. Kasdan, *Raiders of the Lost Ark*, screenplay, 1st draft, June 15, 1978.
3. Kasdan, *Raiders of the Lost Ark*, screenplay, revised 5th draft, April 1980.
4. Kasdan, *Raiders of the Lost Ark*, screenplay, 3rd draft, revised through August 3, 1979.
5. While this chapter focuses mainly upon visual aspects, in a separate essay I discuss how the screenplay affected characterization and the actors' performances in *Raiders*. See Brett Davies, "Characterization, Dialogue and Performance in Lawrence Kasdan's Screenplay for *Raiders of the Lost Ark*," *Bloomsbury Handbook of Global Screenplay Theory* (London: Bloomsbury, forthcoming).
6. The delineation of scene text and dialogue text is borrowed from the works of Claudia Sternberg and Steven Price, and it is a simple but useful prism through which to examine the different aspects of a script. Sternberg in particular uses this paradigm to argue for the screenplay as both a dramatic and narrative medium, suggesting that it can stand as a text in its own right. See Sternberg, *Written for the Screen: The American Motion-Picture Screenplay as Text* (Tübingen, Germany: Stauffenberg, 1997), 26–7; and Price, *The Screenplay: Authorship, Theory and Criticism* (Hampshire, UK: Palgrave Macmillan, 2010), 112–66.
7. Sternberg, *Written for Screen*, 26–7.
8. Osip Brik, "From the Theory and Practice of the Screenwriter" (trans. D. Matias), *Screen: The Journal of the Society for Education in Film and Television* 15, no. 3 (1974 [original article, 1936]), 96.
9. Kasdan's talent for writing dialogue is highlighted by Stephen Prince, *A New Pot of Gold: Hollywood under the Electronic Rainbow, 1980–1989* (New York: Charles Scribner's Sons, 2000), 256.
10. Sternberg, *Written for Screen*, 66 and 73–5.
11. For further analysis of these deleted scenes, see Davies, "Characterization, dialogue."
12. The idea was discussed at length in the story conference. In his *Raiders* first draft, Kasdan has the crew and several passengers, including "a chubby Little Old Lady" who "smiles cheerily" when Indy boards, parachute from the plane as he sleeps. It was deleted by draft three, but a very similar sequence would be realized in the sequel, *Indiana Jones and the Temple of Doom*.
13. Warren Buckland, "A Close Encounter with *Raiders of the Lost Ark*: Notes on Narrative Aspects of the New Hollywood Blockbuster," in *Contemporary Hollywood Cinema*, edited by Steve Neale and Murray Smith (New York: Routledge, 1998), 173.
14. George Lucas, commentary, *Return of the Jedi*, DVD (20th Century Fox), 2004.
15. Steven Spielberg, quoted in Sven Mikulec, "*Raiders of the Lost Ark*: Lucas and Spielberg's Epitome of Action-Adventure Films Still Waiting to be Surpassed," *Cinephilia and Beyond*, undated, https://cinephiliabeyond.org/raiders-lost-ark-lucas-spielbergs-epitome-action-adventure-films-still-waiting-surpassed/ (accessed June 30, 2023).
16. Kasdan, quoted in Joseph McBride, *Steven Spielberg: A Biography*, 2nd ed. (Jackson: University Press of Mississippi, 2010), 317.
17. Kasdan, interviewed by John August and Craig Mazin, "Episode 247: The One with Lawrence Kasdan," *Scriptnotes*, audio podcast, April 26, 2016, http://johnaugust.com/2016/the-one-with-lawrence-kasdan (accessed June 29, 2023).
18. Eric Hynes, "The Other America: Revisiting Lawrence Kasdan's *Grand Canyon*," *The Village Voice*, April 18, 2012, <http://www.villagevoice.com/film/the-other-america-revisiting-lawrence-kasdans-grand-canyon-6434596 (accessed June 30, 2023). Original emphasis.
19. Kasdan, interviewed by August and Mazin, "Episode 247."

20. Aljean Harmetz, "How He Became Hollywood's Hot Writer," *The New York Times*, November 1, 1981, http://www.nytimes.com/1981/11/01/movies/how-he-became-hollywood-s-hot-writer.html?pagewanted=all (accessed June 30, 2023).

21. Kasdan, quoted in Rinzler, *Making Indiana Jones*, 49.

22. Kasdan, interviewed by August and Mazin, "Episode 247."

23. The full list of the "101 Greatest Screenplays," compiled in 2005, can be found at http://www.wga.org/writers-room/101-best-lists/101-greatest-screenplays (accessed June 30, 2023).

PART II

Kasdan the Director: Developing Style(s)

CHAPTER 3

Body Heat: Heightened Style in the Neo-Noir

In the words of William Goldman, the screenplays for *The Empire Strikes Back* and *Raiders of the Lost Ark* established Lawrence Kasdan as American cinema's "best young screenwriter."[1] However, Kasdan says that "I had always had a scheme. [. . .] It took me seven years to sell anything, and yet the goal is not to sell anything. It's to become such a hot writer that they're going to make you a director."

This chapter and the next will examine Kasdan's first two pictures as director, establishing which filmmaking techniques he employed and with what intention. Of course, as he also wrote the screenplays, it is pertinent to discuss the films both in terms of directorial style and narrative form. To achieve this, I will adopt a neo-formalist approach, specifically employing David Bordwell's notion of "historical poetics," in which visual style is analyzed in tandem with story and plot.[2] The section begins, then, with a brief summary of the neo-formalist paradigms, before applying them to *Body Heat* and *The Big Chill*, two very different films.

CINEMATIC FORM

By the time production began on *Body Heat*, Lawrence Kasdan had already sold his original scripts for *The Bodyguard* and *Continental Divide*, as well as writing *Raiders of the Lost Ark* and the Star Wars sequel, *The Empire Strikes Back*. All these screenplays conformed to the parameters of classical Hollywood storytelling, and Kasdan was aware of his predilection for classicism, saying: "Once I was on the inside, I asked myself, *Why am I doing so well?* I realized that I was satisfying [the demand for] classic dramatic structure that had been lost in Hollywood, and that made me valuable."[3]

According to David Bordwell and Kristin Thompson, the preeminent exponents of neo-formalism, classical Hollywood narratives usually feature "individual characters as causal agents," with these characters displaying "desire" that will establish a goal. Within a classical narrative film there is a series of "appointments" and "deadlines" motivating characters toward fulfilling their desires, and this will affect some kind of "change" in the story world until, finally, there is "closure."[4] In addition, Bordwell and Thompson argue that Hollywood films tend to have "a basically 'objective' story reality, against which various degrees of perceptual and mental subjectivity [of the characters] can be measured."[5] Perhaps the easiest way to understand this concept is to consider a film that does not follow the "objective" principles of classical Hollywood narrative. *Rashomon* (1950) is arguably the most famous example, as it re-tells the same incident subjectively from the perspectives of various characters, leaving the audience uncertain of any objective truth. As Lawrence Kasdan has often professed his regard for the films of Akira Kurosawa (as will be discussed in Chapter 7), then it is by no means a given that he should lean toward the classical Hollywood form of storytelling, let alone build a career upon it.

Bordwell states that any film narrative is supported by two systems: *syuzhet* and style. Syuzhet (often translated as "plot") was a term coined by the early-twentieth-century Russian formalists such as Propp and Shklovsky to describe the way in which the *fabula* ("story") is presented and arranged.[6] According to Bordwell, while "the fabula embodies the action as a chronological, cause-and-effect chain of events occurring within a given duration and a spatial field," the syuzhet is what guides the audience to comprehend the fabula.[7] To take an example from Lawrence Kasdan's screenwriting *oeuvre*, the syuzhet of *Raiders of the Lost Ark* introduces the viewer to Indiana Jones through the opening sequence in Peru, before he returns to the US, and is approached by Washington agents who tell him about the Nazis' search for the Ark of the Covenant. Then Indy embarks on his quest, eventually leading to the opening of the Ark, before the syuzhet, or plot, ends with the Ark being hidden away in a huge warehouse. From this syuzhet, the viewer uses, to quote Bordwell, "prototype schemata (identifiable types of persons, actions, locales, et cetera), template schemata (the 'canonic' story), and procedural schemata (a search for appropriate motivations and relations of causality, time, and space)" to construct a fabula, a timeline of events in the order that they "actually" occurred.[8] So, based on the events that we see in the final screenplay or film, we might infer that the fabula of *Raiders* begins with Hitler ordering his army to search the desert for the Ark of the Covenant; then the Germans' unsuccessful excavation efforts (none of which appear in the film itself but are vital to the story). Only then do we come to Indy's adventures in Peru, and the opening sequence of the film's syuzhet. The forming of a fabula, then, is a progressive and retroactive process that, Bordwell states, "requires us to construct the story [. . .] while at the same time framing and testing hypotheses about past events,"[9] such as when Marion apparently dies in a truck explosion after being kidnapped in a basket, as the syuzhet of *Raiders* leads us to believe, before we discover that she has been kept alive. At this point in the film, Indy says "[t]hey must have switched baskets," and we are guided to change our perception of what occurred earlier in the story. This example illustrates how the syuzhet does not simply lay out the fabula before the viewer; instead, it can manipulate our understanding of events through deliberate retardation of information, and by creating gaps in the fabula that may be filled later. It is a dramaturgical construct, then, that prompts us to assemble the story in—the filmmakers would hope—satisfying ways; and one that Kasdan would utilize repeatedly in his own work.

In defining "style," here I will use Bordwell's definition as a "film's systematic use of cinematic devices." He differentiates this from the other common use of the word "style" to discuss recurrent techniques in a filmmaker's body of work; instead, in this context, "style" describes "a steady flow of applications of cinematic techniques" used in a particular film. Bordwell states that a movie's style is usually subservient to the syuzhet, employing camera angles and movements, editing, music, sound design, and mise-en-scène in ways that impart the syuzhet to the viewer, inviting them to construct the fabula.[10]

The analyses in this chapter and the next will follow Bordwell and Thompson's formalist approach by exploring ways in which the styles of *Body Heat* and *The Big Chill*—Lawrence Kasdan's first two movies as writer-director—interact with the syuzhet in order to create engaging, but quite different, film narratives.

THE NEO-NOIR

Following his work with George Lucas and Steven Spielberg, Lawrence Kasdan was receiving numerous offers to become a writer-for-hire on other directors' projects. However, he decided to reject these advances in order to make his own film, realizing the goal when George Lucas agreed to sponsor Kasdan's first feature, offering a quarter of a million dollars as guarantee against overages. This encouraged Alan Ladd Jr., a former Fox executive and ally of Lucas's who was instrumental in greenlighting *Star Wars* (1977), to finance *Body Heat* with Kasdan as director.[11]

Until that point, Lawrence Kasdan's screenplays had been heavily influenced by classic Hollywood, and his directorial debut continued this approach, the script for *Body Heat* drawing inspiration from *Out of the Past* (1947), *Murder, My Sweet* (1944) and *Double Indemnity* (1944).[12] In mimicking and subverting the conventions of 1940s noir, *Body Heat* could more accurately be labeled neo-noir. Steve Neale, in his book on Hollywood genres, includes in this category those films made from the mid-1960s onward which "relate to or draw upon the notion, the image and the putative conventions of *film noir*."[13] The screenplay of *Body Heat* clearly conforms to Neale's neo-noir parameters, with the erotic undercurrent and the imperfect male lead unable to escape the charms of a classic femme fatale.

Additionally, Kasdan injects the script with directions for costume and production design that highlight the out-of-time, noirish tone he clearly intends to evoke: Matty presenting the hapless male lead Ned Racine with a 1940s-style fedora hat; and the description of Matty's house that has "the look of an affluent home of Thirties America."[14]

Ronald Schwartz adds further layers to the definition of neo-noir stating that, unlike classic noir, "there are many plot twists that dazzle and leave the audience limp and breathless."[15] This is certainly the case in *Body Heat*, with its series of revelations in the final scenes that change the audience's perception of the fabula completely. Furthermore, Schwartz suggests that societal changes, post-McCarthy, Vietnam, and Watergate, led to differences in the representation of men and women in noir. By the 1980s, the femme fatale could be victorious:

> Ned Racine's betrayal is classic, a pure noir experience because viewers watch his downfall. What makes *Body Heat* a true neo-noir film are its use of color and CinemaScope, the femme fatale cleverer than every male (or female) who crosses her path, and her triumph over everyone.[16]

Kasdan's screenplay falls into Borde and Chaumeton's paradigm for classic film noir, too, as the sweaty Florida heatwave makes possible the strange, oneiric quality; while the plot is cruel, erotic, and ambivalent, as often displayed through dialogue that is heightened nearly to the point of parody.[17] For example, when Racine is still attempting to seduce Matty:

```
                MATTY
            (laughs)
      Yes. My temperature runs a
      couple degrees high. Around 100
      all the time I don't mind it.
      It's the engine or something.


                RACINE
      Maybe you need a tune-up.


                MATTY
      Don't tell me - you have just
      the right tool.


                RACINE
      I don't talk that way.[18]
```

The syuzhet of the screenplay reveals aspects of the fabula in what first appears quite linear fashion, told almost exclusively from Racine's perspective.

However, in the tradition of the crime story, the fabula will eventually be revealed as something quite different from what we—through Racine's point of view—are first led to believe. Unlike most films in the classical Hollywood mode, such crime stories tend toward a more restricted narration, "controlling knowledge, self-consciousness, and communicativeness [to] create curiosity about past story events [. . .], suspense about upcoming events, and surprise with respect to unexpected disclosures."[19] Thus, while being more restricted and subjective than many classic Hollywood films, according to Bordwell and Thompson's paradigms,[20] *Body Heat*'s narrative remains "classic" in the tradition of other crime and detective films produced by Hollywood studios.

VISUAL STYLE IN *BODY HEAT*

A contemporary essay in *Film Comment* on *Body Heat* uses the word "stylized" three times in the first paragraph alone. It then discusses camera movement at length, stating that "lap dissolves and gliding camera moves shave off the sharp edges" of its densely packed sequences, and "[t]he images have a rounded feeling of completeness."[21] Later in the article, its writer David Chute comments on the subjectivity of the film, which tallies closely with Bordwell and Thompson's notion of the restricted narration prevalent in crime pictures, discussed above. Chute suggests that the subjectivity is a result not only of the syuzhet as written in the screenplay, but also of the style of the finished movie:

> Watching the movie for the first time you're likely to read its events precisely as William Hurt's befogged protagonist does. [. . .] Kasdan's camera never assumes a subjective POV, but it's very responsive to Ned's moods. It pans off in the direction of his gaze; tracks toward a seductive woman as if empathizing with his lust; swoops down solicitously when a hot gust of emotion courses through him. And yet this sympathetic, almost subjective camera is also in cahoots with Kathleen Turner's bristly femme fatale.[22]

This sense of subjectivity is emphasized by the very first shot, after the audience is primed for the noirishness of the film through its atmospheric opening title sequence: oblique, nebulous images of fire, silk, and a woman's naked body, under credits printed in an art deco font. As John Barry's sultry saxophone theme fades, replaced by the wail of police sirens, there is a thirteen-second static shot of Ned Racine (Hurt) watching an old restaurant burn in the distance (Figure 3.1).

The film cuts to the reverse (Figure 3.2), another static shot looking into Racine's bedroom, lasting twelve seconds.

Figure 3.1 The opening shot: smoke and sweat

Figure 3.2 The reverse shot: the lover partially obscured

It is a simple opening to the movie, and rather at odds with what is to follow: the "gliding camera moves" and "swoops" employed by Kasdan's cinematographer Richard H. Kline.[23] It is also quite different in execution from the opening of Kasdan's screenplay, which asks for a camera that pulls back from an exterior shot of town to the interior of Racine's apartment, then moves through rooms, all in a single take.

While these directorial choices may have been made for logistical or technical reasons —two static shots presumably easier to complete than one continuous take as described in the script—they create an atmosphere of stifling closeness, and they reveal many of the themes that the movie would return to repeatedly. There is the orange smoke bellowing from a fire that, according to Racine, has been started deliberately "to clear the lot" and was probably done by one of his clients. This gives us a glimpse into the seediness of his world as a small-town lawyer, and more specifically hints at the crime that he would later commit: burning a body in a fire. With echoes of the title sequence, the smoke—and Racine's fixation on it—possesses a sensuality that portends the events to come. Then the reverse shot into Racine's bedroom (Figure 3.2) develops this notion with the image of a woman dressing after sex, the crumpled bedsheets, and the ineffectual electric fan. Racine remains narcissistically still, the sweat dripping from his body, barely noticing as Angela (Lynn Hallowell) readies to leave.

Kasdan's choice of showing the protagonist off-center in the frame will be repeated in later films, but what makes this shot interesting is the positioning of Angela at the very edge of the picture, while most of the shot is taken up with the bed and fan. In fact, we only catch passing glimpses of Angela's face in this scene, suggesting that she is of little importance to Racine, or to the movie. The relatively long duration of these shots is representative of the entire film. The average take in *Body Heat* lasts 10.7 seconds, much longer than the average for contemporary releases. Such languid pacing could be viewed simply as aesthetic, enabling Kasdan the director to employ the pans and camera swoops that give the picture such a recognizable visual style. However, it also serves two narrative functions: it contributes to the sense of oppressive heat that causes things to go, as Oscar the cop (J.A. Preston) puts it, "just a little askew;" and it allows the audience to fully appreciate Racine's emotional state, as if Kasdan is daring his leading man to blink under pressure. *Body Heat* includes four shots lasting longer than eighty seconds, and each of these comes at a pivotal emotional moment for Racine: when he finally finds Matty for the second time in her local bar, an apparent victory after a long search; when he is uncharacteristically coy about his new lover with his friends Lowenstein (Ted Danson) and Oscar, just after Matty makes him promise not to tell anyone about their relationship; when Matty expresses her fear of her husband, and Racine begins to formulate a plan to get rid of him; and when Lowenstein tells him of Matty's niece's testimony about seeing a "guy" with her aunt, a statement that could have incriminated Racine if the girl had remembered more accurately. In each of these shots, actor William Hurt expresses the changes in Racine's emotional state through subtle eye movements that may not be as apparent in a scene with multiple cuts.

These long-lasting shots also showcase Lawrence Kasdan's (and cinematographer Richard H. Kline's) talent for composition. For example, the scene in the diner, in which Racine refuses to divulge any information about his lover, starts with a close-up of Lowenstein's fingers "dancing" on the counter before he is handed two sweating glasses of iced tea. He swigs one greedily, reminding the viewer of the heat, then he carries these along the counter, the camera panning out so that we can see his face as he stops briefly to exchange pleasantries with a policeman eating his lunch. Lowenstein then joins Racine at a table and

Figure 3.3 The cop ever-present in the background

the camera becomes static. What would be a conventional two-shot (becoming a three-shot when they are joined by Oscar, with Stella the waitress [Jane Hallaren] an occasional participant) is injected with extra dynamism by the use of deep focus, within which the uniformed police officer is constantly visible (Figure 3.3). It is an element not featured in the screenplay explicitly, besides a mention of the "courthouse/cop crowd" in the initial scene description, but it provides both a realistic function (the diner is next to a courthouse, so police officers would likely frequent it) and a metaphorical one, representing the precarious situation in which Racine is becoming entwined. Kasdan's visual style in *Body Heat*, therefore, contributes to the syuzhet, allowing the audience to use a prototype schema (in this instance, the constant presence of a cop) alongside the template and procedural schemata in order to construct a fabula, an understanding of the story being told.

David Chute states that "Kasdan's camera never assumes a subjective POV,"[24] yet it comes very close when introducing the character of Matty (Kathleen Turner). The camera follows Racine as he buys a drink then takes it outside and leans against a fence to watch the band. He stands off-center in the foreground, a composition that recalls the opening shots of the film (Figures 3.1 and 3.2). This time, though, rather than a distant inferno or a barely visible lover, the background element is much clearer: as the orchestra on-stage plays a laid-back jazz tune, the camera focuses on a woman leaving her seat and walking toward Racine (Figure 3.4). Her confident catwalk stride and her pristine white dress make her stand out from the rows of beige-clad spectators fanning themselves in the heat. Racine's gaze is emphasized further by the camera focusing away from him and onto Matty.

As noted previously, Bordwell and Thompson discuss the more restricted narration of detective films,[25] and Kasdan accentuates this subjectivity in *Body*

Figure 3.4 Matty revealed from Racine's point of view

Heat, not only through Racine's almost total presence in the screenplay and movie, but also through the composition of shots such as this: the audience is receiving information not as omniscient "outside" viewers, but at the same time as the protagonist.

Chute adds that the camera "is also in cahoots with Kathleen Turner's bristly femme fatale."[26] While I disagree with this statement for the most part, Kasdan employs a similar composition in reverse during those scenes in which Matty is showing (or faking) her vulnerability. For example, when expressing her fear of being caught cheating on her husband, she asks Racine not to tell anyone about their relationship. As she begs him, "Promise me," the camera looks over her shoulder (Figure 3.5). The viewer, then, is allied briefly with Matty, now apparently in the subservient role while Racine stands insouciantly, his arms folded as he teases her for her over-cautiousness. The scene works as a further example of the visual style, not present in the script, serving the syuzhet and drawing the audience toward a fabula that will later be subverted.

The placement of the "viewer" in the weaker position, while the "viewed" exudes power, is taken further by the movie's sweeping camera movements. These serve a story function in reminding the audience of its position as "viewer," thus, according to the form of this film, at a disadvantage to those in the more dominant "viewed" position. There are echoes here of much of Alfred Hitchcock's work, in which he would employ unconventional camera movements (often through windows) that would force the viewer into becoming a "voyeur." In his monograph on *Rear Window* (1954), John Fawell summarizes previous critics' reading of Hitchcock, in which the director "cultivates a voyeurism in his audience and then punishes them for that voyeurism." In *Rear Window*, Fawell writes, Hitchcock "inculcates a complicity between the audience and Jeff [the central protagonist] while at the same time encouraging

Figure 3.5 Matty shows vulnerability

us not to trust him."[27] Similarly, the camera set-ups in Kasdan's *Body Heat* invite the audience to "peep" at these people, to both empathize with them and judge them. One way that it achieves this is through establishing what Buckland calls an "off-screen presence," as mentioned in Chapter 2. In discussing *Raiders of the Lost Ark*, Buckland states that the film "is operating within a norm that confers definite value to on-screen and off-screen space." In the case of *Raiders*, this off-screen space, and the "presence" of an off-screen character, is created by placing the camera in a "hidden" position just behind jungle foliage or a wooden pillar, suggesting that somebody is watching the on-screen space while trying to remain out of sight themselves. As discussed in Chapter 2, Buckland argues that the off-screen presences in *Raiders* are finally revealed to be diegetic characters.[28] In *Body Heat*, though, these off-screen presences remain unattributed (within the story world, nobody is watching the on-screen characters), yet the placement of the camera in partially obscured positions (Figure 3.6; like Hitchcock, peering through windows) invites the audience to assume the dual role of both viewer and participant. The tension is heightened subliminally, the characters' affair and murder apparently open to exposure at any moment.

Similarly, the audience becomes an off-screen presence in the film's denouement, as Racine, now in prison, begins to piece together the extent of Matty's schemes. Not only is the camera positioned in a partially obscured field, behind bars, but Racine even seems to speak directly to the camera/audience when he has his epiphany: "She's alive."

Body Heat self-consciously references previous works of film noir, playing within what Fredric Jameson calls the "nostalgia mode"[29] with all the stylistic qualities of the genre present. However, Kasdan does more than simply mimic existing films. Even as he employs established noir tropes in narrative

Figure 3.6 The camera peers through windows

Figure 3.7 Obscured behind bars

construction (with its restricted, subjective point of view), mise-en-scène (the costumes and sets not out of place in the 1940s, despite its 1980s setting), and visual style (stark contrasts between light and dark), Kasdan develops and subverts these to make a film that is unique rather than derivative. The distinctive visual style of *Body Heat* is created by careful blocking of scenes, longer-than-average shot duration, foreground-background juxtapositions, and swooping camera shots. In utilizing these techniques, Lawrence Kasdan evokes an atmosphere of eroticism, guilt, and suspicion; he also establishes and subverts power dynamics between the characters; and he reminds viewers of their own roles as voyeur-participants. The formal style of *Body Heat*, then, is not only aesthetic; it simultaneously serves the syuzhet in guiding the audience to understanding the fabula, which, in the tradition of classic Hollywood crime and detective films, is repeatedly realigned through restricted narration, the "objective" truth only fully revealed at the movie's climax.

NOTES

1. William Goldman, *Adventures in the Screen Trade: A Personal View of Hollywood* (London: Macdonald, 1984), 37.
2. David Bordwell, *Making Meaning: Inference and Rhetoric in the Interpretation of Cinema* (Cambridge, MA: Harvard University Press, 1989), 270–1.
3. Lawrence Kasdan, quoted in Rose Eichenbaum, *The Director Within: Storytellers of Stage and Screen* (Middletown, CT: Wesleyan University Press, 2014), 240. Original emphasis and parentheses.
4. Bordwell and Kristin Thompson, *Film Art: An Introduction*, 6th ed. (New York: McGraw Hill, 2001), 76–7. While *The Empire Strikes Back* does not have complete closure, it still follows all other criteria for classical Hollywood narration. Furthermore, as the middle film of the original Star Wars trilogy, there was an expectation at the time that the subsequent and final episode, *Return of the Jedi* (1983, also co-written by Kasdan), would complete the story in a classical way. See Chapters 9 and 10 for further analyses of these screenplays.
5. Ibid., 77.
6. See, for example, Vladimir Propp, *Morphology of the Folk Tale*, translated by L. Scott, 2nd ed. (Austin: University of Texas Press, 2009).
7. Bordwell, *Narration in the Fiction Film* (Oxon: Routledge, 1985), 49–50.
8. Ibid., 49. Original parentheses.
9. Ibid.
10. Ibid., 50–2.
11. Alex Simon, "Chillin' Big with Lawrence Kasdan," *The Hollywood Interview*, December 3, 2012, http://thehollywoodinterview.blogspot.com/2008/03/lawrence-kasdan-hollywood-interview.html (accessed June 30, 2023).
12. See Dan Yakir, "Lawrence Kasdan Interviewed," *Film Comment* 17, no. 5 (1981), 53–4; Roger Ebert, "*Body Heat*," *Roger Ebert*, July 20, 1997, http://www.rogerebert.com/reviews/great-movie-body-heat-1981 (accessed June 30, 2023); Ronald Schwartz, *Noir, Now and Then: Film Noir Originals and Remakes (1944–1999)* (Westport, CT: Greenwood, 2001), xii.
13. Steve Neale, *Genre and Hollywood* (New York: Routledge, 2000), 165. Original emphasis.
14. Kasdan, *Body Heat*, screenplay, 3rd draft, October 6, 1980, 18.
15. Schwartz, *Noir, Now and Then*, 6.
16. Ibid.
17. Raymond Borde and Etienne Chaumeton, *Panorama du film noir américain 1941–1953 (A Panorama of American Film Noir 1941–1953)*, translated by P. Hammond (San Francisco: City Lights Books, 1955 [Reprint, 2002]), 2.
18. Kasdan, *Body Heat*, 15.
19. Bordwell, *Narration*, 65.
20. Bordwell and Thompson, *Film Art*, 77.
21. David Chute, "Tropic of Kasdan," *Film Comment* 17, no. 5 (1981), 49.
22. Chute, "Tropic," 51.
23. Ibid., 49 and 51.
24. Chute, "Tropic," 51.
25. Bordwell and Thompson, *Film Art*, 77.
26. Chute, "Tropic," 51.
27. John Fawell, *Hitchcock's Rear Window: The Well-Made Film* (Carbondale and Edwardsville: Southern Illinois University Press, 2001), 5 and 10.

28. Warren Buckland, *Directed by Steven Spielberg: Poetics of the Contemporary Hollywood Blockbuster* (New York: Continuum, 2006), 146–8.
29. Fredric Jameson has written extensively about the "nostalgia mode," citing Kasdan's work specifically in his seminal essay: *Postmodernism, or, The Cultural Logic of Multinational Capitalism* (Durham, NC: Duke University Press, 1991), 21. Additionally, Christopher Orr cites the nostalgia mode in reference to *Body Heat* in "Cain, naturalism and noir," *Film Criticism* 25, no. 1 (2000), 62.

CHAPTER 4

Classical Structure in the "Perfect Ensemble" of *The Big Chill*

In spite of *Body Heat*'s impressive box-office performance, Lawrence Kasdan had difficulty attracting finance for his next film. With Barbara Benedek, he co-wrote a screenplay about a weekend reunion of old college friends, but, he says, "No-one wanted to make an ensemble film. [. . .] When I presented [producers] with a movie that had eight protagonists, they were only confused."[1]

Eventually produced by talk-show host Johnny Carson's fledgling company, *The Big Chill* would become a critical and financial success, and it remains the most profitable of all Kasdan's movies as writer-director. Far from handicapping the film, the multi-protagonist approach became its central selling point, with the theatrical poster promising: "The story of eight old friends searching for something they lost, and finding that all they needed was each other."[2]

The dynamic between the seven protagonists (or eight if including Chloe, the interloper in the group of old college friends) was discussed in the majority of contemporary reviews. *The Big Chill* was described as "so perfect an example of ensemble playing,"[3] with "an octet of exceptional, perfectly balanced performers."[4] Another review, while criticizing the film for having "no real meat, no depth," praises the "cast of attractive, talented performers" and says that "none gives a bad performance." Despite his reservations, the same critic calls the film "unusual [. . .] in that it attempts to focus on characterization."[5]

In narrative terms, *The Big Chill* seems quite different from *Body Heat*. Kasdan's directorial debut, as demonstrated above, conforms faithfully to the neo-noir genre in a classical storytelling mode, its carefully constructed plot deliberately misdirecting the audience until its final, satisfying reveal. *The Big Chill*, though, has been perceived very differently by critics. According to Stephen Prince, the film "seems very casual in its structure, with loosely connected and seemingly improvised scenes."[6] Kim Newman's contemporary review states that the script is "virtually plotless" and "barely acknowledges the need for any plot elements."[7] Kasdan himself seems to confirm this, stating that

Jean Renoir's *La Règle du jeu/The Rules of the Game* (1939) was a major influence, explaining that "it's about so many things, and evokes so many feelings."[8] *The Big Chill* certainly seems a departure from the "conventional, classic dramatic structure" Kasdan says he was taught in college.[9] However, Kasdan later suggested that his first two films as writer-director actually share thematic, if not necessarily structural, traits:

> Ned Racine in *Body Heat* could have been one of my friends, one of the guys for whom things came easily, he wasn't that smart, and suddenly things get harder, and he gives into a lot of temptation. *The Big Chill* is a much more realistic treatment of the same theme.[10]

There was disagreement among contemporary reviewers about the visual storytelling style in *The Big Chill*. The *Hollywood Reporter* wrote: "For anyone who remembers favorably Lawrence Kasdan's visually exciting, richly textured *Body Heat, The Big Chill* can only be a keen disappointment."[11] Conversely, *The New York Times* noted that "'The Big Chill,' like 'Body Heat,' demonstrates that [Kasdan] is a writer who works as much through images as through words," adding that the film "is packed with frequently witty visual information that sometimes contradicts and sometimes supports what the characters say about themselves."[12]

This section, therefore, will explore whether the less obviously generic film, *The Big Chill*, utilizes a similar style to the deliberately referential *Body Heat*, and whether this style contributes to the audience's understanding of the fabula. Furthermore, it will examine the style and syuzhet relationship to establish if the film really is "virtually plotless" or whether, like Kasdan's other films as writer or director at that stage of his career, it conforms to classical Hollywood narrative norms as defined by Bordwell and Thompson, with "objective" truths, relationships between "appointments" and "deadlines," and story "closure."[13]

VISUAL STYLE IN *THE BIG CHILL*

The Big Chill is often referred to as an "ensemble" film.[14] Indeed, a computer analysis of 500 American screenplays confirms this, with the researchers stating that: "We have yet to find another 'ensemble' or 'multi-character' screenplay with such a tight range of presence levels for this many characters."[15] However, the movie begins in such a way that through visual composition we are led to view one character as the central protagonist. The opening shot is a close-up of a young boy in the bath (played by Kasdan's son and future writing partner, Jonathan). The shot cuts to another close-up of his father Harold (Kevin Kline), who is bathing him. When the telephone rings, Harold looks up. The scene cuts to a reverse shot reminiscent of the opening of *Body Heat*, with Harold in the foreground, off-center, while his wife Sarah (Glenn Close) speaks on the phone (Figure 4.1). Even as Sarah reacts to receiving bad news, the scene is shown from Harold's perspective.

The opening credits montage comes next, in which a series of short shots (mostly static close-ups) introduces us to the other six major characters, plus a well-dressed man whose face we do not see. This prepares us for the ensemble piece that is to follow. But, after the sequence ends with a close-up revealing that the besuited character is in fact a body being prepared for its funeral, the music fades out and the film has its second "opening" shot. As if responding to the claustrophobia of the tight montage images, the camera shows a wide vista of a gray sky over a rural fall landscape. Director of photography John Bailey has the camera tilt down to reveal Harold, again, in the foreground and off-center, again (Figure 4.2). It is a quiet shot symbolizing Harold's reverie.

Figure 4.1 The opening scene: Sarah and Harold

Figure 4.2 Harold's reverie

The camera holds still for approximately nine seconds as Harold turns around; then, in a precisely choreographed crane move, the single shot follows him, and we see that he is in a church parking lot (Figure 4.3). He then waves vehicles into parking spaces as they arrive, subtly placing him in the role of leader, even in this apparently egalitarian piece (Figure 4.4).

This single shot gives far more information than is contained in the screenplay, which says, simply: "Near the entry drive [. . .] stands Harold, directing traffic, as much from nervous energy as actual need."[16] Thus, like in *Body Heat*, the placement and movement of the camera—the visual style—contribute to the syuzhet, informing the audience that Harold is the central protagonist, even if the screenplay is less explicit and computer analysis shows similar presence levels for most characters.[17] Furthermore, this visual placement of Harold at the center of the story affects the audience's understanding of the fabula: it

Figure 4.3 Harold turns toward the camera

Figure 4.4 Harold waves cars into the lot

leads the viewer to presume an especially intimate bond between Harold and his deceased friend, Alex, before the later revelation that Alex had slept with Harold's wife. This deliberate use of restricted narration echoes that found in the crime story of *Body Heat*, and it permits the surprising reveals and causal events that occur later: our realization that Alex had slept with Sarah, then Sarah asking Harold to have sex with Meg. The last development is apparently an act of kindness toward Meg, who is desperate for a baby but has struggled to find a suitable partner; but it also works as an emotional release for Harold, based on his affectionate exchange with Sarah the next morning, offering some sense of closure to that storyline.

The accusation that *The Big Chill* is, in visual terms, "a keen disappointment" after *Body Heat*[18] may stem from its more realistic tone when compared to the heightened, deliberately melodramatic fabula at the center of Kasdan's earlier film. Certainly, there are fewer ostentatious camera movements at key emotional points, like when the audience is made to feel as if it is running after Racine in *Body Heat* as he smashes a chair through a window in order to have sex with Matty the first time. Such camera moves would, of course, be entirely out of place in the lower-key drama of *The Big Chill*. There are, though, interesting visual techniques employed to reveal aspects of individual characters, as well as dynamics within the group. As mentioned above, the opening titles sequence shows a montage of the main characters as they react to the same bad news that Sarah had received over the phone in the pre-credits scene. The montage lasts three minutes and a quarter, and it very economically tells us about the ensemble, not only through performances but also through visual cues created by camera movement and mise-en-scène. For example, when Karen (JoBeth Williams) is shown, we first see only her left hand in extreme close-up (Figure 4.5). It is next to a phone, suggesting that she has just received a call, but now her fingers (complete with a large diamond wedding ring) absent-mindedly rim the edge of an ornate bone-china teacup. As Roger Ebert observed in his contemporary review, "the camera is extremely attentive to details of body language,"[19] and this shot, lasting just over one second, already reveals a lot: Karen is married and, we presume, financially comfortable, but she is utterly stunned by the news she has just heard. This hypothesis is confirmed as we see a reverse shot, a medium-close-up of her sitting at a kitchen counter wearing a preppy tennis sweater. She rests her head on her hands forlornly, and the camera pans out to show that she is in a well-appointed, clinically clean kitchen, a cookbook opened neatly on the sideboard (Figure 4.6). These two shots last twelve seconds in total and there is no sound other than the non-diegetic song, yet, as well as showing Karen's sadness, they reveal her marital status, affluent circumstances, and apparent loneliness, sat off-center in the large, empty kitchen.

These images prepare us for the drama later in the syuzhet, in which— despite taking her husband Richard (Don Galloway) to the funeral and subsequent gathering of old friends (Richard is the only outsider in the group apart

Figure 4.5 Close-up: Diamond ring, preppy sweater, bone china teacup

Figure 4.6 The clinically clean kitchen

from Chloe)—she will declare her unhappiness in her family life and her long-held desire to be with Sam.

While revealing character background, Kasdan also occasionally misdirects the audience in the same montage. For example, Chloe (Meg Tilly) is shown in an aerobics outfit performing stretching exercises, emphasizing her relative youth compared to the other characters, but also suggesting that she is taking the news far more lightly, a misconception that will be held by Alex's friends initially. Soon after these opening credits, we learn that she was Alex's girl-friend, and that she discovered his body after his grisly suicide; the audience will then reformulate the fabula, further perceiving her strangely unaffected by events, an assumption that will prove to be incorrect, as revealed in another wordless scene toward the end of the film in which she moves Alex's clothes out of the closet, tears running down her face.

A more playful use of visual elements to present a restricted narration is when, in the opening montage, we first see Michael (Jeff Goldblum) becoming frustrated as he searches for something in his home office. He is calmed by his partner Annie (Patricia Gaul), who finds the batteries he has been looking for then hugs him affectionately. While this reveals Michael's neurotic nature, as well as his despair and discombobulation, it also suggests that he is in a stable, loving relationship. The notion is tempered in the sequence immediately after the credits by his obvious pleasure in being assigned to take care of Chloe at Alex's funeral. At this point, the audience's perception of Michael within the fabula may shift slightly, although his tactility could still be interpreted as misjudged over-friendliness. But the perception of Michael as someone looking for extra-relationship sex will be confirmed soon afterward when, along with the batteries that his partner had helped him find in the opening montage, he unpacks a stash of condoms from his overnight bag. Again, this is a dialogue-free scene, the syuzhet revealing an aspect of fabula entirely through visual cues.

Another way that the intertwined relationships are established in *The Big Chill* is through shot composition. With so many protagonists, and with most of the action occurring indoors, there is frequent cutting between close-ups and two-shots. However, Kasdan often attempts to include all or most of the characters within the frame, as shown in Figure 4.7.

This would seem a deliberate effort on Kasdan's part to establish and reinforce the bond between these characters. It helps, too, that he insisted on all actors remaining on set throughout the shoot, according to actor JoBeth Williams, allowing characters to appear in the background even when they are not driving the scene.[20] In *Body Heat*, Kasdan had shown a flair for impactful composition, executed through careful blocking and

Figure 4.7 The entire group in frame

camera moves. In *The Big Chill*, Kasdan, alongside cinematographer John Bailey, develops this predilection for striking imagery through the repeated use of deep space, even within relatively confined interiors. The final shot of the film, for example, includes all seven main characters in close proximity, reconfirming their close friendship even after the many dramas of their weekend together (Figure 4.8).

Whereas *Body Heat* frequently uses a moving camera, the dynamism in *The Big Chill*, particularly in these group shots, is created by the actors within the frame. Furthermore, the editing (with more frequent cuts than in *Body Heat*) provides thrust to the scenes and allows for temporal movement and character revelation even if the location does not change. For example, the montage of shots in the kitchen at sixty-two minutes (Figures 4.9, 4.10, 4.11) shows Harold gifting

Figure 4.8 Deep focus: the actors provide the movement

Figure 4.9 The sneaker montage begins

Figure 4.10 The camera remains static

Figure 4.11 Sarah struggles with a hangover

running shoes to his guests, an act that reinforces Ryan and Kellner's reading of the film that Kevin Kline's character is the "leader and provider" of the group.[21] Yet it also reveals aspects of the other protagonists' personalities and relationships, such as the childlike glee that Nick (William Hurt) takes in trying on his new sneakers, and the friction between Meg (Mary Kay Place) and Karen regarding Sam (Figure 4.9); Chloe's growing acceptance within the group (Figure 4.10); and Sarah's inability to cope with an alcohol-and-cocaine hangover, her tolerance weakened in the decade or more since college (Figure 4.11).

The physicality of this sequence is perhaps born of Kasdan's rehearsal process with his actors, where, he says, he encourages "an atmosphere in which they have enormous freedom to act" through performance rather than just dialogue.[22] This allows the film to retain a cinematic quality even as the camera remains static. Rather than being "a keen disappointment" visually after *Body Heat*, this suggests more restrained direction from Kasdan within the grounded fabula of his second movie. It seems that, rather than forcing a visual style onto the story, he allows the actors' performances to inform the camera movement and placement. In fact, cinematographer John Bailey confirmed that he positioned the camera in the montage described above only after the scenes had been blocked by Kasdan and the actors.[23] By doing this, the camera remains unobtrusive and the action within scenes retains a realism more in keeping with the character-driven piece.

Another aspect in which *The Big Chill*'s visual style differs from *Body Heat*'s is through the objectivity of the camera. Perhaps due to its relative lack of mobility, the camera stays neutral, especially in the interiors of the house. Except in the opening sequences, as discussed previously, it tends not to favor any one character over the others and rarely takes any subjective point of view. This is what makes Harold's placement as the apparent protagonist in the opening scenes so powerful: even as the rest of the 105-minute film strives to give the ensemble equal prominence, the audience has been primed to see the film as Harold's.

The camera's objective point of view also obviates any suggestion of an off-screen presence. Unlike in *Body Heat*, where the partially obscured views and moving camera suggest that we are watching events surreptitiously, *The Big Chill* allows viewers a sense of omniscience as they are drawn close into the conversations without ever feeling like voyeuristic participants. This directorial decision complements the less generic style of the film, with the closeness of the camera matching the intimacy of the old friends' exchanges; but it also reduces the tension, even in more private discussions. It contributes to the more "casual" style of the movie, and may partially explain why, even as secrets are revealed, arguments occur, and six of the party sleep with new partners, some critics still read *The Big Chill* as being "virtually plotless."

CLASSICAL STRUCTURE IN *THE BIG CHILL*

David Bordwell and Kristin Thompson argue that classical Hollywood narration tends to have "a basically 'objective' story reality, against which various degrees of perceptual and mental subjectivity can be measured."[24] If, as discussed above, the visual style of *The Big Chill* marks it as less subjective than *Body Heat*, then it may be a more classical narrative than Lawrence Kasdan's debut film. On the other hand, its less plot-driven, less generic structure would suggest the opposite. Therefore, I will next analyze the structure of *The Big Chill*, as presented through syuzhet and visual style, to establish whether it conforms to the "conventional, classic dramatic structure" that Kasdan says he usually favors,[25] or if it is truly as "casual in its structure, [. . .] loosely connected and seemingly improvised" as Prince contends.[26]

Some critics have argued that the "New Hollywood" of the 1960s and 1970s helped propagate a post-classical mode of storytelling in popular American films, in which the classical traits—cause and effect, clear psychological reasoning, and objective clarity—were phased out. Kristin Thompson, while arguing against this post-classical theory, summarizes some of the arguments that have been put forward to support the idea. On the one hand, some critics, such as Thomas Elsaesser, saw a more daring, experimental trend becoming dominant, a "new realism" apparent in movies such as *Five Easy Pieces* (1970) and *American Graffiti* (1973), gradually replacing the "affirmative-consequential" model.[27] In contrast, others attribute post-classicism to market conditions, with writer Justin Wyatt suggesting that "high concept" cinema is "one central development—perhaps *the* central development—within post-classical cinema, a style of filmmaking molded by economic and institutional forces."[28]

Thompson, though, argues against post-classicism, stating that, while the 1970s rise of the "movie brats" such as Francis Ford Coppola, Brian De Palma, and George Lucas had a strong impact on marketing (with studios realizing the appeal of certain directors' names on posters) and on the "juvenilization" of cinema (with the proliferation of nostalgic throwbacks to B-movie adventures), they did not change the dominant narrative style of Hollywood filmmaking. She contends that the three most commercially popular films of the 1970s—*The Godfather* (1972), *Jaws* (1975), and *Star Wars* (1977)—demonstrate that "[t]he ideal American film still centers around a well-structured, carefully motivated series of events" including "fast-paced action and characters with clear psychological traits."[29]

Where Thompson diverges from many other theorists is in her assertion that classical Hollywood narratives can usually be broken into four acts rather than the ¼–½–¼ three-act structure popularized by Sid Field and subsequently touted by many screenwriting manuals.[30] Thompson divides the long second act—the "½" of Field's schema—into two distinct parts, creating four roughly equal sections in an entire movie. Another way in which Thompson deviates from Field's concept is by basing the structure not around story action but around the lead character's motivations. The rationale for this is that "the most frequent reason a narrative changes direction is a shift in the protagonist's goals."[31] In summary, she describes these sections as:

1. *The setup*
   The "initial situation is [. . .] established." The protagonist's goals are conceived, or circumstances are created that will lead to these goals.
2. *The complicating action*
   This is either "the hero pursuing a goal conceived in the setup but having to change tactics dramatically;" or a "counter-setup, building a whole new situation with which the protagonist must cope."

3. *The development*

The "protagonist's struggle toward his or her goals typically occurs," even if "very little progress is actually made." This section "ends at the point where all the premises regarding the goals and the lines of action have been introduced."

4. *The climax*

"[T]he action shifts into a straightforward progress toward the final resolution."[32]

If, as noted earlier, the visual style, especially in early scenes, places Harold as the protagonist of *The Big Chill*, then it may be possible to map this pattern onto the film without difficulty. However, if—as many contend, including Kasdan himself[33]—*The Big Chill* does not have a sole protagonist, then it is presumably more problematic to apply Thompson's paradigm than if it were a conventional narrative. However, Thompson does allow for dual- or multiple-protagonist films, and in more detailed analyses of ten movies, she includes three that have groups of three or more lead characters. The closest of these in style and structure to *The Big Chill* is *Hannah and Her Sisters* (1986). Not only is it an adult-oriented, dialogue-reliant ensemble piece, but it is also made by a writer-director, Woody Allen, so a close relationship between syuzhet and visual style can be expected. For example, Thompson posits that Allen uses cinematic style to show which characters are protagonists and which are supporting players; then Allen uses the camera to establish the protagonists' equal importance to the fabula, emphasizing them as groups by keeping the actors in frame together, rather than relying upon the more conventional shot/reverse-shot technique utilized in many Hollywood films.[34]

Thompson makes a bold choice in selecting *Hannah* as one of just ten exemplars of classical Hollywood narrative since the mid-1970s, as, on face value, it is far less goal-oriented than the majority of mainstream American movies. Still, Thompson is very persuasive in mapping her goal-driven paradigm onto the film, with the shifts from one act to another occurring at points that fulfil her criteria. For instance, Thompson has the break from Act One (set-up) to Act Two (complicating action) in *Hannah* at the moment when Holly has started a catering business with her friend, even as she continues pursuing a career in acting. Thompson justifies the act break by saying that "this is the first time any of the characters has taken a step toward achieving a goal," meeting the standard that the protagonist change tactics at this stage of a classical Hollywood narrative.[35]

In *Hannah and Her Sisters*, as in *The Big Chill*, there is some ambiguity in who the protagonists actually are, which could make Thompson's goal-centered approach to structure difficult to apply. However, she examines both syuzhet and style to identify the five protagonists among the ten major players in the narrative of *Hannah*, noting that these characters "have clear-cut traits and pursue personal goals." Additionally, the film uses many of the same classical narrative strategies as the other films she discusses in the same volume, such as appointments, dialogue hooks, and causal progression.[36]

Thompson's analysis of *Hannah and Her Sisters* is a useful template when examining a similarly multi-protagonist piece in *The Big Chill*. In fact, after her analyses of ten films from the modern era, Thompson lists a selection of ninety films from the 1910s to the 1990s, chosen to represent "a considerable variety of directors, genres, studios, and budgets,"[37] and she includes *The Big Chill* in the sub-list of ten movies from the 1980s. She suggests that it follows her paradigm for classical narrative structure, with four identifiable acts: "setup, 28 [minutes]; complicating action, 24.5; development, 25.5; climax and epilogue, 24 (epilogue alone, 4); end credits 3."[38] As Thompson's timings are only approximate, it is not always certain precisely which points in the film she is referring to, but this overview is a useful starting point for discussion of *The Big Chill* in terms of classical structure.

During what Thompson identifies as the "setup," there is the aforementioned pre-credits scene of Harold bathing his son, then the titles montage; next is Alex's funeral, in which the old friends are reunited; and the funeral cortège is when we begin to see minor ruptures between members of the group. The wake builds on this, and we learn more about Alex and Chloe's relationship (and hints of disapproval from Sarah) before the decision is made for the group to stay the weekend at Sarah and Harold's home. Surprisingly, the decision is made off-screen and with little dramatic motivation. We simply see Sarah and Harold each saying that they have invited people to stay, even though they had not discussed or planned it previously. In this storytelling choice, there is a lack of the kind of causal motivation one would expect in a classical Hollywood narrative and certainly no dialogue hook to prepare us for their decision on which the entire film is predicated.[39]

The set-up ends when, after the sequence establishing that the friends are going to stay, Sarah (who, we will discover later, once had a brief affair with the deceased Alex) is shown hugging herself and crying in the shower. Not only is this the most dramatic beat in the syuzhet thus far, it is noticeably different in visual terms from much of what has occurred previously. It is the only time during the entire movie, aside from the pre-credits scene and opening credits montage, when the camera overtly "reveals" somebody: The upbeat music (*Tell Him* by The Exciters), capturing the giddy excitement of the friends reuniting, plays over shots of the guests unpacking. Then the music fades out, and we are left with the sound of water gushing from a shower. The camera moves slowly through the bathroom and into the shower compartment, where we see Sarah sitting on the floor, sobbing uncontrollably. The visual style signals a major plot point and a very definite change in our perception of the fabula: the realization that Sarah was much closer to Alex than previously understood. The act break is entirely appropriate whether viewing the film as an ensemble piece or, as the visual style intimates, Harold's story, with this surprising revelation of his wife's grief signaling a "complicating action" within their marriage, a "counter-setup, building a whole new situation with which the protagonist must cope."[40]

While the first act works to introduce the protagonists and move them into place, this second act is when the characters begin revealing their agendas: Meg's hope to have sex with one of her old friends in order to conceive, Karen's frustrations with her husband, Sam (Tom Berenger) searching for meaning away from his Hollywood-TV-star life, and Michael escalating his attempts to sleep with Chloe. We learn that Nick is unable to have sex since Vietnam, a revelation in the syuzhet that forces the audience to reinterpret their understanding of the fabula: the earlier scenes of his drug use while driving a high-octane sports car now have more poignancy; rather than being the care-free, irresponsible character we may have imagined, we know now that Nick has suffered a horrific trauma. It is during this "complicating action" section that Harold talks to Nick about Sarah and Alex's affair, even if the married couple appears reconciled now. Harold also suggests that Nick buy shares in his company, which is about to be bought out by a major corporation—an illegal act of insider trading, but one that shows that Harold is worried about Nick and wants to help him. While the film's style shows less favoritism toward Harold by this point, if the viewer interprets him as the sole protagonist, then this section has him trying to exert influence on others in the group as the "leader and provider."

According to Thompson, the second act break—the transition from "complicating action" to "development"—occurs 24.5 minutes after the first. This is a more problematic fit, with the act ending as the group watches Sam's television show, a comedic scene that reveals scant new information. If following Thompson's paradigm, though, the third act—the "development"—starts in the next scene, with the eight protagonists eating dinner and discussing how their lives have changed since college. Sam says, "I lost my idea of what I should be," and Sarah laments that "I'd hate to think that it was all just fashion. [. . .] Our commitment." Harold, irritated by the consensus that they have become worse people since university, asks, "What's the thrust here? We were great then and we're shit now?" This seems a more suitable moment for the transition than the previous scene of them watching TV, a more obvious complicating action: the escalation of conflict between Harold's current entrepreneurial values and the group's former idealism. However, even if the dinner scene is a dramatic passage, I would argue that it is simply an articulation of much of the subtext throughout the film. If this were the prelude to major plot developments—a rift between characters, for example—then it could be interpreted as a major turning point; but any tension is dissipated in the very next sequence, when the group dances together while cleaning up after dinner, apparently unaffected by their brief disagreement. Therefore, it is difficult to argue strongly for this being an obvious act break. In fact, in this respect it could be posited that *The Big Chill* fits Field's three-act structure better, with Thompson's two central acts more unified than she suggests.

While the act break is debatable, within Thompson's four-act schema the third act of *The Big Chill* fulfils her demand that the protagonist "struggle toward his or her goals [. . .], often involving many incidents that create action, suspense, and delay."[41] Certainly, Meg's attempt to have a baby escalates in this section: first she is politely rejected by Sam; then she is propositioned by Michael, but this time she refuses; and by the end of the act, she is on the point of giving up on the idea. Karen reveals her feelings for Sam more strongly, though not yet explicitly; Sam elucidates on his loneliness since his divorce; and Nick, who seems the closest to their late friend Alex, becomes closer to Chloe. From Harold's point of view, though, there is little change, until he is forced to protect Nick from the police, an exemplar of how his values, as the upstanding local businessman, have diverged from Nick's and his former self's. Thompson has the third of the four acts ending on seventy-eight minutes, which is just as this scene ends. Nick has been caught running a red light, suspected of using drugs, but Harold smooths things over with the police officer. Nick seems surprised that Harold is so liked and respected by the cop, and the scene ends when Harold tells Nick: "You know, I live here, this place means something to me, I'm dug in. I don't need this shit." From Harold's perspective, this moment certainly works as a turning point, his frustration with Nick, whom he has been trying to help, finally boiling over. However, if viewing the narrative as multi-protagonist, I would suggest that a more appropriate scene to announce the beginning of the climax begins slightly later, when Chloe is being interviewed on a home video camera by Nick. It is one of the few times that Chloe speaks at any length, and she is unwittingly cutting when she says, "I don't like talking about my past as much as you guys do." She then tells Nick about her time with Alex, humanizing him more than in any other exchange during the film. While his old college friends seem to have lionized Alex as the only one who stayed true to his principles, we get little sense of him as a real person until this exchange, and it is an affecting moment. Almost off-handedly, she mentions that Alex had said "maybe he should have accepted that Rutledge Scholarship," a prestigious grant that would have enabled him to continue his education. The last revelation is shown within the TV screen as the other friends watch the video tape, and their reactions—particularly Michael's, lowering his head as if stunned—show their shock. This precise moment could be read as the beginning of the "climax," with the characters' attitudes toward Alex, the personification of their old ideals, now altered.

To follow Thompson's paradigm, the third act "ends at the point where all the premises regarding the goals and the lines of action have been introduced,"[42] and regardless of the exact transition point, then this criterion has been fulfilled around this section of the film. The premises have been set, and the friends follow this in the climax by acting upon their impulses and the echoes of their 1960s selves: Karen tells Sam that she is going to leave her husband, and they have sex; Sarah suggests that Harold sleep with Meg (an act by Sarah that could be seen as "counterbalancing" her affair with Alex, bringing equilibrium to the marriage; while also enabling Meg to achieve her goal); and Nick and Chloe find solace in one another. Only Michael has no clear "climax," other than repairing his mildly fractious relationships with the others by the final scene.

Whether accepting *The Big Chill* as a single-protagonist or multi-protagonist film, then, it conforms broadly to Thompson's four-act structure based around protagonists' goals. However, elements of the film do not fit Thompson's definition of classical Hollywood narrative. She states that "[t]he most basic principle of the Hollywood cinema is that a narrative should consist of a chain of causes and effects that is easy for the spectator to follow," and that they tend to be "lacking [. . .] ambiguities."[43] Yet the final scene has Karen talk very casually about the others coming to visit Richard and her sons, an about-turn after previously saying that she was leaving her husband. Sam looks comfortable with this revelation, even though he had previously appeared to be seeking a partner rather than a one-night stand, and it is a very ambiguous denouement to this storyline involving apparently unmotivated actions with no clear cause-and-effect pattern. In other words, it works against classical Hollywood narrative structure as defined by Thompson. Furthermore, Meg's situation is not resolved: Will she be able to conceive? And what will be Harold and Sarah's relationship with the baby if she does? A further dangling cause pertains to Harold and his goal to help Nick: while revealing that Nick will stay with Chloe, presumably rent-free, to fix up the old house on their land, there is no resolution to Harold's offer for Nick to buy shares in his company (and no comment on the illegality of the act, which would go against the group's left-leaning 1960s idealism, as well as imperiling Harold's present status as a pillar of his community).

Most strikingly, there is a revelation in the same scene which changes the fabula markedly, yet it is so hidden by both the style—the scene dominated by an "objective" wide shot of the group—and the dense dialogue that it can easily be missed. In fact, I have not found any review, critique or synopsis that even mentions it: Nick shows the others the article in the college newspaper that Michael had written about Alex that "made him famous" on campus. The headline reads: "Get Yourself Another Boy! He Says 'No, In Thunder' to Rutledge Foundation," the article lauding Alex for turning down the fellowship. The reveal, of course, dovetails with the earlier claim by Chloe that Alex had expressed regret for this action, suggesting that this moment from their university days had reverberated throughout Alex's life. More revelatory, though, is that Nick also mentions finding Alex's induction notice, the letter drafting him into the US military. This is the first mention in the syuzhet that Alex may have fought in the armed forces; so, in the very last scene, Kasdan reveals a possible cause-and-effect reason for Alex's suicide: he regretted not taking the scholarship, not only because of the educational opportunities it may have presented, but because it would have precluded him from being drafted to fight in Vietnam. Given Nick's scars from that war, and the apparent similarity between Nick and Alex (according to Chloe), then a clearer picture emerges, of both men's pain. It is interesting that Lawrence Kasdan chose not to highlight this information more explicitly, either through syuzhet (a clearer explanation in the dialogue, for instance, of the exact consequences of his Rutledge Fellowship refusal) or through style (such as a close-up on Nick when he reveals this fact, or on the reactions of his friends). Instead, the moment is laughed off before the conversation topic changes. In the role of writer-director, Kasdan made a conscious choice to keep this detail ambiguous, and he told me that it was his instinct to have the audience "work" to understand the movie: "I don't want to make a big thing out of the big things."[44] The choice to make this revelation so subtle is unusual in a mainstream Hollywood film. This, along with the other dangling causes as the film ends, conforms more to the post-classical notion of "new realism" described by Thomas Elsaesser, that eschews the "affirmative-consequential model of narrative."[45]

The Big Chill, then, broadly meets the structural criteria that Thompson posits are the basic elements of classical Hollywood storytelling, with four acts consisting of a set-up, complicating action, development, and climax. However, compared to Kasdan's other work during the same period, as well as most contemporary American films, it does not contain what Thompson calls "[t]he most basic principle" of Hollywood cinema: the "chain of cause and effects that is easy for the spectator to follow."[46] Instead, it is perhaps more in keeping with Renoir's *La Règle du jeu/The Rules of the Game*, which Kasdan cites as an inspiration precisely because "it's hard to put your finger on what [it] is about."[47] Little is explained for certain by the end of *The Big Chill*, and, particularly with the revelation regarding Alex's induction notice, the epilogue—rather than "tie up any loose ends," as Thompson says most Hollywood epilogues do[48]—actually raises tantalizing new questions.

These findings point to an attempt by Lawrence Kasdan to make a film that avoids Hollywood tropes. However, his admitted preference for classicism prevails in the story structure, even if the protagonists' goals are less explicit than in most contemporary American films. Such a balance between classicism and ambiguity may be the very reason why audiences and critics responded positively to Kasdan's "leisurely weekend party"[49] with its "loosely connected [. . .] scenes."[50] *The Big Chill* provided adult audiences with an alternative to the fast-expanding blockbuster market, allowing for a more nuanced drama than was common at the time; yet on a subconscious level it still satisfied a desire for classical structure that has underpinned American cinema throughout its history.

Lawrence Kasdan achieved considerable success in his first two films as writer-director, his predilection for classic structure complemented by an ability to adapt his directing style to meet the contrasting narrative needs of the films. Kasdan utilized aspects of cinematic style, such as camera angles and editing, in order to lead the viewer toward the construction of a cohesive fabula. In line with Bordwell's paradigm of classical Hollywood storytelling, Kasdan's "style" remained subservient to the narrative, information disclosed or withheld subjectively until an overall objective story reality was ultimately revealed.[51] Although *Body Heat* and *The Big Chill* belonged to different genres, certain patterns emerged, such as Kasdan's penchant for witty dialogue and character ambiguity, as well as a preference to focus on actors' performances rather than ostentatious camerawork, with long rehearsal sessions contributing to the engaging interplay between characters.[52] However, the theme that would be discussed most frequently, and that would inflect much of his later work, was his representation of middle-class Americans in their thirties as they left behind their 1960s idealism and entered the Reagan era. These two films marked the beginning of a career in which Lawrence Kasdan would become known as a spokesperson for the baby-boom generation.

NOTES

1. Lawrence Kasdan, interviewed for *The Directors: Lawrence Kasdan*, DVD (American Film Institute), 1997.
2. The poster for *The Big Chill* can be found at http://www.impawards.com/1983/big_chill_ver1.html (accessed July 3, 2023).
3. Marjorie Bilbow, "Marjorie Bilbow's Reviews: *The Big Chill*," *Screen International (Archive: 1976–2000)* (January 21, 1984), 20.
4. Kim Newman, "*The Big Chill*," *Monthly Film Bulletin* 51, no. 600 (1984), 42.
5. Rob Edelman, "*The Big Chill*," *Cineaste* 13, no. 2 (1984): 41–2.
6. Stephen Prince, *A New Pot of Gold: Hollywood Under the Electronic Rainbow, 1980–1989* (New York: Charles Scribner's Sons, 2000), 254.
7. Newman, "*Big Chill*," 41–2.
8. Kasdan, quoted in Alex Simon, "Chillin' Big with Lawrence Kasdan," *The Hollywood Interview*, December 3, 2012, http://thehollywoodinterview.blogspot.com/2008/03/lawrence-kasdan-hollywood-interview.html (accessed July 3, 2023).
9. Kasdan, quoted in Rose Eichenbaum, *The Director Within: Storytellers of Stage and Screen* (Middletown, CT: Wesleyan University Press, 2014), 240.
10. Kasdan, quoted in Simon, "Chillin' Big."
11. Arthur Knight, "*The Big Chill*: THR's 1983 Review," *The Hollywood Reporter*, 1983 [Republished September 30, 2018], https://www.hollywoodreporter.com/review/big-chill-review-1983-movie-1147771 (accessed July 3, 2023).

12. Vincent Canby, "Screen: *The Big Chill*, Reunion of 60's Activists," *The New York Times*, September 23, 1983, https://www.nytimes.com/1983/09/23/movies/screen-the-big-chill-reunion-of-60-s-activists.html (accessed July 3, 2023).

13. David Bordwell and Kristin Thompson, *Film Art: An Introduction*, 6th ed. (New York: McGraw Hill, 2001), 76–7.

14. Bilbow, "Marjorie Bilbow's Reviews," 20; and Michael Wilmington, "*Big Chill* Still a bit Chilly at 15," *Chicago Tribune*, November 6, 1998, https://www.chicagotribune.com/news/ct-xpm-1998-11-06-9811060485-story.html (accessed July 3, 2023).

15. Eric Hoyt, Kevin Ponto, and Carrie Roy, "Visualizing and Analyzing the Hollywood Screenplay with ScripThreads," *Digital Humanities Quarterly* 8, no. 4 (2014), 26, http://www.digitalhumanities.org/dhq/vol/8/4/000190/000190.html (accessed July 3, 2023).

16. Lawrence Kasdan and Barbara Benedek, *The Big Chill*, screenplay 1st draft, July 16, 1982, 4.

17. Hoyt, Ponto, and Roy, "Visualizing and Analyzing," 26.

18. Knight, "*Big Chill*."

19. Roger Ebert, "*The Big Chill*," *Roger Ebert*, September 30, 1983, https://www.rogerebertristin T.com/reviews/the-big-chill-1983 (accessed July 3, 2023).

20. JoBeth Williams, interviewed for "*The Big Chill*: A Reunion," *The Big Chill*, DVD (Columbia TriStar), 1998.

21. Michael Ryan and Douglas Kellner, *Camera Politica: The Politics and Ideology of Contemporary Hollywood Film* (Indiana University Press, 1988), 277.

22. Kasdan, quoted in Carole Zucker, *Figures of Light: Actors and Directors Illuminate the Art of Film Acting* (New York: Plenum Press, 1995), 289.

23. John Bailey, interviewed for "*The Big Chill*: A Reunion," *The Big Chill*, DVD (Columbia TriStar), 1998.

24. Bordwell and Thompson, *Film Art*, 77.

25. Kasdan, quoted in Eichenbaum, *Director Within*, 240.

26. Prince, *New Pot of Gold*, 254.

27. Kristin Thompson, *Storytelling in the New Hollywood: Understanding Classical Narrative Technique* (Cambridge, MA: Harvard University Press, 1999), 2–3. The contrast between the affirmative-consequential model of classical cinema and the new realism prevalent in many American films of the 1970s was posited by Thomas Elsaesser in "The Pathos of Failure: American Films in the 70s—Notes on the Unmotivated Hero," *Monogram* 6 (1975), 14.

28. Justin Wyatt, *High Concept: Movies and Marketing in Hollywood* (Austin: University of Texas Press, 1994), 8. Original emphasis.

29. Thompson, *Storytelling New Hollywood*, 5–6.

30. Sid Field, *Screenplay: The Foundations of Screenwriting*, 3rd ed. (New York: Dell, 1979 [Reprint 1994]), 9.

31. Thompson, *Storytelling New Hollywood*, 27.

32. Ibid. 27–9.

33. Kasdan, interviewed for *Directors: Lawrence Kasdan*.

34. Thompson, *Storytelling New Hollywood*, 308–9.

35. Ibid., 319.

36. Ibid., 314–5.

37. Ibid., 37.

38. Ibid., 361.

39. Scenes were filmed in which both Harold and Sarah invited others to join them, but were cut from the finished picture.

40. Ibid., 28.

41. Ibid.

42. Ibid., 29.

43. Ibid., 10–11.

44. At the end of the screenplay is a 14-page sequence showing the friends, including Alex, preparing a Thanksgiving dinner in 1969. Kasdan confirmed to me that "it was one of the first ideas I had for the movie," and that it was shot, but that it was cut early in post-production when he realized that "it just confuses the mood." As written in the script, the sequence elucidates very briefly on Alex's refusal of the scholarship, with Meg confirming that it would come with an "assured deferment." (See Kasdan and Benedek, 116.) However, Kasdan told me that he always intended that connection between the scholarship refusal and army induction to be played subtly.

45. Elsaesser, "Pathos of Failure," 14.

46. Thompson, *Storytelling New Hollywood*, 10–11.

47. Kasdan, quoted in Simon, "Chillin' Big."

48. Thompson, *Storytelling New Hollywood*, 12.

49. Newman, "*Big Chill*," 42.

50. Prince, *New Pot of Gold*, 254.

51. David Bordwell, *Narration in the Fiction Film* (Oxon: Routledge, 1985), 52.

52. Zucker, *Figures of Light*, 285, 291.

PART III

Voice of the Largest Generation

Altruism and Otherness in *The Big Chill*, *The Accidental Tourist*, and *Grand Canyon*

awrence Kasdan's *Rotten Tomatoes* biography begins with the words: "The archetypal Hollywood baby boomer."[1] In countless interviews and reviews, too, he is associated with the generation perhaps more than any other filmmaker.[2] Kasdan often talks about his own work within the context of his age group; for example, on discussing *Body Heat*, he said that "we were a generation who had been given a great deal, who believed that the world was ours and that what we wanted to do was what we *would* do."[3] And, over thirty years later, Kasdan stated: "*The Big Chill* people were in their 30s when we were, and *Grand Canyon*'s were in their 40s, and so were we. It's an instinct, to look around and see what's happening."[4] However, he has also said that "I had no desire to make a summing-up film about baby boomers."[5] Why is it, then, that Lawrence Kasdan's movies have been described as "the original film anthem of the baby-boomers," or as examples of "boomer pulse-taking"?[6]

Born in 1949, Kasdan was part of the early wave of post-war births. His description of his childhood in West Virginia sounds almost like a 1950s stereotype, growing up in a "neighborhood that looked like *Leave it to Beaver*. [. . .] I had a small-town American upbringing."[7] Kasdan's childhood memories reflect the prominence of movies for his generation: "where I grew up, there were five or six theaters [. . .]. I couldn't wait for the next show to come in. I would see them once, twice, three times."[8] This appreciation of cinema continued when he entered college. Again, Kasdan's memories read like an encapsulation of the era:

> I was at the University of Michigan which was at the absolute white-hot center of American student radicalism. That's where SDS [Students for a Democratic Society] started. That's where the Weathermen started. The entire time I was there [1966–72] was the hottest moment in American student radicalism. The movies were absolutely

the thing that was happening culturally. The anti-war movement was happening politically, but there was plenty of mixing and crossing over in terms of what the zeitgeist was. The zeitgeist was: the world is changing. We're going to change it. And look: the movies are different to how they've ever been.[9]

After gaining his master's degree, Kasdan spent five years as an advertising copywriter in Detroit then Los Angeles. Clearly, this was a period of dissatisfaction, as life changed from one where Kasdan felt "a sense of importance" to one where he realized that his cohort "didn't have much impact on the world" after all, where "you go out in the real world and it was kind of dull."[10] This sense of disappointment is one that Kasdan would explore in *Body Heat* and, more directly, *The Big Chill*, and it reflects another boomer stereotype, according to the cultural theorists Cogan and Gencarelli: "their gradual abandonment of the very same principles they themselves established and stood for and that defined them during the 1960s."[11]

Kasdan's background certainly suggests that he is typical of his generation; but, then again, most successful American filmmakers active during the 1980s and 1990s were from the same cohort. In what ways, then, does Kasdan's body of work represent his demographic more than those of other writers and directors? In order to establish this, I will examine some of his films to which critics have applied the "baby-boomer" label and consider three questions: Whose point of view is favored? What problems are raised? How are these problems resolved within the narrative? By exploring these points, it may be possible to understand the social and political leanings that underpin the individual films; and by looking at the movies in the wider context of his career, it may explain just why Lawrence Kasdan is known as the "archetypal Hollywood baby boomer."

THE BIG CHILL

On the release of his first film as director, *Body Heat*, Lawrence Kasdan suggested that it was a film about his generation. Now in his early thirties, he expressed a sense of jadedness with the realities of adult life, when the idealism of the 1960s was becoming a memory. He says that *Body Heat*:

really started with my feeling about my friends and contemporaries — that we were a generation who had been given a great deal [. . .]. And then we came out and discovered it wasn't true: we had to take work we didn't believe in, very much like other generations did. The reaction to that was a sort of searching around for a quick score.[12]

Most contemporary critics, however, appeared to miss this aspect of the picture, instead focusing on its evocative, noirish style. Only Marina Heung, in her essay on Kasdan's early work, recognized that *Body Heat* is less about the past than the present, saying that "the steamily languid *mise-en-scène* and the hardboiled dialogue plausibly enact Kasdan's parable of survival in the '80s."[13]

It was with his second movie as writer-director, *The Big Chill*, "the original film anthem of the baby-boomers,"[14] that Kasdan's reputation was firmly established as "a spokesman for our contemporary social predicament."[15] But Kasdan, who co-wrote with Barbara Benedek, was initially coy about suggestions that the picture was representative of his generation, stating that:

> I never wanted this to be a movie about baby boomers. [. . .] The issues here are things people of all ages go through [. . .] the ways in which people rationalize their behavior, and the choices they make so they can make a living.[16]

Even in refuting the baby-boomer label, though, Kasdan presents a situation in *The Big Chill* that is more closely associated with that generation than any other: the dichotomy between the idealism of the youthful self and the pragmatism required later in life as adults with families and more material concerns. And in another interview, given just two months later, Kasdan appears to contradict his claim that *The Big Chill* is not about his cohort, stating that the central theme is "the need for meaningful, satisfying work. [. . .] [M]y parents' generation had no expectations that they would be happy in their work. But our generation thought we would be happy in everything."[17] Kasdan later expanded on this, saying:

> We were the children of the sixties. *The Big Chill* is about ten years after the fact and what happens when they get together and are reminded of what they thought ten years earlier and what their hopes were and what they had thought their lives would be like.[18]

The film is not only perceived as a baby-boomer picture, then; it was conceived as one too. But how does it present the generation's experience, and why did it resonate so strongly with contemporary audiences? And why is it still viewed today as a movie that encapsulates the experience of America's largest demographic? The formal analysis in Chapter 4 shows that, in spite of its multi-character approach, *The Big Chill* has a main protagonist in Harold. His is an interesting choice given that he is the member of the ensemble who appears to have changed most dramatically in the ten years since college; at least, he is the most willing to admit that life is not as simple as they had all once presumed. For example, in a key scene at the mid-point, the friends take turns lamenting the loss of their former ideals, the self-loathing directness of the exchange almost a parody of nostalgia for the 1960s. Sam says, "I lost my idea of what I should be." Michael, now a tabloid reporter, adds, "There was something in me then that, you know, made me want to go to Harlem and teach those ghetto kids." Meg, a real estate lawyer, says, "I was gonna help the scum, as I so compassionately refer to them now," and later adds that "sometimes I think [. . .] I pretended [college] wasn't real just so I could live with how I am now." Only Harold rails against the self-pity by asking, "What's the thrust here? We were great then and we're shit now?" He then implores Nick to "help me with these bleeding hearts." Not only does *The Big Chill* describe the experience of middle-class boomers in the decade after college, then, but it also favors the viewpoint of a character who appears cynical about their previous naïve idealism. This may be why Ryan and Kellner assert that the film is "subliminally survivalist and individualist [. . .] celebrating the burial of sixties radicalism and the passage to a more 'mature,' self-interested, upwardly mobile outlook on life."[19] Similarly, Barry Langford posits that in *The Big Chill* "the 1960s are figured as a period of trauma and schism in American life whose reparation is the primary duty of the present."[20]

I would argue that the film is more nuanced than these critiques suggest. Certainly, the central problem in *The Big Chill* is about the compromises made by 1960s radicals after they entered the "cold world" to which the title alludes; and the main protagonist appears critical of his friends for preferring the younger, more progressive versions of themselves. But it is telling that the only other character to echo Harold's sentiments is Nick, the least materially successful of the group, who says: "It was easy back then. No one ever had a cushier berth than we did. [. . .] It's only out here in the world that it gets tough." Rather than criticizing the early-boomer generation and the idealistic '60s, Nick's declaration is an admission that this particular group was far more privileged than it was willing to admit, and that its professed progressive values were not necessarily sincere. In fact, Sarah even ponders: "I'd hate to think that it was all just fashion."

Similarly, where Ryan and Kellner call the film "rightist" in showing characters subsume their former radicalism in material success,[21] it is the more progressive characters who are shown most positively. The deceased friend Alex, whom the audience never sees, is elevated to almost saintly status, acting as a proxy for the group's 1960s values. Harold says at his funeral that "Alex drew us together from the beginning. Now he brings us together again." Then he adds that "there was always something about Alex that was too good for this world." Nick is most closely aligned to Alex and the only other in the group who we know was drafted to Vietnam (and affected horribly by the experience). Like Alex, Nick did not complete his University of Michigan education, and he struggled to hold down a permanent job; yet he is shown to be the most principled of his cohort. On some level, he clings to his radical past, talking back to a policeman (Ken Place) who stops him for running a red light. When the officer asks Sam to perform a stunt from his TV show in return for letting Nick off, most of the group is eager to appease him, while Nick balks against the authority figure's demand: "Don't do it, Sam." He then chides Harold: "Since when did you get so friendly with cops?" In addition to this anti-authoritarian posturing, though, he reveals that he had quit his job as a radio psychologist because he felt that he was deceiving his listeners—showing far more principle than any of his friends who exchanged their ideals for financial gain—then learns that he had been more useful than he realized, when Chloe tells him that his radio show had helped her when she was a teenager. This contrasts with most of the other characters, who repeatedly voice their disappointment at the unfulfilling careers they have followed, but never suggest that they might go as far as actually giving them up.

The thematic core of *The Big Chill*, then, is the question of how 1960s liberals can retain their ideals as they move toward middle age. The answer for most of the characters is that they cannot. Instead, they pine nostalgically for their former lives while enjoying the material rewards gained as real-estate lawyers, Hollywood stars, and tabloid reporters; all except Harold, who is comfortable in his position as a successful business owner, and Nick, who ends the film by taking Alex's place, almost literally. Not only does he move into his deceased friend's home, but he also begins a relationship with Alex's girlfriend Chloe, accentuating Nick's closeness to Alex and establishing a connection between the past and the present, with Chloe the age that the rest of the group would have been when they were at college together. The denouement, then, manages to reconcile the sense of nostalgia prevalent in Kasdan's work (and often associated with the baby-boomers) with the assertion that the values of their generation might just remain relevant, even in the less-than-idealistic 1980s.

THE ACCIDENTAL TOURIST

Lawrence Kasdan returned once again to the allusion mode associated with the baby boomers when he directed the Western *Silverado* in 1985, co-writing the script with his brother Mark. The film was steeped in nostalgia, inspired by the cowboy pictures that the siblings had watched as children. Kasdan said that he and Mark "just loved Westerns, and we wanted to do all those things. Let's put this in. Let's put that in." As a broad, bold adventure film, then, designed as the antithesis of the more elegiac Westerns of the time, *Silverado* does not explore any specific generational concerns. In contrast, Kasdan's next movie was an adaptation of Anne Tyler's 1985 novel, *The Accidental Tourist*, a story rooted in gritty, present-day reality.

Even in this, just his fourth film as director, Kasdan's predilection for working repeatedly with certain actors was well-established. *The Accidental Tourist* would be William Hurt's third appearance for Kasdan, and the very fact that the protagonist, Macon Leary, was played by the actor from *Body Heat* and *The Big Chill* would act as a prototype schema for many viewers, the actor closely associated with Kasdan's adult-oriented work. The connection would be emphasized further by the appearance of Kathleen Turner, who portrayed Matty in *Body Heat*, as Macon's wife Sarah. As Bordwell states when describing his Constructivist view of the audience's activity, in which "perceiving and thinking are active, goal-oriented processes," when watching a film "we draw on schemata derived from our transactions with the everyday world, with other artworks, and with other films."[22] Therefore, Kasdan's employment of these actors may shape a viewer's perception of the movie within the first few minutes (or, more likely, before watching, if the viewer has prior knowledge of the cast). Audiences, then, would have been primed to expect a film more directly aligned with the contemporary baby-boomer concerns of *Body Heat* than, say, *Return of the Jedi* or *Silverado*. The allusion to previous Kasdan works is emphasized further by the scene under the opening credits, in which a man's hands are shown in close-up as they pack a carry-on case for travel. It is very similar to the credits montage in *The Big Chill*, and might act as a subliminal reminder that this is part of Kasdan's more personal canon, even if it is his first adapted work. In fact, *The Accidental Tourist* is only one of two times in eighteen features as writer or director that Kasdan has worked with previously published material. Anne Tyler's book was released three years prior to the film, meaning that Kasdan was likely writing the screenplay (after earlier drafts by Frank Galati) very soon after the novel had received a Pulitzer Prize nomination and the National Book Critics Circle Award. It is interesting, then, to examine both the film's "success" as an adaptation along with the ways in which it appears to reflect Kasdan's world view as seen in *Body Heat* and *The Big Chill*.

The film academic Karen Kline discusses *The Accidental Tourist* by utilizing four critical paradigms that she asserts may be adopted to gauge a movie's success as an adaptation. First, the "translation" paradigm "judges the film's [. . .] 'fidelity' to the novel, particularly with regard to narrative elements, such as character, setting, and theme." Next, the "pluralist" paradigm examines how well the film exists "in its own right" while conveying "such qualities as the novel's mood, tone and, values." Thirdly, the "transformation" paradigm "consider[s] the novel raw material which the film alters significantly, so that the film becomes an artistic work in its own right," essentially favoring the adaptation over the source. Finally, the "materialist" paradigm considers the context in which the film is made; for example, the commercial requirements of the studio system in which it was produced, or the pressure exerted by fans of the original work.[23] Kline finds that the most appropriate paradigm in this case is as a "translation," with Lawrence Kasdan's film mostly remaining true to the letter of the book. Certainly, as Kline demonstrates, some scenes stay entirely faithful to Tyler's original dialogue, even if the novel's exchanges are trimmed slightly.[24] In terms of its fidelity to "character, setting, and theme," then Kasdan's film is even more successful, with the key elements from the book all present: the major characters, the Baltimore locations, and the tragicomic tone as it deals with Tyler's core issues of grief and the protagonist's misguided efforts to regain control in a time of uncertainty. As Kasdan explains, the story in both the novel and the movie explores the ways that "no matter what planning we do, whatever desire we have for life to be predictable and safe, it's not."[25]

Such respect for the source material is perhaps to be expected in an adaptation of a recently published novel that had enjoyed considerable critical and commercial success, and that was reliant on the strength of its characters rather than plot twists or action sequences. The sense that Kasdan was attempting to serve the original text can be inferred from his comments in publicity interviews: "I spent a lot of time with Anne Tyler [. . .]. We went to all the locations in Baltimore that she had been writing about in the book, and we shot there. That sort of set the tone for the whole filmmaking."[26] So Kasdan had clearly developed a relationship with the author and appeared keen to reflect the tones and themes that she had established. The extent to which Kasdan's version remains faithful can be measured in what he chooses to omit, which is very little. This includes further details about why Macon's siblings are so controlling regarding apparent trivialities (for example, alphabetizing their groceries), as well as giving Macon more pronounced quirks after his wife leaves him. However, none of these details strongly change our perception of the characters, and Kasdan's choice to cut them was probably to pare down the story for the reduced timeframe of a Hollywood studio film.

Regardless of the specific reasons, the film does not stray far from the letter and spirit of Anne Tyler's book. Therefore, while there may be traces of the pluralist, transformation, and materialist influences that Kline discusses, I would argue that these are unavoidable consequences of adapting any work of art between media, and Kasdan's primary goal was to translate the novel from page to screen. In this sense, *The Accidental Tourist* is an effective adaptation, and it garnered mostly positive contemporary reviews as well as Oscar nominations for Best Adapted Screenplay and Best Picture, even if this fidelity to the source led to some criticism. Janet Maslin, for instance, argues that the film "merely restages some of the events from Miss Tyler's novel without giving them a genuinely cinematic flavor."[27]

Despite being a rare adaptation for Lawrence Kasdan, *The Accidental Tourist* shares clear similarities with his previous, more personal works, which probably explains his attraction to the book in the first place. In fact, Kasdan has said that the novel has "an enormous amount of humor and sadness, and all the things that are in life that interest me and that I try to get into my movies."[28] Like in *Body Heat* and *The Big Chill*, the protagonist of *The Accidental Tourist* is a middle-class professional who is only now beginning to face the consequences of his previous life choices. While there is an obvious outside influence on his current reverie—the murder of his son before the events of the film begin—most of Macon's traits are a result of decisions made even earlier, such as that to "endure, [. . .] holding steady," as he puts it. His wife Sarah, in explaining her reason for wanting a divorce, interprets it differently: "There's something so [. . .] muffled about the way you experience things. It's as if you were trying to slip through life unchanged." As with William Hurt's previous characterizations for Kasdan, there is a complacency in Macon that is only punctured by external forces, and a continuation of Kasdan's concerns expressed in *Body Heat* and *The Big Chill*: the realization that for all his generation's sense of potential and wish for control, "you didn't have much impact on the world."[29]

But, whereas the two earlier films explored the private lamentations of the radicals-cum-yuppies within a self-contained bubble, *The Accidental Tourist* provides a working-class counterfoil in Muriel (Geena Davis). This choice gives the story greater universality, a sense that these people live in the "real" world, accentuated by the authentic Baltimore settings, the damp, gray weather, and John Bailey's saturated cinematography, all serving to make the film less glossy than its predecessors. Through his relationship with Muriel—the single parent to a sickly, vulnerable child, Alexander (Robert Gorman)—Macon is compelled to consider a different perspective outside the organized, sterile existence that he has tried to create for himself. Much of the drama stems from this clash of class and culture: the stark difference between the spirited, emotional Muriel and Macon's more composed wife Sarah; Macon's comically middle-class siblings' disapproval of his new relationship; not to mention the central relationship itself between the suppressed, buttoned-up Macon and the more spontaneous Muriel.

However, just as *The Big Chill* favored the perspective of the "male [. . .] leader and provider,"[30] *The Accidental Tourist* reveals Muriel and her inner-city neighborhood entirely from Macon's point of view. Although he will eventually become a kind of surrogate father to Alexander, the focus is less on Muriel and Alexander's lives and more on how they affect Macon's emotional awakening. Indeed, Kasdan says that Muriel "intuits what Macon needs. [. . .] Someone to take a firm hand and help him tame this grief so he can go on with his life."[31] So, rather than exploring the female lead's hardships or her fortitude in raising her disadvantaged child alone, the story focuses on how she can help the male protagonist find redemption.

It is important to consider the historical context, of course, and the fact that Kasdan chose to make a film based on a female writer's work and featuring women in two of the three main roles would still be a rarity today, with females making up only thirty-five per cent of major characters in popular Hollywood films,[32] let alone in 1988. However, the main protagonist is evidently the affluent male, Macon, with the female leads there primarily to support his character development. In utilizing Muriel in this way, Kasdan is remaining faithful to Anne Tyler's source novel, in which Macon considers "he knew that what mattered was the pattern of [Muriel's] life; that although he did not love her he loved the surprise of her, and also the surprise of himself when he was with her."[33] Therefore, Kasdan cannot be accused of deviating from the original author's intentions, but the fact that he was attracted to the work in the beginning, and remained so faithful to it, may be because the book reflected his world view so closely.

Kasdan was at this time a well-regarded Hollywood filmmaker, after a successful career in advertising, which followed five years at the University of Michigan. It is unsurprising, then, that he tended toward films that see the world through the eyes of a financially stable, professional male with liberal sympathies. In this sense, Macon represents that perspective very succinctly as he sees himself as a savior to Muriel. In a passage of dialogue almost identical to the novel, Macon says that he will pay for Alexander to go to private school. Muriel responds by saying, "Alexander's got ten more years of school ahead of him. Are you saying you'll be around for all ten years? You can't just put him in a private school and take him out again at every passing whim of yours." These moments of conflict elevate *The Accidental Tourist* above the level of condescension, but the audience is still led to see events from Macon's perspective, with a camera that "almost stalks him," according to its director of photography John

Figure 5.1 Close-up on Macon in Muriel's neighborhood

Bailey.[34] And, even while using real inner-city Baltimore locations, there is an implied understanding that the audience is from Macon's world, entering the run-down street with an initial wariness, the camera in close-up on his uneasy expression. But, just as Muriel helps to heal Macon, this street also becomes less frightening to him, even appealing. Again, this is representative of the book, which calls Muriel's neighborhood "the foreign country that was Singleton Street [where] he was an entirely different person."[35]

So, while Kasdan was heavily influenced by Anne Tyler's source, it is probably because it tallied so closely with his own outlook. Like his earlier works as writer-director, it centered upon an outwardly successful but spiritually unfulfilled professional who had come to realize that he and his generation were not going to change the world after all. Instead, Macon was stuck in what the character calls "the Leary groove." In both *Body Heat* and *The Accidental Tourist*, the protagonist is awoken from his stasis by a new woman in his life. Whereas in the heightened, genre-driven *Body Heat*, this leads to adultery and murder, in the more grounded fictive world of *The Accidental Tourist*, it predicates an emotional rebirth, with Muriel giving Macon, he concedes, "another chance to decide who I am."

GRAND CANYON

In discussing his reasons for making *The Accidental Tourist*, Lawrence Kasdan says that:

> There's a central issue in the book, and in the movie, which I think is absolutely essential to all my movies, which is that the world is a dangerous, chaotic place, and people will do anything to try to control their fears about that.[36]

This notion was explored further, and more directly, in his next film as writer-director (with his wife, Meg Kasdan, as co-writer), *Grand Canyon*. In fact, while *The Accidental Tourist* examined the dichotomy between fear and control obliquely, the very first utterance in *Grand Canyon* has Davis, Steve Martin's Hollywood-director character, launch apropos of nothing into a speech aimed at Mack, the film's protagonist, within which he says:

> Control, control, control. When are you gonna realize? Nothing can be controlled. We live in chaos. The central issue in everyone's life. Mack, look around you, everyone in this parking lot is struggling for control, and you know what it is they're trying to control, each and every one of them? Fear, they're trying to control their fear.

It is a remarkably emphatic tirade with which to begin the story, and it serves as a thesis statement for the entire film, with the rest of its 135-minute running time spent explaining and exemplifying Davis's proclamation.

While Kasdan's earlier directorial works used middle-class boomer concerns as underlying themes, this film addresses social issues much more explicitly. As if to emphasize this, in the very next sequence, we see Mack become lost in the streets of Los Angeles as he drives home. Our empathy with the protagonist and his increasing anxiety is strengthened by the fact that Mack is played by Kevin Kline, in his fourth film for Kasdan. Mack is of similar temperament and social status to his character Harold in *The Big Chill*, and he even taps his steering wheel and sings along to the radio in a manner reminiscent of Kline's earlier performance. In the same way that knowledge of William Hurt and Kathleen Turner's work on *Body Heat* may have affected an audience's perception of *The Accidental Tourist*, this is a further instance in which viewers might use a prototype schema in order to make judgments about a character and story, with Kasdan's use of the same actor guiding them to align themselves with Mack. When his car breaks down in a poor neighborhood, he—a white lawyer in a stylish suit and expensive vehicle—is set upon by a gang of black men threatening him with a gun, perfectly illustrating Davis's opening remark about our lack of control in life.

After Mack is rescued by the arrival of the roadside mechanic, Simon (played by Danny Glover, another returnee to Kasdan's work following his part in *Silverado*), this exchange occurs:

> *Mack:*   What's going on in this world?
> *Simon:* This neighborhood is gone to shit.
> *Mack:*   This country's gone to shit.

Again, this is a far more vehement declaration of the film's themes than in the early scenes of, for example, *The Big Chill*, and it gives extra meaning to what Davis just said in his opening comments about controlling fear. In fact, Davis's very first words in the movie are: "You know what your problem is? You're always talking about X, but you're thinking about Y. You got to learn to talk about Y. Forget about X. X is gonna take care of itself." *Grand Canyon* imparts in the viewer the feeling that Kasdan has decided to "talk about Y" more directly, rather than through the prism of film noir in *Body Heat*, or softened by the occasionally comedic tone of *The Big Chill* and *The Accidental Tourist*. The sense of urgency may have stemmed from its timing, with the film released during a period of simmering racial tension in the United States, and Los Angeles in particular, less than five months before the police beating of Rodney King and the ensuing riots. Kasdan concurred in a later interview: "Anyone walking around LA at that time could feel [the rage and threat of violence]. The riots were a natural kind of explosion that anyone could have predicted."[37]

This willingness to address social issues brought mostly positive reviews, the film praised for the way it "taps into the Zeitgeist"[38] and for "gliding gracefully among a representative set of [Los Angeles] characters," leaving the viewer with "no idea what will happen next and many reasons to care."[39] However, there was criticism for its white middle-class viewpoint, with one reviewer positing that, "although Grand Canyon attempts to span all social strata, its viewpoint is anchored in Mack's white liberal guilt;"[40] while another complained about the "sanctimonious yuppie angst" of its characters.[41] This may be a case of critics using prototype schemata to negatively affect their understanding of the movie: a Lawrence Kasdan film set in modern-day America, with Kevin Kline at the center of an ensemble, is likely to put an audience in mind of *The Big Chill*; indeed, *Grand Canyon*'s publicity poster leads with the tagline: "In the 80's he brought us 'The Big Chill.' Welcome to the 90's."[42] While the marketing team likely saw this as a favorable connection, it may also have encouraged similar criticisms to its predecessor, with *The Big Chill* sometimes referred to as a "yuppie" story.[43] The trend continued with *Grand Canyon* and, soon after the initial wave of reviews, Kasdan complained in *The New York Times* that "[yuppie] is a very superior, derisive, derogatory, condescending phrase. [. . .] It's often used by movie reviewers to distance themselves from middle-class life, as though they weren't part of the middle-class."[44] While he makes an astute point regarding critics' hypocrisy, Kasdan's decision to place Kevin Kline as a successful upper-middle-class man at the center of both *The Big Chill* and *Grand Canyon* probably contributed to people making the connection. The earlier film's cast of well-educated, high-achieving professionals exemplified the "yuppie" image in the 1980s. Therefore, it is not surprising that the word was forefront in people's minds when watching Kline in *Grand Canyon*. Furthermore, the choice to make Mack an immigration lawyer—showing us his expansive high-rise office, but none of his clients—certainly hints at a wish to portray a financially successful but socially liberal protagonist, very much like the friends in *The Big Chill*, and archetypally "yuppie."

Another reason why some reviewers criticized the film's white liberal perspective may have stemmed, perversely, from its attempt to represent characters from a diverse array of backgrounds. The publicity suggests an ensemble film reminiscent of *The Big Chill* but with a multi-racial cast. Both the poster and trailer cite Kasdan's earlier work and list the names of the six main cast members in alphabetical order, inviting the target audience to draw upon their prototype schemata and expect a similar experience to *The Big Chill*. Certainly, *Grand Canyon* is an ensemble, with each of these characters having, according to David Bordwell, "their wants [. . .] developed beyond the limits of a conventional subplot, providing thematic echoes and counterpoints." Bordwell states that the couple of Mack and his wife Claire (Mary McDonnell) and that of

Simon and his sister Deborah (Tina Lifford, not featured on the poster) are clearly favored, their stories receiving "roughly equal emphasis" and following Thompson's goal-oriented four-act template (as discussed in Chapter 4).[45] However, a computer analysis of *Grand Canyon*'s screenplay by Hoyt, Ponto, and Roy has suggested that these two pairings are not equally present throughout the film. Their statistics-led approach shows that Mack is present in fifty per cent more scenes than any other character, with Claire next, then Simon third; and Deborah is present in fewer scenes than either Davis or Mack's son Roberto (Jeremy Sisto),[46] both of whom Bordwell labels "subsidiary characters."[47] Of course, there is a difference between character presence as defined by computer analysis and the "equal emphasis" that Bordwell posits. Hoyt et al address Bordwell's assertion directly by conceding that, in spite of the discrepancy in screen time, "The screenplay's two major spotlighting maneuvers, which occur at the beginning and end, further encourage us to perceive Mack [. . .] and Simon [. . .] as equal in narrative importance," namely Simon rescuing Mack when he is being threatened by a gang, then the climax at the Grand Canyon itself.[48] Thus, it appears that the film strives to give equal emphasis to white middle-class and black working-class protagonists, while affording more screen time to the former.

That a white filmmaker was attempting to address issues of race and class in a Hollywood studio release was a rarity in the early 1990s. Similarly, an ensemble cast that consisted of five white people and four black people, all of whom encounter obstacles and goals, was unusual at a time when African-Americans made up twelve per cent of the US population yet, according to the director-producer of *House Party* (1990), Reginald Hudlin, "very few of our [black people's] stories have been told."[49] Kasdan said that "[t]he premise of the movie is pain hurts, no matter what your circumstances;"[50] and, as well as the central friendship between Mack and Simon, the visual style deliberately connects characters from both sides of the race and class divide. For example, just after Simon rescues Mack, there is a scene showing Deborah's son Otis (Patrick Malone) coming home late at night. As Deborah goes to bed, Otis turns on the television and watches highlights of the basketball game that Mack had just attended (in the most expensive courtside seats). We see a close-up of the NBA action on the TV screen, then the camera pans away to reveal the same broadcast being watched in a different house by Roberto, who we will soon learn is Mack's son. Otis and Roberto will not share any scenes together until the climax at the Grand Canyon, but they are connected through camera moves and subtle editing. This establishes a "network narrative" ensemble for *Grand Canyon*,[51] in which—unlike *The Big Chill*, where characters are anchored to a specific location, with long histories between them—the protagonists are joined by theme and a single "event frame," Mack and Simon's chance meeting in the first act.[52]

Kasdan uses recurring images to connect different characters, regardless of their backgrounds. As noted above, basketball appears repeatedly, a benign link between classes and cultures. A more ominous visual motif, though, is the police helicopter. It appears initially in the opening montage of a pick-up basketball game in South Central LA, where we first see Simon, then Otis, who leaves his group of friends and looks up at the chopper resentfully. We next see it after Mack says goodbye to Davis in the parking lot of the LA Forum, just before his near-carjacking. Later, a helicopter flies by as Otis is going out at night to meet "some people," causing Deborah and Simon concern; and, again, immediately after the house is destroyed in a drive-by shooting. The motif is twisted when the helicopter swoops past at the start of Mack's dream of flying that soon becomes a nightmare. It is a harbinger of fear, representing the lack of control discussed in the film's opening lines, and an effective method for linking apparently disparate lives.

The helicopter motif, however, became a target of criticism regarding the points of view presented in *Grand Canyon*. Peter Travers observes that "shots of a police chopper [. . .] draw unfortunate comparisons to John Singleton's much grittier and truer *Boyz n the Hood*."[53] Given that *Boyz n the Hood* (1991) was released only five months prior to *Grand Canyon*, Kasdan would not have seen the film before shooting his own. Instead, it could be argued that this similarity suggests a truth to both movies. Each was reporting upon the state of Los Angeles at that time, and it is telling that two writer-directors from different social backgrounds would use the police helicopter as a symbol of underlying dread and the threat of violence. However, Travers's criticism does allude to the fact that Kasdan, an affluent white man, was attempting to portray the experiences of black people in the most deprived areas of the city. Conversely, Singleton was born and raised in South LA, the very neighborhood central to both movies, and his debut film, made when he was twenty-three years old, possesses a verve that Kasdan's lacks even in its most dramatic moments. Furthermore, *Boyz n the Hood* was part of a wave of "black film properties," nineteen of which were released in 1991, more than in the entire previous decade, according to *The New York Times*.[54] This gives credence to the argument that Kasdan had tapped into the cultural zeitgeist— when Hollywood studios were finally seeing value in making films featuring black protagonists—but also put his film at odds with pictures made by black filmmakers that were "stridently confrontational in their depiction of a problem-riddled urban culture in conflict with a white mainstream."[55] Rather than adopting a similarly confrontational approach, *Grand Canyon* has at its center a burgeoning friendship between its black and white protagonists. The decision to focus on the interpersonal rather than political led to later criticism from the sociologist Norman K. Denzin that the film is "whimsical and [. . .] utopian," and "refuses to connect race with politics, and politics with power and corruption;"[56] and that it trivializes complex issues by suggesting that problems can be resolved if the races simply learn to work together.[57] The exchange of favors between characters—Simon saving Mack from a potential robbery, then Mack helping Simon's family move to a less dangerous neighborhood—is undeniably neat, and at face value it could be read as patronizing. However, immediately after Mack fulfils his promise to help Simon, Otis faces assault then unfair arrest on his first night in the new "safer" area. This narrative choice rather negates Denzin's argument that Kasdan shows "the good white man [. . .] help the black man get out of the nightmare of the hood,"[58] as the film immediately follows up Mack's so-called "white savior" act with a young black man suffering as a result.

In 1991, Lawrence Kasdan was a white, middle-aged man directing a film that featured wealthy white people and working-class black people. In writing the screenplay, he and Meg Kasdan aimed to, in his words, "raise, but not resolve, certain questions, including what kind of personal values to adhere to in deteriorating cities, and how to cope with constant jeopardy, the fragility of relationships and, for that matter, life."[59] In that sense, *Grand Canyon* is a film of its time, with the protagonists belonging to his baby-boomer cohort and the leads displaying the liberal ideals and concerns that audiences had come to expect from a Kasdan ensemble. Its portrayal of the black experience in urban America may lack the first-hand subjectivity of *Boyz n the Hood*, but it also deserves credit as a major studio release that puts black people at the heart of a contemporary human story, not as sidekicks in action movies or comedies, or shown through the filter of historical drama. It also criticizes the clumsiness of Mack's "white man's burden" act, even if the film can be labeled "a story about what the hood means for life in the white ghettos," rather than about the lives of black people themselves, as Denzin contends.[60] *Grand Canyon*, though, with its affluent lead and its elements of magic realism, was not aiming to strike the same tone as the films of, say, John Singleton or Spike Lee. Kasdan states that "the middle ground was where I lived, and it didn't seem to me to be equivocating. It seemed to me to take in the confusion of life." He was making, then, a piece of social commentary born out of his progressive point of view, and a film that, he argues, was more daring than it may have appeared. Responding to reviewers who criticized the film's "yuppie angst," he says:

> If you make a movie about some subject that's distant from our lives, a movie about a spaceship or a gangster or a serial killer, something that people don't experience on an everyday basis, then nobody challenges that reality. But there are certain subjects, like everyday life in urban America, where everybody is an expert. Suddenly your view is put up against everyone else's view. So you're open to criticism.[61]

By choosing to write and direct such films ten years after his debut, Lawrence Kasdan was continuing to report on the state of the nation. While his movies still tended to focus upon the tribulations of professional white people, in *Grand Canyon* he developed themes explored in *The Accidental Tourist* by placing his alter ego in unfamiliar territory, physically and metaphorically, and showing an empathy for people from different backgrounds. In each case, the protagonist's willingness to let go of the need for control is what leads to his final epiphany: that uncertainty and chaos should be accepted rather than feared.

NOTES

1. "Lawrence Kasdan," *Rotten Tomatoes*, 2020, https://www.rottentomatoes.com/celebrity/lawrence_kasdan (accessed July 3, 2023).
2. See, for example, Josh Rottenberg, "Diane Keaton and Kevin Kline Sign on for the Baby Boomer-Centric *Darling Companion*," *Entertainment Weekly*, September 22, 2010, http://ew.com/article/2010/09/22/diane-keaton-and-kevin-kline-sign-on-for-the-baby-boomer-centric-darling-companion/ (accessed July 3, 2023); Melissa Anderson, "*Darling Companion*," *The Village Voice*, April 18, 2012, http://www.villagevoice.com/film/darling-companion-6434614 (accessed July 3, 2023); Chuck Wilson, "Lawrence Kasdan Interview," *LA Weekly*, April 19, 2012, https://www.laweekly.com/lawrence-kasdan-interview/ (accessed July 3, 2023).
3. Lawrence Kasdan, quoted in Dan Yakir, "Lawrence Kasdan Interviewed," *Film Comment* 17, no. 5 (1981), 53. Original emphasis.
4. Kasdan quoted in Wilson, "Kasdan Interview," 2012.
5. Kasdan, quoted in an unpublished interview with James Russell (2013).
6. JoAnn Balingit, "Review of Grand Canyon," in *Magill's Cinema Annual: 1992: A Survey of the Films of 1991*, edited by Frank Magill (Englewood Cliffs, NJ: Salem, 1992), 158; and Wilson 2012.
7. Kasdan, quoted in Russell, unpublished.
8. Ibid.
9. Ibid. Original emphasis.
10. Kasdan, quoted in James Russell and Jim Whalley, *Hollywood and the Baby Boom: A Social History* (London: Bloomsbury, 2018), 182.
11. Brian Cogan and Thom Gencarelli (eds.), *Baby Boomers and Popular Culture: An Inquiry into America's Most Powerful Generation* (Santa Barbara, CA: Praeger, 2015), x.
12. Lawrence Kasdan, quoted in Dan Yakir, "Lawrence Kasdan Interviewed," *Film Comment* 17, no. 5 (1981), 53.
13. Marina Heung, "The Big Score: Work and Survival in the Films of Lawrence Kasdan," *Michigan Quarterly Review* 24, no. 4 (1985), 545, https://quod.lib.umich.edu/m/mqrarchive/act2080.0024.004/49:3?page=root;rgn=full+text;size=100;view=image (accessed July 3, 2023).
14. Balingit, "Review of *Grand Canyon*," 158.
15. Heung, "Big Score," 548.
16. Kasdan, quoted in Dale Pollock, "Kasdan: A 'Chill' of His Very Own," *The Los Angeles Times*, September 18, 1983; cited in Heung, "Big Score," 545–6.
17. Kasdan, quoted in Pat H. Broeske, "Chill Director-Writer Lawrence Kasdan: 'I Make the Kind of Pictures I Like to See,'" *Hollywood Drama Logue* 45 (November 10–16, 1983), 14.

18. Kasdan, quoted in Robert J. Emery, *The Directors: Take One*, read by John Bell (New York: Allworth Press, 2002), audiobook.

19. Michael Ryan and Douglas Kellner, *Camera Politica: The Politics and Ideology of Contemporary Hollywood Film* (Indiana University Press, 1988), 277.

20. Barry Langford, *Post-Classical Hollywood: Film Industry, Style and Ideology Since 1945* (Edinburgh University Press, 2010), 227.

21. Ryan and Kellner, *Camera Politica*, 279.

22. David Bordwell, *Narration in the Fiction Film* (Oxon: Routledge, 1985), 31–2.

23. Karen Kline, "*The Accidental Tourist* on Page and on Screen: Interrogating Narrative Theories about Film Adaptation," *Literature/Film Quarterly* 24, no. 1 (1996), 70–2.

24. Ibid., 77.

25. Kasdan, interviewed for "It's Like Life," *The Accidental Tourist*, DVD (Warner Bros.), 2003.

26. Kasdan, interviewed for "Reflections of *The Accidental Tourist*," *The Accidental Tourist*, DVD (Warner Bros.), 2003.

27. Janet Maslin, "A Tourist Lost En Route to the Screen," *The New York Times*, January 15, 1989, https://www.nytimes.com/1989/01/15/movies/film-view-a-tourist-lost-en-route-to-the-screen.html (accessed July 3, 2023).

28. Kasdan, "Reflections."

29. Kasdan, quoted in Russell and Whalley, *Hollywood and Baby Boom*, 182.

30. Ryan and Kellner, *Camera Politica*, 277.

31. Kasdan, "Reflections."

32. Martha M. Lauzen, "It's a Man's (Celluloid) World, even in a Pandemic Year: Portrayals of Female Characters in the Top U.S. Films of 2021," *Center for the Study of Women in Television and Film*, 2022, 5, https://womenintvfilm.sdsu.edu/wp-content/uploads/2022/03/2021-Its-a-Mans-Celluloid-World-Report.pdf (accessed July 10, 2023).

33. Anne Tyler, *The Accidental Tourist* (New York: Random House, 1985), 241.

34. John Bailey, quoted in Nora Lee, "*The Accidental Tourist* is No Accident: Novel to Film Translation Challenges All," *American Cinematographer* 69, no. 11 (November 1988), 49.

35. Tyler, *Accidental Tourist*, 241.

36. Kasdan, "Reflections."

37. Kasdan, quoted in Emery, *Directors*.

38. Joe Brown, "*Grand Canyon*," *The Washington Post*, January 10, 1992, http://www.washingtonpost.com/wp-srv/style/longterm/movies/videos/grandcanyonrbrown_a0add9.htm (accessed July 3, 2023).

39. Janet Maslin, "The Accidents and Miracles in Everyday Life," *The New York Times*, December 25, 1991, https://www.nytimes.com/1991/12/25/movies/review-film-the-accidents-and-miracles-in-everyday-life.html (accessed July 3, 2023).

40. Brian D. Johnson, "City of Catastrophe," *Maclean's*, January 13, 1992, 50.

41. Peter Travers, "Movies—*Grand Canyon* Directed by Lawrence Kasdan," *Rolling Stone*, January 23, 1992, 49.

42. The publicity poster can be found at http://www.impawards.com/1991/grand_canyon.html (accessed July 3, 2023).

43. See Ryan and Kellner, *Camera Politica*, 277; and Alan Nadel, "1983: Movies and Reaganism," in *American Cinema of the 1980s: Themes and Variations*, edited by Stephen Prince (New Brunswick, NJ: Rutgers University Press, 2007), 103.

44. Kasdan, quoted in Bernard Weinraub, "Director Criticizes *Grand Canyon* Critics," *The New York Times*, January 16, 1992, https://www.nytimes.com/1992/01/16/movies/director-criticizes-grand-canyon-critics.html?searchResultPosition=1 (accessed July 3, 2023).

45. David Bordwell, *The Way Hollywood Tells It*, Berkeley, CA: University of California Press, 2006), 96. Kristin Thompson's four-act structure can be found at *Storytelling in the New Hollywood: Understanding Classical Narrative Technique* (Cambridge, MA: Harvard University Press, 1999), 28–9.

46. Eric Hoyt, Kevin Ponto, and Carrie Roy, "Visualizing and Analyzing the Hollywood Screenplay with ScripThreads," *Digital Humanities Quarterly* 8, no. 4 (2014), 33, http://www.digitalhumanities.org/dhq/vol/8/4/000190/000190.html (accessed July 3, 2023).

47. Bordwell, *Way Hollywood Tells It*, 96.

48. Hoyt, Ponto, and Roy, "Visualizing and Analyzing," 34. Deborah is absent from this climactic scene, but her son Otis is there with Simon and his new girlfriend Jane (Alfre Woodard).

49. Reginald Hudlin, quoted in Karen Grigsby Bates, "They've Gotta Have Us," *The New York Times Magazine*, July 14, 1991, https://www.nytimes.com/1991/07/14/magazine/theyve-gotta-have-us.html (accessed July 3, 2023).

50. Kasdan, quoted in Weinraub, "Director Criticizes."

51. Bordwell, *Way Hollywood*, 99.

52. Ibid., 97.

53. Travers, "Movies—*Grand Canyon*," 49.

54. Grigsby Bates, "They've Gotta."

55. Ibid.

56. Norman K. Denzin, *Reading Race: Hollywood and the Cinema of Racial Violence* (London: Sage, 2002), 51–2.

57. Henry A. Giroux, *Disturbing Pleasures* (New York: Routledge, 1994), 81.

58. Ibid., 51.

59. Kasdan, quoted in Weinraub, "Director Criticizes."

60. Denzin, *Reading Race*, 51.

61. Kasdan, quoted in Weinraub, "Director Criticizes."

CHAPTER 6

Cowboys, Aliens, and Sixtysomethings: Age and Nostalgia in Kasdan's Later Films

WYATT EARP TO *DREAMCATCHER*

L awrence Kasdan's first ever script sale, *The Bodyguard*, was finally made in 1992. Directed by Mick Jackson, it became a massive commercial success, even if Kasdan says that "I didn't think it was very well directed, and I can't watch it to this day." He then followed up his directorial work on *Grand Canyon* by trying again to revive that most nostalgic of genres for US baby-boomer males: the cowboy picture. His first Western, *Silverado*, had been an affectionate homage to the films that he had enjoyed in his youth, but *Wyatt Earp* (1994) was a comprehensive biopic of the famed lawman, a "three-hour movie about a very difficult character," in Kasdan's words, which reveled in the epic myths of the American West. Unfortunately for Kasdan, the film suffered from negative comparisons to *Tombstone* (1993), a lighter retelling of the same story released just a few months prior. Roger Ebert said that *Wyatt Earp* "took 'Tombstone' and pumped it full of hot air;"[1] while *The New York Times* complained that "the film's literal-minded approach to the hero's dark soul is one of its terrible problems," its 190-minute running time "slow" and "labor[ed]."[2] Kasdan's longtime collaborator, editor Carol Littleton, summarizes the situation succinctly: "*Tombstone* hurt us because it's a completely different kind of film [to *Wyatt Earp*], and it was a little more hip and it was not quite as serious."[3] *Tombstone*'s success showed that cowboy pictures could still attract a large audience, but it seemed that the stately, "handsome [and] grandiose"[4] iteration was not *en vogue*. Just as *Grand Canyon* suffered from comparisons to the freshness and urgency of *Boyz n the Hood*, so *Wyatt Earp* felt old-fashioned in the wake of *Tombstone*.

The moderate financial success of his next film, *French Kiss*, in 1995, helped to revive Kasdan's stock in Hollywood. This time he directed Adam Brooks's original screenplay, and Kasdan brought a clean, breezy pace to the romantic comedy—a genre that certainly was in fashion in the mid-1990s—even if

French Kiss has a rather retrograde view of its location: Kevin Kline's Gallic accent is dubious, stereotypes of snobbish locals are rife, and Paris and Cannes look postcard perfect. However, unlike *Wyatt Earp*, this attempt at a classic genre managed to find an audience, grossing over a hundred million dollars worldwide and becoming Kasdan's highest earning film as director since *The Big Chill*.[5]

For all his transitioning between genres, a common theme of Kasdan's films during this period was a predilection for homage. As discussed earlier, nostalgia has been cited as a facet of the baby-boomer experience, and one that is often attached to Lawrence Kasdan specifically.[6] However, his three films after *Silverado* were set in the present day and did not allude to any previous work or genre; rather, they commented on the contemporary concerns of American society. *The Accidental Tourist* and *Grand Canyon* addressed the struggle to adapt in a chaotic, dangerous world; while the screwball black comedy, *I Love You to Death* (1990; written by John Kostmayer), was based upon a true story about a woman's failed attempts to murder her unfaithful husband. However, Kasdan chose to follow these with three movies that harked back to "old" Hollywood: an expansive Western, a glamorous Europe-set romantic comedy, then, in 1999, *Mumford*, a small-town ensemble that reviewers likened to the work of Frank Capra.[7]

Mumford is, like its eponymous protagonist (played by Loren Dean), somewhat inscrutable, "a movie that prides itself on its quirks."[8] It is a gentle comedy that explores the dissonance between the external and internal self. As Sofie (Hope Davis), a patient with whom "Doctor" Mumford falls in love, says, "You feel like a fake, an impostor, as if you don't know what you're doing. Everybody feels that way sometimes, like we're not who we're supposed to be." This is a theme that resonates throughout Kasdan's work, and something he has even said about himself: "There's a secret life going on with everybody all the time. And it's the one that feels like, I'm a fake. I'm a sham. How am I going to get through this?"[9] From Ned Racine in *Body Heat*, whose alpha-male swagger is offset by his incompetence as a lawyer and a murderer, and the friends in *The Big Chill*, who lament the disconnect between their past and present selves; all the way through to the young Han Solo's combination of bravado and uncertainty in *Solo: A Star Wars Story*, Kasdan's protagonists are frequently plagued by self-doubt while struggling to maintain a veneer of confidence. In *Mumford*, though, the contrast is especially jarring, between the character's current standing as a respected (but, it transpires, entirely unqualified) therapist in a cozily tight-knit community, and his former life as a corrupt, drug-addicted IRS investigator who had an affair with his partner's wife and whose actions pushed another man to suicide. In a mainly positive review, Owen Gleiberman asks, "Who is Mumford, and will he get away with being the most deceptive and unethical shrink this side of Hannibal Lecter?"[10] The question speaks both to the film's strength and its weakness: the gap between Mumford's present (shot in bright sunshine and high-key colors) and his gritty past (filmed in grainy, washed-out sixteen-millimeter) is certainly revealing; but, like the characters in *The Big Chill*, for all the talk, the protagonist makes no genuine attempt at redeeming himself. Mumford's secret backstory, and his premeditated and potentially dangerous deception of the entire community, is only revealed to the town by the broadcast of a television program that discusses his hidden past; and it is only then, when he has already been exposed, that he admits his fraudulent behavior to the town and to the woman he loves.

A common criticism of the baby boomers is that, growing up in an era of relative stability and prosperity, they are prone to a sense of entitlement. Bruce Gibney, author of *A Generation of Sociopaths: How the Baby Boomers Betrayed America*, characterizes them as "a spoiled generation assuming things would be easy and that no sacrifices would have to be made."[11] While this accusation is wildly hyperbolic, there are traces of this attitude in some films of the era, and exemplified in *Mumford*: despite lying to his patients about his qualifications as a psychologist, falling in love with one of his patients, and repeatedly and deliberately breaching doctor-patient confidentiality, the protagonist displays almost no contrition. Furthermore, Kasdan's denouement seems designed to make his lead's comeuppance as painless as possible. Mumford receives a three-month prison sentence at a correctional facility that his lawyer (Martin Short) tells him is more like "a country club," before saying that he will "have him out in half the time," and Sofie promises to wait for him so that they can be together on his release. While it is interesting to see a Hollywood studio picture that refuses to moralize, the decision to have Mumford avoid any serious retribution for his crime does suggest a lack of concern with the potential consequences of such a deceit. Instead, it seems that the audience should be rooting for this rather bland, conservatively dressed man who has lied and endangered his patients' mental health entirely for his own gain—a problem that is, admittedly, tempered by the heightened, comedic tone of the movie.

A more benign aspect of baby-boomer culture that plays a central role in much of Kasdan's work is the television set. The symbol of 1950s affluence and aspiration, the TV is, of course, the medium through which Kasdan's generation consumed much of its entertainment. It is a frequent player in *The Big Chill*, its characters both watching it and appearing on-screen (Sam on his detective show, and various other friends through their mock interviews on the camcorder); it is utilized as a device to establish a "network narrative" in *Grand Canyon* as it connects families across lines of affluence and race; and, here, a TV program serves as the disruptor that unmasks the "real" Mumford, eventually leading to his redemption of sorts.

Lawrence Kasdan's next picture was an homage to the kinds of movies he probably watched on TV in his youth. *Dreamcatcher* (2003) is a schlock-horror with a B-movie sensibility that harks back to 1950s science fiction, such as *Invasion of the Body Snatchers* (1956) or *The Thing from Another World* (1951).[12] It is based on the novel by Stephen King, a writer often seen as an exemplar of the American baby boomers.[13] Therefore, it is not especially surprising that Kasdan would choose to make only his second literary adaptation from a King novel, and he said while shooting the film:

> The material sounded like something I could relate to. You know, friends who were sort of dissatisfied with their life, married to an extraordinary Stephen King development [. . .]. I thought, that's like one of my movies but with the thing I really want to do now, which is something more, something bigger.[14]

Dreamcatcher is certainly bigger than anything Kasdan made before or since, its $68-million budget more than double that of *Mumford*'s $28.7 million.[15] The decision to make this kind of large-scale sci-fi movie was surprising given Kasdan's usual choice of film. Of his previous directorial work, only *Silverado* had been in the vein of the screenplays he had written for George Lucas— a spirited action-adventure. Otherwise, Kasdan had usually focused on more reflective, adult-oriented pictures. Interviewed on the release of *Body Heat*, Kasdan said: "I fell into the world of mega-hits by accident. It doesn't interest me and I don't think it has been a productive thing for Hollywood."[16] Of course, it is the artist's prerogative to change his mind, especially more than two decades later, but Kasdan had never expressed any desire to make a "mega-hit" in the years since he began directing, until *Dreamcatcher*, when he said in a publicity interview: "I've written effects movies and never made one. So I had directed nine movies without ever doing an effects movie, and I wanted to do it."[17] Twenty years later, Kasdan was able to be more candid, admitting that, after the disappointing commercial performances of *Wyatt Earp* and *Mumford*, "I know why I was doing it, I was doing it for money."[18]

Stephen King's source material (which had been adapted by William Goldman before Kasdan's rewrite) includes themes that are prominent in Kasdan's work, most obviously the group of old friends who harbor a shared secret, and, as he explained in a contemporary interview, "about the way in which where we grow up is always with us [. . .] and about how it is threatened by the world outside."[19] Unfortunately, *Dreamcatcher* is also one of Stephen King's less successful books, the novelist saying: "I don't like *Dreamcatcher* very much. *Dreamcatcher* was written after the accident [when King was hit by a van]. I was using a lot of Oxycontin for pain. [. . .] I was pretty stoned when I wrote it."[20]

Aside from the ensemble dynamic, the most obvious aspect that connects *Dreamcatcher* to Kasdan's previous films is the spirit of nostalgia, especially when the characters remember their childhood in Derry, King's archetype for small-town America that echoes Kasdan's own upbringing in West Virginia, where, "we owned the town with our bikes."[21] In an analysis of King's works on screen, Regina Hansen notes that *Dreamcatcher*—the novel and the movie— depicts the frequent King trope of "nostalgia for being the odd person (usually man) out" and for being "the sensitive underdog who will eventually conquer the bully/monster." She adds that, while "King's allegiance with socially marginalized people" is admirable, these "social outsiders are white, straight, able-bodied males" that "maintain a hierarchy among losers."[22] In Kasdan's adaptation, none of the friends are obvious action-hero types, but their reduc- tion of relationships with women to "fuckarow" (when they are refused sex) and "fuckaree" (when they have sex) makes their sexuality abundantly clear, even in a film with almost no female characters. The libidinous theme contin- ues in the shared memory from their childhood in which they fulfilled the male fantasy of standing up to the bullies, their adventure instigated by a pubescent desire to see a picture of a naked girl. Furthermore, the blend of gross-out comedy and body horror—with the alien "shit weasels" hiding in toilets, caus- ing flatulence, attacking their victims' crotches, and entering and emerging from the anuses of their hosts—plays on starkly male, heterosexual fears.

More troubling, though, is that this deliberately outrageous fantasy-horror is juxtaposed against the story of Duddits (Donnie Wahlberg), mentally dis- abled and suffering from terminal cancer. Even though the group call Duddits their friend, his otherness is apparent both by his separation from them (he is not invited to their annual reunion, despite their declared love for him) and then, more directly, by the revelation that he is actually an alien—this final twist a departure from King's novel, which never explains the reason for Duddits's supernatural powers—and eventually becoming a Christ-like savior. Hansen likens this representation of the "magical goodness/innocence" of the sole dis- abled character to the "Magical Negro" trope that Stephen King uses in *The*

Figure 6.1 Duddits the savior

Green Mile.[23] In terms of Lawrence Kasdan's work, there are similarities to the way that he utilizes the working-class female in *The Accidental Tourist*, with Muriel there "to take a firm hand and help [Macon] tame this grief so he can go on with his life;"[24] and, to a lesser extent, the black working-class male in *Grand Canyon*, with Simon teaching Mack to appreciate the beauty in uncertainty. Kasdan frequently employs non-white, non-middle-class, non-able-bodied characters; but they are often there to support the white male lead, sacrificing themselves in order to help the central character become a better man.

While the big-budget sci-fi movie, based on an existing source, was an unusual choice for Kasdan to direct, the film conformed to many of the typically baby-boomer themes that are prevalent throughout his career: the nostalgia mode (for 1950s invasion sci-fi, as well as for childhood in small-town USA), the quick-witted exchanges between an ensemble of old friends, and the sympathetic but unintentionally condescending use of the "outsider" (from the perspective of a middle-class male) to help resolve the problems of the lead characters. The film performed poorly at the box office, with Roger Ebert labeling it "a monster movie of stunning awfulness."[25] The failure of the film to make a profit left Lawrence Kasdan, in his words, "wounded careerwise,"[26] and there was perhaps a sense that the writer of some of the most popular blockbuster films of the 1980s and 1990s was now out of step with many cinemagoers, especially with the younger viewers that usually consume this kind of big-budget spectacle. Kasdan himself alluded to this when he said that "there was a period when I became very discouraged about movies [. . .] because they just stopped making the kind of movies that I had thrived on."[27] Similarly, Kasdan had stopped making the kind of movies that appealed to large audiences, and he would have to wait nine years before he was able to direct his next film.

DARLING COMPANION

Lawrence Kasdan wrote *Darling Companion* with his wife Meg, their second collaboration, having worked together on *Grand Canyon*. Released in 2012, the film is markedly different in style and scope to *Dreamcatcher*'s expansive CGI-heavy action. A comedy-drama about an extended family's search for a lost dog, *Darling Companion* was independently financed on a budget of five million dollars,[28] less than ten per cent of *Dreamcatcher*'s production costs. For most filmmakers, such a career turn would appear to be an enforced reduction in their ambitions; certainly, as Kasdan concedes, his status in Hollywood was at a low ebb. However, due to his eclectic choice of subject and genre, *Darling Companion* is no less anomalous than his decision to make the Western *Silverado* immediately after *The Big Chill*, or to follow the broad comedy of *I Love You to Death* with an exploration of race and class in *Grand Canyon*. The film, too, shares many characteristics of Kasdan's more celebrated works as writer-director; in fact, some critics position *Darling Companion* as the third of a baby-boomer trilogy after *The Big Chill* and *Grand Canyon*.[29] The prototype schema that the viewer might employ in watching the movie's early scenes, with Kevin Kline anchoring an ensemble cast in a contemporary drama, certainly suggests as much. Furthermore, the genesis of this film was clearly personal, based on the Kasdans' own experience of losing their pet dog, in a way that mirrors the other films that are most overtly about his generation. Kasdan said of *The Big Chill* in a 1983 interview that, "Absolutely, it's very personal. [. . .] These are issues that are very real in my life;"[30] and of *Grand Canyon*, "This movie was written from my gut. It's about my own surprise about the way the world is, as opposed to the way I thought it was going to be."[31] Similarly, Kasdan stated that "*Darling Companion* is meant to be light, but there's no question that there's a tinge of mortality throughout, one that comes more naturally into your conversation as your friends get older and you get older, too."[32]

So, once again, Kasdan was examining his generation's current concerns explicitly, not through the haze of nostalgia as in his preceding four films, nor obliquely as he had done with *Body Heat* and *The Accidental Tourist*. The difference with *Darling Companion*, compared to the first two parts of his "trilogy," was that in 2010, when the film was shot, the early boomers were no longer in their thirties or forties, but entering their sixties. This immediately placed it outside the studio mainstream, with Kasdan remarking that "Hollywood certainly isn't making movies about sixty-year-old people and thirty-year-old marriages."[33] In this respect, *Darling Companion* was a bold choice of project: a personal story in which the protagonists do not fit the conventional movie-star template. Kasdan was aware of the commercial risk, stating on its release:

> Truffaut said that when what you're interested in matches up with the public, it's an accident. It's so true. It's all timing and gestalt. If you've had the luxury of expressing something personal, and no one goes, that's not a shock. If it's personal, and people go, that's the shock.[34]

Darling Companion reports on the experiences of upper-middle-class baby boomers as their children are leaving home and getting married, and the difficulties adapting to shifting family dynamics. As with his earlier personal films, Kasdan employs an ensemble of characters with intertwined histories. However, unlike *The Big Chill* or *Grand Canyon*, or Kasdan's other works as writer-director, for that matter, there is almost no social comment, nor even an acknowledgment of life outside the protagonists' affluent bubble. This could, of course, be an observation in itself, with the themes of Kasdan's films reflecting the changes in attitude of his cohort as they get older: first, his characters in *The Big Chill* voiced frustration at the loss of 1960s idealism in the post-Vietnam era; then *Grand Canyon* explored the fear of chaos and change that many of Kasdan's contemporaries were experiencing as parents in urban America; finally, *Darling Companion* describes the empty-nest syndrome of later years, when married couples are forced to look at their own relationships in a new light, to worry about themselves again now that their children no longer need them. It is necessarily a more melancholic, inward-looking condition, so it is perhaps unfair to criticize the film's lack of urgency, but it does mark it as different to its predecessors with their socio-political undertones.

Another way that *Darling Companion* deviates from *The Big Chill* and *Grand Canyon* is in its reliance on a clearly established story premise: the search for the missing dog. The previous instalments in the "trilogy" were described as "virtually plotless" and deceptively casual,[35] and in interviews Kasdan tended to discuss their themes more than the actual plots. But, even if *Darling Companion* focuses on human relationships, the Kasdans talked about this film much less ambiguously; for example, Meg Kasdan said that:

> The story is about a couple who have been married for a long time. The wife rescues a dog and they become attached to the dog. And the husband [. . .] loses the dog, and the movie is about the search that ensues.[36]

This synopsis marks the film as separate from *The Big Chill* and *Grand Canyon*, with their more nebulous plots, far harder to summarize concisely. Furthermore, by relying on such a clearly defined goal—finding the dog—the narrative is much more conventional. Even if the other movies broadly fit the classic dramatic structure at which Kasdan is so adept, the turning points are less obvious (as demonstrated by my partial disagreement with Kristin Thompson's analysis of *The Big Chill*'s acts, discussed in Chapter 4). In *Darling Companion*, conversely, it is much simpler to identify the transitions between acts, whether basing it upon a traditional three-act structure or on Thompson's four-act paradigm.[37] This more conventional, plot-driven mode of storytelling means that it is no surprise when the protagonists are finally reunited with the dog; and, consequently, the character developments are easier to predict, too: that the married couple Beth (Diane Keaton) and Joseph (Kline) will be reconciled through the search, that Penny's (Dianne Wiest) apparently unsuitable new partner Russell (Richard Jenkins) will earn acceptance into the family, and that Bryan (Mark Duplass) and Carmen (Ayelet Zurer) will be drawn together romantically.

Where *Darling Companion* is similar to the earlier movies is in its emphasis on relationships and dialogue over set-pieces. In publicizing the film, Kasdan said that:

> The truth of our lives is not car chases and rocket ships. The truth of our lives for most of us is we sit in a room with people we care about, or have just met, or want to care about, and we talk, and that's what human beings do. And I like to see it in movies.[38]

Indeed, the film's more labored moments, and the times when the small budget becomes most apparent, are the action sequences, such as when Bryan and Russell fight off a "mountain man," or the aircraft's emergency landing during the climax. Otherwise, Kasdan utilizes his experienced cast effectively, with clear parallels to *The Big Chill*, especially during the interior scenes, when the camera often remains static, allowing the actors' exchanges to provide the dynamism within the frame. Even in the exteriors, with the snow-capped mountains and lush forests reminiscent of *Silverado*, the camera usually remains in tight one- or two-shots, the emphasis on the characters' interactions, despite Kasdan's obvious attraction to the scenery. A key point here is that the film is less about individual performances than the to-and-fro between characters, even if Kevin Kline serves again in the role of main protagonist, based on screen time, as well as the opening shot in which we take his point of view before he turns to the camera in close-up. Kasdan makes the distinction between characters and relationships, saying that "you have a character but he doesn't have any shape. There's no molding. There's no contrast until there's the light of another character shown on him."[39] When I interviewed him, he said, "I like the audience to think, 'Well, is that really the truth, what he's saying about himself?' and let other characters give you a different perspective on it." *Darling Companion* exemplifies this philosophy, the members of each pair in the search party forcing the other to examine their own weaknesses, most prominently in the disconnect between Joseph, the aloof surgeon, and his wife Beth as she struggles to come to terms with the "loss" of her grown-up daughters and now her dog. Therefore, while *Darling Companion* lacks the elements of social criticism present in *The Big Chill* and *Grand Canyon*, and the idyllic setting and lighter tone make it a gentler film, it is perhaps more scathing of its characters—all the harsher as, in their advanced years, there is less scope for change.

The movie did not recoup its costs, and it received mostly negative reviews, a fact that contrasts sharply with the commercial and critical success of Lawrence Kasdan's earlier "boomer" films. It suffered from a central story device that failed to capture the zeitgeist in the way that its predecessors had, Kasdan admitting to me that "my wife and I had had this experience [of losing a pet dog], and we didn't realize that no-one else in the world would give a shit about it." *Darling Companion* was the first of his more personal works to be released at a time when baby boomers no longer dominated Hollywood (with only two of his cohort directing any of the ten highest-grossing films of the 2010s; compared to the previous decade when eight of the top ten were directed by boomers), and when actors of his generation were no longer the desired age to lead studio pictures. Kasdan was aware of this fact, and in portraying a thirty-year marriage and focusing primarily on sexagenarian characters, then *Darling Companion* serves as a flawed but sincere attempt at completing the "trilogy" about his generation, with all its attendant physical, spiritual, and emotional aches and pains; and it contributes further to Lawrence Kasdan's reputation as the spokesperson for the baby boomers.

SPOKESPERSON FOR A GENERATION?

When the film academic Marina Heung called Lawrence Kasdan "a spokes-man for our contemporary social predicament,"[40] only one of his seven releases as writer or director up to that time had been overtly about his own genera-tion's concerns. Contemporary critics recognized that *The Big Chill* was not simply a film about an old friends' weekend reunion, but a commentary on a wider malaise among Kasdan's cohort that tries "to make up for the American cinema's dismal failure to deal adequately with the late 1960s while they were happening;"[41] and "an unusual film for the 1980s [. . .] about a generation."[42]

That Kasdan has become so associated with the baby boomers may sim-ply be a matter of timing. Aside from John Sayles's *Return of the Secaucus 7* (1980)—an independent release, to which *The Big Chill* has often been compared—there had been few films that discussed the early boomers' experi-ence post-Vietnam (aside from those specifically about military veterans) and none that had received the backing of a major studio. Whereas in the late 1960s, movies such as *Midnight Cowboy* (1969) and *Easy Rider* (1969) were made for Kasdan's generation, by the 1980s it was his generation that was making the pictures themselves, with the demographic gaining power in Hollywood and in American society at large. But, rather than reporting upon the boomers' con-temporary condition, much of the popular cinema created by Kasdan's peers, and sometimes by Kasdan himself, tended toward nostalgia for childhood and adolescence, or for the entertainment of those times: Steven Spielberg had just directed *Raiders of the Lost Ark* (with Kasdan as screenwriter) and *E.T.: The Extra-Terrestrial* (1982), while writing and producing the TV-fixated *Polter-geist* (1982); Barry Levinson (born slightly earlier, in 1942) had just made *Diner* (1982); and George Lucas (another "victory baby," like Levinson) had followed *American Graffiti* (1973) by creating the Star Wars trilogy and *Raiders*, again with Kasdan involved. Eight of the ten highest-grossing films of the decade would be directed by boomers, and the list would be dominated by youth-oriented fantasy and sci-fi pictures.

The Big Chill, then, was the first Hollywood studio release made by and about the baby boomers as young professionals, the film "a symbol of the yuppification of '80s America."[43] Kasdan dislikes the term "yuppie," but the movie does represent that moment at which the radical generation of the 1960s and 1970s, a group shaped by its anti-authoritarianism, was now becoming the establishment, its members' lives no longer defined by their stance on Vietnam but by business deals, babies, and liberal guilt. And *The Big Chill* addresses this transition head-on by having its characters discuss the uncomfortable juxta-position of their past and present selves, while making it palatable for a wider audience through the warmth of the relationships and its soundtrack of crowd-pleasing 1960s hits. Even if *The Big Chill* did not make it into the top ten of highest-grossing US films of the year, its cultural impact was far more power-ful than most of those that did, as it invented the "quarter-life crisis film"[44] that inflected future mumble-core dramas, as well as ensemble comedies such as *Four Weddings and a Funeral* (1994) and even *The Royal Tenenbaums* (2001). Its influence was perhaps felt even more strongly in television, with the Emmy-winning *Thirtysomething* (1987–91) clearly inspired by *The Big Chill*, its ensemble of formerly idealistic middle-class couples dealing with early-mid-life angst. This in turn led to an increase in dialogue-heavy TV dramas like *My So-Called Life* (1994–5),[45] and even more recent ensemble shows, such as *Girls* (2012–17), with creator Lena Dunham writing an essay about *The Big Chill*'s influence on her generation's view of their parents.[46]

In spite of this impact, if, after *The Big Chill*, Lawrence Kasdan had con-tinued to make films such as his next, the nostalgic Western *Silverado*, then he may have become part of the group of populist directors like Joe Dante, Ivan Reitman, and Robert Zemeckis, all baby boomers, but rarely labeled as such. Zemeckis is an interesting comparison, given that, like Kasdan, he was a writer-director who had worked for Steven Spielberg while making his own more personal films, *I Wanna Hold Your Hand* (1978) and *Used Cars* (1980). After these failed financially, Zemeckis directed the Indiana Jones-inspired action-adventure *Romancing the Stone* (1984), then, under the mentorship of Spielberg, the *Back to the Future* trilogy (1985, 1989, and 1990) and *Who Framed Roger Rabbit* (1988), all of which were heavily imbued with nostalgia and stunningly successful at the box office. However, while Zemeckis contin-ued to exemplify his generation's predilection for looking back, Kasdan after *Silverado* returned to contemporary, adult-focused stories, directing *The Acci-dental Tourist*, *I Love You to Death*, and *Grand Canyon*. Rather than telling fan-tastic tales, Kasdan explored issues of grief, divorce, infidelity, race relations, and existential ennui. This helped to secure Kasdan's status as the "archetypal Hollywood baby boomer," even if, ironically, he may have been more arche-typal had he continued in the vein of Zemeckis, who stayed primarily in the nostalgia mode his entire career.

Further positioning Kasdan as representative of his cohort is his contin-ued interest in "boomer pulse-taking,"[47] not just when his generation was the dominant creative force in Hollywood and provided the majority of movie stars, but even into the 2010s when, with *Darling Companion*, he focused upon the travails of his peers as they entered their sixties. His filmography, then, offers audiences a longitudinal study of his age group that few of his con-temporaries have attempted. Interestingly, the earliest of Kasdan's present-day dramas share characteristics with the most recent, showing a generation that is inward-looking and unintentionally self-absorbed. Conversely, his films in the intervening years had the leads feeling similarly discombobulated but find-ing solace in assisting others, such as Macon helping Muriel in *The Accidental*

Tourist, or Mack's connection with Simon and his family in *Grand Canyon*. This points to Kasdan's evolving world view, from seeing white middle-class baby boomers as up-and-coming professionals concerned with their own situations; to presenting them in positions of stability, parenthood, and community service; before a return to a more self-centered condition as financially comfortable but emotionally uncertain empty-nesters, an evolution that mirrors his cohort's status in American life.

After growing up in a period of unprecedented economic growth, Kasdan's generation was at the forefront of massive cultural upheaval through adolescence and early adulthood, contributing to an era of growing liberalism, and these early boomers are still more likely to vote Democrat, according to the Pew Research Center.[48] The attitude is personified through most of Kasdan's films set in the present day, in which the protagonists are nearly always financially comfortable professionals who strive to do the decent thing in helping those they perceive as less fortunate: the characters in *The Big Chill* who lament the lapse of their more altruistic selves, Macon trying to help Muriel and her sick son in *The Accidental Tourist*, Mack moving Simon's family to a better neighborhood in *Grand Canyon*, the friends in *Dreamcatcher* who rescue Duddits from bullies. While these efforts to help could be read as patronizing toward the recipient, there is an inherent idealism at their core, and an acceptance of people from different backgrounds that is not always present in films made by Kasdan's peers. Even in his screenplays and movies set in different times and places, Kasdan often positions marginalized people at the center of the narrative, including a black co-protagonist in the ensemble of *Silverado*, a rarity in the genre; making the Egyptian Sallah more prominent than discussed in the story conference in *Raiders of the Lost Ark* (while also facing criticism for the treatment of peripheral Arab characters[49]); boosting Leia's importance in *The Empire Strikes Back*; then choosing to use non-white and female leads in *The Force Awakens*.[50]

It would be absurd to suggest that any single filmmaker could speak for an entire generation, and it is important to emphasize that the baby-boomer archetype is actually a relatively small subset of that group: the white, college-educated strand of Americans who came of age in the second half of the 1960s. But if we accept this narrower definition, then Lawrence Kasdan is the Hollywood filmmaker who has portrayed on-screen the concerns of his demographic more than any other. Both through making socially conscious movies about middle-class professionals, and in creating screenplays and films that hark back to the Westerns and adventure serials that his cohort watched on television as children, Kasdan has repeatedly chronicled and spoken to the experience of the baby boomers, the generation that outnumbered all others for over half a century and continues to dominate many aspects of American society today.

NOTES

1. Roger Ebert, "*Wyatt Earp*," *Roger Ebert*, June 24, 1994, https://www.rogerebert.com/reviews/wyatt-earp-1994 (accessed July 4, 2023).

2. Caryn James, "Review/Film: *Wyatt Earp*; Into the Heart and Soul of Darkness," *The New York Times*, June 24, 1994, http://www.nytimes.com/1994/06/24/movies/review-film-wyatt-earp-into-the-heart-and-soul-of-darkness.html (accessed July 4, 2023).

3. Carol Littleton, quoted in Tim Greiving, "It Happened That Way," *Wyatt Earp Original Motion Picture Soundtrack*, Sleeve notes, La-La Land Records, 2013.

4. Todd McCarthy, "Review: *Wyatt Earp*," *Variety*, 1994, http://variety.com/1994/film/reviews/wyatt-earp-1200437510/ (accessed July 4, 2023).

5. "*French Kiss*: Grosses," *Box Office Mojo*, 2020, https://www.boxofficemojo.com/release/rl794134017/weekend/ (accessed July 4, 2023).

6. For example, Marina Heung, "The Big Score: Work and Survival in the Films of Lawrence Kasdan," *Michigan Quarterly Review* 24, no. 4 (1985), 546, https://quod.lib.umich.edu/m/mqrarchive/act2080.0024.004/49:3?page=root;rgn=full+text;size=100;view=image (accessed July 4, 2023); Christopher Orr, "Cain, Naturalism and Noir," *Film Criticism* 25, no. 1 (2000), 62; and David R. Shumway, "Rock 'n' Roll Soundtracks and the Production of Nostalgia," *Cinema Journal* 38, no. 2 (1999), 36.

7. Stephen Holden, "Sure, the Doctor is in: In Demand and in Trouble," *The New York Times*, September 24, 1999, https://www.nytimes.com/1999/09/24/movies/film-review-sure-the-doctor-is-in-in-demand-and-in-trouble.html (accessed July 4, 2023).

8. Ann Hornaday, "The Misfits of *Mumford*; Review: A Psychologist Administers to a Small Town's Many Eccentrics in Lawrence Kasdan's New Ensemble Comedy," *The Baltimore Sun*, September 24, 1999, https://www.baltimoresun.com/news/bs-xpm-1999-09-24-9909240361-story.html/ (accessed July 4, 2023).

9. Lawrence Kasdan, interviewed by John August and Craig Mazin, "Episode 247: The One with Lawrence Kasdan," *Scriptnotes*, audio podcast, April 26, 2016, http://johnaugust.com/2016/the-one-with-lawrence-kasdan (accessed June 29, 2023).

10. Owen Gleiberman, "*Mumford*," *Entertainment Weekly*, September 24, 1999, https://ew.com/article/1999/09/24/mumford-2/ (accessed July 4, 2023).

11. Bruce Gibney, quoted in Sean Illing, "How the Baby Boomers—not Millennials—Screwed America," *Vox*, October 26, 2019, https://www.vox.com/2017/12/20/16772670/baby-boomers-millennials-congress-debt (accessed July 4, 2023). See also Bill Keller, "The Entitled Generation," *The New York Times*, July 29, 2012, https://www.nytimes.com/2012/07/30/opinion/keller-the-entitled-generation.html (accessed July 4, 2023). Also, Rachel Hosie, "Baby Boomers more Entitled than Millennials, says Study," *The Independent*, May 18, 2017, https://www.independent.co.uk/life-style/baby-boomers-millennials-more-entitled-older-generation-savings-homeowner-income-study-house-car-a7742411.html (accessed July 4, 2023).

12. See Michael Sragow, "High-end Horror? Keep Dreaming," *The Baltimore Sun*, March 21, 2003, https://www.baltimoresun.com/news/bs-xpm-2003-03-21-0303210131-story.html (accessed July 4, 2023); and Mark Browning, *Stephen King on the Big Screen* (Bristol, UK: Intellect, 2009), 139.

13. See, for example, Patrick McAleer, "I Have the Whole World in my Hands. . . Now What?: Power, Control, Responsibility and the Baby Boomers in Stephen King's Fiction," *The Journal of Popular Culture* 44, no. 6 (2011); Sonny Bunch, "In Film, '*It*' Tosses Out the Most Powerful Part of Stephen King's Novel," *The Washington Post*, September 8, 2017,

https://www.washingtonpost.com/news/act-four/wp/2017/09/07/in-film-it-tosses-out-the-most-powerful-part-of-stephen-kings-novel/ (accessed July 4, 2023). Stephen King has called himself a "typical" baby-boomer; see "Stephen King on the Laziness of the Baby Boomers," *Entertainment Weekly*, February 1, 2007, https://ew.com/article/2007/02/01/stephen-king-laziness-baby-boomers/ (accessed July 4, 2023).

14. Kasdan, interviewed for "DreamMakers—A Journey Through Production," *Dreamcatcher*, DVD (Warner Bros.), 2003.

15. Box office data from "*Dreamcatcher*," 2020, *Box Office Mojo*, https://www.boxofficemojo.com/release/rl3092153857/ (accessed July 4, 2023); and "Mumford (1999)," *The Numbers*, 2020, https://www.the-numbers.com/movie/Mumford#tab=summary (accessed July 4, 2023).

16. Kasdan, quoted in Dan Yakir, "Lawrence Kasdan Interviewed," *Film Comment* 17, no. 5 (1981), 52.

17. Kasdan, interviewed for "DreamWeavers—The Visual Effects of *Dreamcatcher*," *Dreamcatcher*, DVD (Warner Bros.), 2003.

18. Kasdan, quoted in Jim Hemphill, "Lawrence Kasdan," *Academy of Motion Picture Arts and Sciences: Oral History Collection* (Los Angeles: AMPAS, 2022), transcript, 44.

19. Kasdan, quoted in John Whitley, "Filmmakers on Film: Lawrence Kasdan," *The Daily Telegraph*, April 27, 2002, http://www.telegraph.co.uk/culture/film/3576515/Filmmakers-on-film-Lawrence-Kasdan.html (accessed July 4, 2023).

20. King, quoted in Andy Greene, "Stephen King: The Rolling Stone interview," *Rolling Stone*, October 31, 2014, https://www.rollingstone.com/culture/culture-features/stephen-king-the-rolling-stone-interview-191529/ (accessed July 4, 2023).

21. Kasdan, quoted in an unpublished interview with James Russell (2013).

22. Regina Hansen, "Stephen King's *IT* and *Dreamcatcher* on Screen: Hegemonic White Masculinity and Nostalgia for Underdog Boyhood," *Science Fiction Film and Television* 10, no. 2 (2017), 161–2. Original parentheses.

23. Hansen, "Stephen King's *IT*," 171.

24. Kasdan, interviewed for "Reflections of *The Accidental Tourist*," *The Accidental Tourist*, DVD (Warner Bros.), 2003.

25. Roger Ebert, "*Dreamcatcher*," *Roger Ebert*, March 22, 2003, https://www.rogerebert.com/reviews/dreamcatcher-2003 (accessed July 4, 2023).

26. Kasdan, quoted in Chuck Wilson, "Lawrence Kasdan Interview," *LA Weekly*, April 19, 2012, https://www.laweekly.com/lawrence-kasdan-interview/ (accessed July 4, 2023).

27. Kasdan, interviewed by August and Mazin, "Episode 247."

28. Ray Morton, "Darling Companions: A Conversation with Lawrence and Meg Kasdan," *Script*, April 26, 2012, https://scriptmag.com/features/darling-companions-a-conversation-with-lawrence-and-meg-kasdan (accessed July 4, 2023).

29. For example, Andrew O'Hehir, "*Darling Companion*: A Death Knell for the Baby Boom?" *Salon*, April 18, 2012, http://www.salon.com/2012/04/18/darling_companion_a_death_knell_for_the_baby_boom/ (accessed July 4, 2023).

30. Kasdan, interviewed on "Lawrence Kasdan for *The Big Chill* 1983," Bobbie Wygant Archive, June 2, 2020, https://www.youtube.com/watch?v=iT1WnT3uA-Q (accessed July 4, 2023).

31. Kasdan, interviewed for "*Grand Canyon*: Featurette," *Grand Canyon*, DVD (20th Century Fox), 1992.

32. Kasdan, quoted in Wilson, "Lawrence Kasdan Interview."

33. Kasdan, interviewed for "*Darling Companion*: Behind the Scenes," *Darling Companion*, DVD (Metrodome), 2013.

34. Kasdan, quoted in Wilson, "Lawrence Kasdan Interview."

35. Kim Newman, "*The Big Chill*," *Monthly Film Bulletin* 51, no. 600 (1984), 42; and Janet Maslin, "The Accidents and Miracles in Everyday Life," *The New York Times*, December 25, 1991, https://www.nytimes.com/1991/12/25/movies/review-film-the-accidents-and-miracles-in-everyday-life.html (accessed July 4, 2023).

36. Meg Kasdan, interviewed for "*Darling Companion*: Behind the Scenes," *Darling Companion*, DVD (Metrodome), 2013.

37. Kristin Thompson, *Storytelling in the New Hollywood: Understanding Classical Narrative Technique* (Cambridge, MA: Harvard University Press, 1999), 28–9.

38. Kasdan, "*Darling Companion*: Behind the Scenes."

39. Kasdan, interviewed by August and Mazin, "Episode 247."

40. Heung, "Big Score," 548.

41. Kim Newman, "*The Big Chill*," *Monthly Film Bulletin* 51, no. 600 (1984), 41.

42. Rob Edelman, "*The Big Chill*," *Cineaste* 13, no. 2 (1984), 42.

43. Phil Maciak, "We're Not Leaving. We're Never Leaving: *The Big Chill* and the Enduring Power of Quarter-life Crisis Movies," *Slate*, July 29, 2014, https://slate.com/culture/2014/07/the-big-chill-and-the-quarter-life-crisis-film.html (accessed July 4, 2023).

44. Ibid.

45. See Scott Collins, "Eightiessomething," *The Los Angeles Times*, August 23, 2009, https://www.latimes.com/archives/la-xpm-2009-aug-23-ca-thirtysomethingmain23-story.html (accessed July 4, 2023); Soraya Roberts, "The Big Thaw: Togetherness and What *Thirty-something* Means Now," *Los Angeles Review of Books*, March 8, 2015, https://lareviewofbooks.org/article/big-thaw-togetherness-thirtysomething-means-now/ (accessed July 4, 2023).

46. Lena Dunham, "*The Big Chill*: These are Your Parents," *The Criterion Collection*, July 29, 2014, https://www.criterion.com/current/posts/3250-the-big-chill-these-are-your-parents (accessed July 4, 2023).

47. Melissa Anderson, "*Darling Companion*," *The Village Voice*, April 18, 2012, http://www.villagevoice.com/film/darling-companion-6434614 (accessed July 4, 2023).

48. "The Whys and Hows of Generation Research," *Pew Research Center*, September 3, 2015, 14, https://www.people-press.org/2015/09/03/the-whys-and-hows-of-generations-research/ (accessed July 4, 2023).

49. Frank Tomasulo, "Mr. Jones goes to Washington: *Raiders of the Lost Ark*," *Quarterly Review of Film Studies* 7, no. 4 (1982), 335.

50. J. J. Abrams said: "From the beginning of discussions [with writer Lawrence Kasdan], the notion of a woman at the centre of the story was always something that was compelling and exciting to me. And not just at the centre. We knew that, in addition to Leia who was a critical piece of this puzzle, we wanted to have other women—not necessarily human, but female—characters in the story." Quoted in Andrew Pulver, "Star Wars Director JJ Abrams: We Always Wanted Women at the Centre of *The Force Awakens*," *The Guardian*, December 17, 2015, https://www.theguardian.com/film/2015/dec/17/star-wars-director-jj-abrams-women-the-force-awakens-daisy-ridley-lupita-nyongo-carrie-fisher, accessed July 4, 2023. Original parentheses.

PART IV

Influences, Without and Within

CHAPTER 7

From Noir to Kurosawa: Allusion and Homage in Lawrence Kasdan's Films

Lawrence Kasdan's early-career success working alongside George Lucas and Steven Spielberg was followed by his emergence as a writer-director of adult-oriented dramas, interspersed with comedy, sci-fi, and Westerns. While many aspects of his filmography appear quite disparate, it may be possible to reconcile Kasdan's varied choice of project by examining his major influences. In interviews, he is more apt than most to cite the filmmakers that have inspired him, and his output has often been allusive. *Raiders of the Lost Ark* is the obvious early example, with the story conference (discussed in Chapter 1) revealing some of the touchstones in constructing the plot and main character, such as Republic adventure serials, samurai movies, Spaghetti Westerns, and the James Bond pictures. Kasdan's directorial debut *Body Heat* has parallels with classic film noir, such as *Double Indemnity* (1944) and *Out of the Past* (1947); and his cowboy pictures, *Silverado* and *Wyatt Earp*, are unashamedly old-fashioned in their construction and execution, the antithesis of the revisionist Westerns of the period. Even a less conventionally generic work such as *Mumford* borrows thematic elements from elsewhere, described in one review as "a Frank Capra-style social fable."[1] A tendency toward homage is common among writers and directors of his generation, as noted in Chapter 6, but Kasdan's proclivity for pastiche has been especially noted by critics, his "'movie-movie' style of film-making" often quoting from previous works and genres.[2] Kasdan makes no secret of his influences, and regards allusion not as something to suppress, but as an intrinsic part of creation. He states that:

> so many directors inspire you. Sometimes they only made one film that inspired you but you don't judge that, you say, "I loved that movie. And that changed my life seeing that movie." [. . .] [A]nd people say, "Well, you know, it's a little bit like such and such and a little bit like that, something else, you know." It's supposed to be. That's how art moves

through the ages. We don't make it up brand new at the time. We put it together in different ways. And the world is pushing us to see it in different ways. But basically the stories are the same. And they are enormously satisfying. So, when someone says, "Well, it's a little bit like such and such." I say, "Great. I like that. I like that kind of thing."[3]

For Lawrence Kasdan, existing works are the building blocks for creating new stories. That is not to say that he merely mimics or remakes old films; rather, he takes inspiration from a variety of writers and directors in order to mold new, distinctive, contemporary narratives. By analyzing the influence of other filmmakers upon his career, the viewer can understand more fully Kasdan's choices of topic and theme. In doing so, this chapter will demonstrate the ways that an "archetypal" baby-boom filmmaker reconstitutes existing movies to create new and original works.

NOSTALGIA AND COMMENT

Kasdan credits his wide appreciation of cinema to the access gained to various types of film during his college days; and, in turn, he connects cinema to the political and social radicalism of that era. It may be the case that, by drawing upon classic works, Kasdan is doing more than simply displaying the common boomer trait of cine-literate nostalgia. Instead, he is subtly aligning himself with the liberal ideals of his time at the University of Michigan, "the hottest moment in American student radicalism" when "movies were absolutely *the* thing that was happening culturally."[4] Certainly, Kasdan's use of intertextuality often acts as a prism through which he comments upon current issues, as the investigations into his boomer films in the preceding section established. Kasdan's application of pastiche is never gratuitous or merely stylistic; instead, it is always in the service of his movies' thematic concerns. For example, in *Body Heat*, the costumes and settings would not be out of place in the 1930s: Matty's elegant white dress and southern gothic mansion; Ned's nondescript suit and tie, and the poky office that could have belonged to Sam Spade; the ageless, faceless diners and bars; not to mention the heightened melodrama and rapid-fire repartee. While these choices evoke the spirit of film noir and contribute to the sleazy, sultry ambience, they also remind the viewer of an apparently simpler time, as Ned Racine, a product of the 1980s, looks to get what he believes the world owes him: the woman with movie-star looks and riches, the money and the mansion. Kasdan has revealed that the film is as much about his generation as *The Big Chill*, and William Hurt's protagonist exemplifies the well-educated graduate of the late 1960s (a lawyer, no less), who is now beginning to feel disappointment at his apparently terminal mediocrity, with his colleague joking darkly: "You've started using your incompetence as a weapon." He wants the success that was promised to him as a child of the post-war economic boom and a member of the generation that was going to change everything, even if he is not necessarily willing to work for it.

Continental Divide was the first of Kasdan's spec scripts to go into production, with Michael Apted directing. It was released just three weeks after *Body Heat*, and it has a similarly retro feel despite its modern-day setting, but this time in the vein of screwball comedy rather than noir. John Belushi plays a cynical Chicago reporter who, after exposing the shady dealings of a local politician, is forced into hiding in the Rockies. There, he seeks to interview a reclusive researcher of bald eagles, a woman who is the very antithesis of the hard-bitten journalist. It is a classic "odd couple" pairing in the spirit of *It Happened One Night* (1934) or *Bringing Up Baby* (1938), but it also comments upon the contemporary American relationship with work. The conflict is centered upon each lead's dedication to their career, and the dissonance between the life of a big-city reporter and an ornithologist who is more at home in nature. While this kind of rift is typical in such a film, in which opposites always attract eventually, the denouement is surprisingly ambiguous: even though Ernie and Nell overcome their differences to fall in love and get married, the movie ends with them deciding to live separately, their respective jobs prioritized over their being together. This demonstrates Kasdan's penchant for uncertainty, which subverts the unequivocal happy ending one would expect in the genre. It also speaks to the era, in which both sexes were identifying themselves more with their work than their relationships, and when it was becoming more common for women to follow their careers, rather than remain in thrall to their partners' needs.

Kasdan says that the chocolate-box-perfect town of *Mumford*, with its tree-lined avenues and primly whitewashed houses, is similar to the West Virginia towns where he grew up in the 1950s and '60s.[5] The location would not be out of place in a Frank Capra comedy; yet the small-town archetype stands in jarring opposition to the existential problems of its characters. That is even before we learn about "Doctor" Mumford's dark backstory, which pulls us out of the 1950s aesthetic and into a hard-edged version of modern day. While Kasdan has described himself as someone who prefers classic dramatic structure,[6] there is a postmodernist bent to his use of pastiche. In *Mumford*, he employs various types of film stock to differentiate between the primary-colored "real" world, the film noir fantasies of one of Mumford's patients, and the gritty, drug-addled memories of the eponymous lead. Through such techniques, Kasdan illustrates the identity crises of the characters in the film; but it also works as parody, with the picture gently poking fun at the mythical idyll of a Rockwell-esque America, as well as the overly heightened tropes of Hollywood movies themselves.

Figure 7.1 Mumford's dark backstory

Lawrence Kasdan uses intertextuality as a prism through which he examines modern society, while simultaneously commenting on the medium of film itself. But there is also some pragmatism in Kasdan's utilization of homage, especially in his earlier work, with the established styles and tropes of certain genres aiding the construction of his pictures. He told me that his choice of film noir for *Body Heat*, his first movie as director, was partly practical:

> I was thinking, what could I direct first when my technical skills are not developed at all? Well, there's this genre which gives you enormous license to do anything you want because these movies had been radically stylized, and the lighting and the action, the dialogue, all so stylized, and it gave you enormous freedom. And I thought "I'm going to do one of those."

Similarly, the third film that he directed, *Silverado*, was an unabashed tribute to the classic Western that was entirely out of fashion in the mid-1980s. He and his brother Mark created the screenplay by incorporating their favorite elements from old cowboy pictures, much in the way that *Raiders of the Lost Ark* was structured around six action set-pieces inspired by 1930s adventure serials. Regardless of genre, Kasdan often looks to "Golden Age" Hollywood for inspiration, then, and the majority of filmmakers that he discusses are those who made their most celebrated pictures within the American studio system of the 1930s to 1950s. For example, in our interview, he said:

> I was so drawn to Hawks. That clearly had influenced me in many ways. And Ford, and to screwball comedy, and to George Cukor. It was like, what is it that I love so much? And those things all got distilled into the movies that I made.

Kasdan's screenplay for *Continental Divide* was very much in that screwball comedy mode, and it was the "Hawksian" relationship between the two leads that attracted Steven Spielberg to Kasdan's work. Not only did Spielberg buy the screenplay (it would become Amblin Entertainment's very first release), but he then showed the script to George Lucas. This led to Kasdan's being hired for *Raiders of the Lost Ark*, the job that established him as a professional screenwriter and made him Hollywood's "overnight sensation."[7] Allusion does not just inflect Kasdan's work, then; it helped build his reputation at the beginning of the 1980s, that decade in which referential filmmaking would gain increasing popularity, and, according to Fredric Jameson, become a dominant trope in pop culture, leading to the "colonization of the present by the nostalgia mode."[8] There is some circularity in Kasdan's attraction to homage. He has cited *The Big Sleep* (1946) as an influence,[9] and one of its screenwriters was Leigh Brackett, whom Kasdan would eventually replace on *The Empire Strikes Back*, thanks to his ability to channel the same kind of snappy dialogue and battle-of-the-sexes banter. His aptitude for writing in that mode, then, allowed him to directly succeed one of its early exponents.

Another oft-cited influence is the director John Sturges. Kasdan has spoken frequently of his admiration for *The Magnificent Seven* (1960), in particular, a movie that he watched as a child and "represented so many paradigms of heroism and manhood and the pull between darkness and light and courage and fear."[10] Kasdan flags Sturges's "knack for dealing with ensembles of men," as well as the dynamism of his work, with its "characters who were flawed and were not superheroes but were fearless."[11] These would become characteristics in Kasdan's movies, both in his Westerns, *Silverado* and *Wyatt Earp*, and in any of his scripts about men torn between self-preservation and the desire to serve some greater cause, like *Raiders of the Lost Ark*, *The Bodyguard*, and *Solo: A Star Wars Story*. There is a constant pull from two sides, the "duality" that Kasdan cites as an engaging character trait, and one that he instils repeatedly in his own protagonists.[12]

Kasdan's influences are not confined to Hollywood directors, though. During his college years, he was exposed to the movies of international filmmakers, and he says that he aspired to "the Truffaut-Bergman ideal, a very personal piece of work that comes out of your life and your feelings and your philosophy." He expresses high regard for Jean-Luc Goddard and Luis Buñuel, and, as mentioned in Chapter 4, he credits Jean Renoir's *La Règle du jeu/The Rules of the Game* (1939) as an inspiration for *The Big Chill*, with its apparently loose, nebulous structure.[13] However, the filmmaker to whom Lawrence Kasdan refers consistently, both in interviews and through his pictures, is the man he calls "the greatest director that ever lived, [. . .] one of the greatest writers that ever lived," and "the Shakespeare of movies."[14]—Akira Kurosawa.

"SENSEI" KUROSAWA

An appreciation for the work of Akira Kurosawa is not surprising given Lawrence Kasdan's age and background. In the US, Kurosawa's filmography is closely associated with the baby-boom generation, his films gaining prominence in the 1950s and '60s, when they came to represent a "radical alternative" to mainstream Hollywood.[15] They appealed, in particular, to the first wave of film school graduates in the 1960s, and they spoke obliquely to the social tensions of the era, as many of Kurosawa's post-war pictures dealt with issues of class, poverty, and inequality. The nihilism that pervades much of his output, as well as his occasionally frenetic camerawork and staccato editing, appealed to the more hard-edged sensibilities gaining prevalence in Hollywood throughout the turbulent decade, especially with the demise of the Motion Picture Production Code and its restrictive censorship rules (finally abandoned in 1968). Kurosawa's visual style, too—the use of telephoto lenses, multi-camera set-ups, and over-the-shoulder shots—was frequently reconstituted by American directors. Arthur Penn credited Kurosawa's techniques for dictating the rhythm of the climactic gun battle in *Bonnie and Clyde* (1967), while Sam Peckinpah, director of *The Wild Bunch* (1969), said that he wanted to make Westerns like Kurosawa's films.[16] The veneration by established Hollywood figures made Kurosawa's *jidaigeki* ("period plays") even more popular among the cine-literate wave of writer-directors who emerged in the 1970s. As well as offering different ways of telling stories, Kurosawa's stylistic choices appeared to satisfy a demand among this cohort of young filmmakers for alternative cinematic techniques. Francis Ford Coppola recycled aspects of Kurosawa's staging in *The Bad Sleep Well* (1960) for the wedding scene in *The Godfather* (1972);[17] and George Lucas used a lance duel in *The Hidden Fortress* (1958) as a template for the lightsaber battle in *Star Wars*.[18] Paul Schrader's screenplay for *Taxi Driver* (1976) paints Travis Bickle as a *ronin*-like loner, the Vietnam vet in search of new direction now that he is "master-less;" and Martin Scorsese, who calls Kurosawa "our sensei,"[19] imbues the film's nighttime New York scenes with the nightmarish quality of the slum sequences in *High and Low* (a.k.a. *Heaven and Hell*, 1963).

Lawrence Kasdan is one of many American devotees of the works of Akira Kurosawa, then, and he cites *Seven Samurai* as "the greatest example for anyone who is trying to learn about movies,"[20] and *Yojimbo* (1961) as "the most entertaining movie ever made."[21] The latter comment highlights an under-discussed reason for Kurosawa's international popularity: his samurai films are so accessible and so thrilling, their characters bold and vividly drawn, and the action faster than in most American pictures of the time. According to Kasdan, Kurosawa said that he aimed to make "a movie that's delicious enough to eat,"[22] and he admits to drawing upon his canon directly, stating that "there's a lot of Kurosawa" in his own most entertaining screenplay, *Raiders of the Lost Ark*.[23]

Where Kasdan differentiates from his compatriots is in which elements of Kurosawa's films appeal to him. While many Hollywood filmmakers tend toward emulating the visuals of Kurosawa as a director, Kasdan is more interested in his themes and characters. In discussing the origins of Yoda in *The Empire Strikes Back*, for instance, Kasdan says that he modeled the Jedi Master's priest-like meditative quality on Kambei Shimada, the leader of the *Seven Samurai*, played by Takashi Shimura, who "always sees the big picture and is slower to react because he's figured it out."[24] Neither filmmaker leans on grandstanding speeches, instead preferring shorter utterances in which subtext is revealed through economical dialogue—a result, perhaps, of a shared admiration for film noir and hardboiled detective novels.[25] These parallels inflect (and are inflected by) the kinds of characters and relationships that each filmmaker creates, leading to deeper thematic correlations that have shaped Kasdan's movies, and his entire career.

KASDAN AND KUROSAWA

Lawrence Kasdan says: "What has always interested me is also what *Seven Samurai* is about—the fear of the universe intruding into our life and destroying it and the way that we work out strategies to deal with this."[26] Kurosawa's 1954 film was the basis for John Sturges's *The Magnificent Seven*, of course, one of Kasdan's favorite movies as an adolescent. When he and his brother Mark were writing the screenplay for *Silverado*, Kasdan explains, "We just loved Westerns, and we wanted to do all those things. Let's put this in. Let's put that in." In commandeering the cowboy-movie tropes—wagon trains, a box canyon, a jail break, galloping horses—the picture paid tribute to any number of classic Westerns, but its lineage could be traced to Kurosawa's *jidaigeki* also, either explicitly or via the American and European remakes of his samurai films. *The Magnificent Seven* mimics the plot of *Seven Samurai* remarkably closely, and stands both as a cover version of its predecessor (though completely uncredited at the time) and as a classic of its own genre. However, while the characters are charismatic and the set-pieces raucously fun, it lacks the existential angst that plagues Kurosawa's samurai. The mercenaries are types rather than people, and in the position of hired hands more by choice than duty. This softens the emotional punch, even as four of the ensemble are killed during the events of the story. In *Seven Samurai*, Kambei's final words, after vanquishing the bandits that had terrorized the village, are searingly nihilistic: "We've lost yet again. With their land, the farmers are the victors, not us." A close facsimile of the line ends *The Magnificent Seven*, but Elmer Bernstein's soaring score and the inclusion of children at the gravesides give the film a more hopeful endnote. *The Magnificent Seven* has a deliberately lighter touch, then, which explains its enduring popularity, but it means that the characters' choices do not resonate as fiercely as those made by the seven samurai, belonging, as they do, to a caste from which they can never free themselves. In this respect, I argue that Lawrence Kasdan's *Silverado* veers closer to Kurosawa's work than Sturges's, with the characters drawn more vividly than in *The Magnificent Seven*, and the emotional stakes higher.[27] As the writer-director of *The Big Chill*, Kasdan was already known as the maker of ensemble films, and this is apparent in *Silverado* too, with each member of the gang given ample screen time in which characterizations are allowed to develop fully. However, Kasdan's approach to revealing each protagonist is quite different from his previous picture. *The Big Chill* had opened with a titles montage that wordlessly introduced the characters in turn, but *Silverado* follows the technique employed in *Seven Samurai*, each new "recruit" first seen through the perspective of the leader. This is achieved through Kurosawa-like camera placement; for example, watching Mal (Danny Glover) fighting in the saloon from just over the shoulders of Emmett (Scott Glenn) and Paden (Kevin Kline). The camera is not omniscient, but subjective, and this immediately invites the audience to align itself with the diegetic viewer, appraising each new character one-by-one, just as the protagonist does.

There are shades of the samurai themselves in *Silverado*'s ensemble, with Emmett a world-weary leader, like Kambei, jaded by violence but inexorably drawn toward it. He is introduced inside a barn, fighting off unseen enemies even after first being without his gun—that most potent symbol of the cowboy. Kambei, in a remarkable act of self-sacrifice, cuts off his top-knot—the signifier of his samurai status—in order to trick his way into a barn, where he dispatches a thief who has taken a child hostage. Both are forced into action by circumstance, both highly skilled fighting men who will lead teams in protecting communities from bandits. Then there is Jake in *Silverado*, the youngest of the ensemble and a version of Kikuchiyo (Toshiro Mifune) from *Seven Samurai*. Played with obvious glee by Kevin Costner in one of the most overtly physical roles of his career, Jake is an effervescent ball of energy, somersaulting, leaping, and yipping his way through the piece, at once entertaining and annoying his comrades just as Mifune's character did in *Seven Samurai*, an innocent looking to prove himself a warrior.

With Westerns so spiritually connected to samurai pictures, the associations between *Silverado* and *Seven Samurai* are perhaps to be expected. However, it is not only the samurai pictures that attract Kasdan, but also Kurosawa's contemporary-set works: the crime dramas and character studies. In our interview, Kasdan said that not only did Kurosawa direct "the best action movie ever made," but "he did *Ikiru*, too, [. . .] *Stray Dog*. And people say, well, wait, that's equal to the best of that genre." The themes and characters in these two films reverberate through Kasdan's filmography. Shades of *Ikiru* (1952), in particular, are present in *Darling Companion*, as Joseph (Kevin Kline) begins to understand that his position in the family is not as secure as he had perceived, his daughters no longer needing him, and his wife appearing to love their dog more than she loves him. His uncertainty comes with a tinge of mortality, a paler version of what *Ikiru*'s Watanabe (Takashi Shimura) experiences as he realizes the apathy of his own family. This dissonance, between the way that we present ourselves to the world and the way that the world sees us, is a common thread through both filmmakers' work. It is present in Kurosawa's *Drunken Angel* (1948), in which a gangster thinks he is on the up in the yakuza, only to learn that he is just a pawn in a bigger game; and in *Stray Dog* (1949), when paranoia grips a police detective who, humiliatingly, has had his service pistol stolen by a pickpocket. And the same disconnect between one's self-identity and the perceptions of others dominates *Body Heat*, *The Accidental Tourist*, *The Force Awakens*, and *Solo: A Star Wars Story*. In each case the protagonist begins with a clear sense of who they are, only to see that image stripped away by others. For example, in *Body Heat*, the femme fatale eventually disabuses Ned Racine of his presumed agency in their affair and the ensuing murder; while in *The Accidental Tourist*, Macon's attempt to close himself off from the world and circumvent the risk of further pain after his son's murder is criticized by his wife, Sarah, then exposed and rejected by Muriel, almost against his will: to change would be a tacit acceptance that he had been mistaken in his approach, and the loss of pride that comes with such an admission would be nearly as difficult to live with as his emotional stuntedness.

Kasdan repeatedly creates narratives in which, like in Kurosawa's films, characters have secrets that they are desperate to protect. The fear of being found out is closely bound to the question of identity, whether it is the hidden backgrounds of characters—the farm boy Kikuchiyo passing himself off as a samurai; the criminal pasts of Matty in *Body Heat* and the "Doctor" in *Mumford*—or the exposure of incompetence or inexperience, as with the tuberculosis-stricken yakuza stooge in *Drunken Angel*, or Han as he gets in over his head among all the schemes and counter-schemes of *Solo*. The undercurrent of paranoia courses through both filmmakers' pictures, driving their protagonists to rash behavior, often against their own best interests. It is these imperfections that make the characters so engaging, as they struggle with both external and internal conflicts. Kasdan has quoted Kurosawa in noting "that villains have arrived at what they're going to be. . . that's their flaw, but that heroes evolve—they're open to change and growth."[28] So even as, for example, George Lucas originally saw Indiana Jones as a "super-man," Kasdan added vulnerability and even weakness. Rather than detract from his action-hero image, the choice allows for character development, and it makes Indy far more relatable than if he were the Bond-style infallible hero that had initially been conceived.

Akira Kurosawa's work is, above all, humanist. His pictures chronicle and criticize social inequalities, whether it is the caste system of feudal Japan in so many of his *jidaigeki*, or his commentaries on modern injustices in, for example, *The Bad Sleep Well* and *High and Low*. His films imbue people from all classes with dignity and fortitude at a time when, for the most part, Japan was struggling to rebuild after the trauma of World War Two and its subsequent occupation. Throughout this period, Kurosawa was subject to censorship—first by the militaristic imperial government, then by the American occupiers—yet he managed to explore injustices and spotlight the problems of the most disadvantaged. Even his propaganda film *The Most Beautiful* (1944) manages to criticize obliquely, and it celebrates the endurance of female factory workers in wartime Japan while surreptitiously lamenting the futility of their efforts as his country edged toward defeat. *Drunken Angel*, made just after the war, avoided showing bombed-out buildings, as per government censorship, but the poisonous sump in the street could easily be a bomb crater, and it physicalizes the abject squalor of the slum district that Dr. Sanada (Takashi Shimura) serves. *High and Low* similarly exemplifies the differences between rich and poor, with the gleaming white mansions on the hillside literally looking down upon the shanty towns of Yokohama. Akira Kurosawa says that he had belonged to an underground left-wing group in his youth more out of a sense adventure than strong political conviction.[29] Whatever the reasons, though, his pictures reveal an obvious sympathy for the less privileged in society, even in the more entertaining action movies such as *The Hidden Fortress* or *Yojimbo*, in which the lower castes become important players and rise up against those more powerful. As explained in Chapters 5 and 6, Lawrence Kasdan frequently empathizes with marginalized groups, having the protagonists help Muriel and Alexander in *The Accidental Tourist* or Simon's family in *Grand Canyon*; and even the uprising of the wookiees in *Solo* can be compared to the riot of the peasants in Kurosawa's *The Hidden Fortress*, both taking place at mines in which they are enslaved. Kasdan's background was one of uncertainty, his family moving often, and his father dying at a young age. Like Kurosawa, the politics of his formative adult years were left-leaning, and his films mirror his progressive values. Whereas Kurosawa would often be directly critical, Kasdan favors a more idealistic vision of society in which people of different backgrounds work together: Leia, Lando, Chewbacca, and the droids taking the lead at the climax of *The Empire Strikes Back*; the disparate group of cowboys and farmers teaming up in *Silverado*; and the networks of characters of different class and race in *Grand Canyon*, *Mumford*, and *Darling Companion*. Both Kurosawa and Kasdan worked in cultures and eras in which disadvantaged people were given very little agency in studio releases, and both strove to create scenarios in which such characters could thrive, or, at the very least, be seen and heard.

Lawrence Kasdan calls Akira Kurosawa a "genius, genius, genius." Though born nearly four decades apart in strikingly different cultures, Kurosawa's inspiration has remained strong throughout Kasdan's career. Some aspects may be the result of shared influences, with the taut, staccato rhythm of dialogue in both writers' screenplays possibly inspired by the 1940s Westerns and hard-boiled detective thrillers that Kurosawa admired and Kasdan emulated. However, there are more explicit connections, too, particularly regarding character and theme. Each creates protagonists that suffer from internal conflicts as much as external, scared of being caught out, either imposters or struggling with imposter syndrome. They are often lonely, unable to confide their most private secrets in anyone else, for fear of exposing their insecurities. This condition often leads to poor choices, but this in turn makes them more realistic characters than most created by contemporary filmmakers, especially in genre movies. The imperfect heroes must learn to evolve, especially when their flaws are exposed by others, as they so often are, with both Kurosawa and Kasdan frequently making two-handers and ensembles. But even within the duality that drives such characters, there is nobility: Sanjuro (Toshiro Mifune) in *Yojimbo* begins by causing trouble between rival crime lords almost just for fun, yet his actions lead to gains for the entire town—something that he surely understood; while in *Raiders of the Lost Ark*, Indiana Jones is introduced as something of a graverobber-for-hire, but he will eventually try to save the world from the Nazis, persevering even when all seems lost.

Throughout his career, Lawrence Kasdan has been very open in citing filmmakers that inspire him, and his interviews reflect his predilection for borrowing from and gently subverting established conventions through his "movie-movie" approach to storytelling. The works of John Sturges and John Ford are present in Kasdan's Westerns, as is the epic scope of David Lean, particularly in the stately *Wyatt Earp*. The rapid-fire back-and-forth of Howard Hawks's and George Cukor's farces is evident in so much of Kasdan's dialogue, especially in his comedies and action pictures. However, for all his admiration for a diverse range of writers and directors, it is the movies of Akira Kurosawa to which Kasdan most often refers. It seems that Kurosawa provides Kasdan with the ideal of a filmmaker who controlled the process from story through to editing, and who was able to explore many of the themes that most interest him: identity, character revelation, and class differences. Kurosawa did this while managing to "delight" viewers,[30] something that Kasdan has always striven toward, telling accessible, engaging stories that appeal to wide audiences but also reflect the filmmaker's deeper, more personal concerns.

NOTES

1. Stephen Holden, "Sure, the Doctor is in: In Demand and in Trouble," *The New York Times*, September 24, 1999, https://www.nytimes.com/1999/09/24/movies/film-review-sure-the-doctor-is-in-in-demand-and-in-trouble.html (accessed July 4, 2023).

2. Jimmy Summers, "Reviews: *Silverado*," *Box Office (Archive: 1920–2000)* 121, no. 9 (1985), R-104.

3. Lawrence Kasdan, quoted in Jim Hemphill, "Lawrence Kasdan," *Academy of Motion Picture Arts and Sciences: Oral History Collection* (Los Angeles: AMPAS, 2022), transcript, 60.

4. Kasdan, quoted in an unpublished interview with James Russell (2013). Original emphasis.

5. Kasdan, quoted in Alex Simon, "Chillin' Big with Lawrence Kasdan," *The Hollywood Interview*, December 3, 2012, http://thehollywoodinterview.blogspot.com/2008/03/lawrence-kasdan-hollywood-interview.html (accessed July 4, 2023).

6. Kasdan, quoted in Rose Eichenbaum, *The Director Within: Storytellers of Stage and Screen* (Middletown, CT: Wesleyan University Press, 2014), 240.

7. Aljean Harmetz, "How He Became Hollywood's Hot Writer," *The New York Times*, November 1, 1981, http://www.nytimes.com/1981/11/01/movies/how-he-became-hollywood-s-hot-writer.html?pagewanted=all (accessed July 4, 2023).

8. Fredric Jameson, *Postmodernism, or, The Cultural Logic of Multinational Capitalism* (Durham, NC: Duke University Press, 1991), 20.

9. Kasdan, quoted in Hemphill, "Lawrence Kasdan," 25.

10. Kasdan, quoted in James Russell and Jim Whalley, *Hollywood and the Baby Boom: A Social History* (London: Bloomsbury, 2018), 61.

11. Kasdan, quoted in Hemphill, "Lawrence Kasdan," 2.

12. Ibid., 16.

13. Simon, "Chillin' Big."

14. Kasdan, interviewed by John August and Craig Mazin, "Episode 247: The One with Lawrence Kasdan," *Scriptnotes*, audio podcast, April 26, 2016, http://johnaugust.com/2016/the-one-with-lawrence-kasdan (accessed June 29, 2023).

15. Catherine Russell, *Classical Japanese Cinema Revisited* (London: Continuum, 2011), xi.

16. Stephen Prince, *A New Pot of Gold: Hollywood under the Electronic Rainbow, 1980–1989* (New York: Charles Scribner's Sons, 2000), 349–50.

17. Fred Shimizu, "Directors: Akira Kurosawa," in John Berra (ed.), *Japan: Directory of World Cinema* (Bristol, UK: Intellect, 2010), 31.

18. Lucas also famously copied the synopsis of *The Hidden Fortress* (1958) when writing his early treatments of *Star Wars*. I discuss these similarities in further detail in Brett Davies, "Droids and Peasants: Akira Kurosawa's Thematic Influence on the Star Wars Saga," *The Kyoto Conference on Arts, Media & Culture 2021: Official Conference Proceedings* (January 2022), 51–3, http://papers.iafor.org/wp-content/uploads/conference-proceedings/KAMC/KAMC2021_proceedings.pdf (accessed July 4, 2023).

19. Martin Scorsese, interviewed for "Anaheim University Akira Kurosawa 100th Anniversary Memorial Tribute," Anaheim University, June 13, 2013, https://www.youtube.com/watch?v=ErelcWcNelQ (accessed July 4, 2023).

20. Kasdan, quoted in John Whitley, "Filmmakers on Film: Lawrence Kasdan," *The Daily Telegraph*, April 27, 2002, http://www.telegraph.co.uk/culture/film/3576515/Filmmakers-on-film-Lawrence-Kasdan.html (accessed July 4, 2023).

21. Luke Goodsell, "Five Favorite Films with Lawrence Kasdan," *Rotten Tomatoes*, April 20, 2012, https://editorial.rottentomatoes.com/article/five-favorite-films-with-lawrence-kasdan/ (accessed July 4, 2023).

22. Ibid.

23. Kasdan, quoted in John Baxter, *George Lucas: A Biography* (London: HarperCollins, 1999), 259.

24. Kasdan, interviewed by John August and Craig Mazin, "Episode 452: *The Empire Strikes Back* with Lawrence Kasdan," *Scriptnotes*, transcript, May 26, 2020, https://johnaugust.com/2020/scriptnotes-ep-452-the-empire-strikes-back-with-lawrence-kasdan-transcript (accessed July 4, 2023).

25. I discuss this, as well as further thematic connections between Kurosawa and Kasdan, in an earlier article: Davies, "Kurosawa to Kasdan: Storytelling Influences," *Journal of Screenwriting* 10, no. 2 (2019).

26. Kasdan, quoted in Whitley, "Filmmakers on Film: Kasdan."

27. For more analysis of *Seven Samurai*'s influence on *Silverado*, see Davies, "*Seven Samurai* in *Silverado*: Kurosawa's Influence on Lawrence Kasdan's Revival Western," *Global Japanese Studies Review* 9, no. 1 (2017).

28. Elaine Dutka, "Lawrence Kasdan's Grand Balancing Act," *The Los Angeles Times*, December 24, 1991, http://articles.latimes.com/1991-12-24/entertainment/ca-947_1_grand-canyon/3 (accessed July 4, 2023).

29. Akira Kurosawa, *Something Like an Autobiography*, trans. A.E. Bock (New York: Vintage, 1983), 77–9.

30. Kasdan, interviewed by John August and Craig Mazin, "Episode 247: The One with Lawrence Kasdan," *Scriptnotes*, audio podcast, April 26, 2016, http://johnaugust.com/2016/the-one-with-lawrence-kasdan (accessed June 29, 2023).

CHAPTER 8

Kasdan's Collaborations: Creation and Performance

Even while taking inspiration from filmmakers of the past, Lawrence Kasdan's films are remarkably contemporary, reporting on the present in movies such as *The Big Chill*, *Grand Canyon*, and *Mumford*, up until his most recent directorial feature, *Darling Companion*. Perhaps more than any other Hollywood filmmaker of the era, his personal concerns are apparent in works spanning several decades, a longitudinal commentary that demonstrates his liberal sensibilities, and his continued disquietude regarding the state of the nation.

As discussed in the previous chapter, Kasdan often uses allusion as a medium through which to reflect and comment upon modern America; but pastiche is just one element guiding his creative choices. Kasdan is also a filmmaker motivated by the world around him. His debut as writer-director, *Body Heat*, is steeped in the style and mythology of film noir, but its themes developed out of Kasdan's seeing his contemporaries flail for meaning in the decade after college, when they realized that the world was not as malleable, nor as welcoming, as they had believed. Since then, most of his movies have spoken to that same condition: how the chaos and uncertainty of external forces push against us, and how we respond to that stress through reaction, reinvention, defiance, or submission. *The Big Chill*, *The Accidental Tourist*, *Grand Canyon*, *Wyatt Earp*, *Mumford*, *Darling Companion*: all deal with variations of this idea; and even the pictures that Kasdan did not write himself—*I Love You to Death* (from a script by John Kostmayer) and *French Kiss* (screenplay by Adam Brooks)—feature protagonists whose apparently settled lives are changed by sudden, stunning revelations. There are consistent motifs running through his filmography, then, even if Kasdan's directorial style is more difficult to characterize than that of many of his peers. In our interview, I asked him whether he considered himself to have a "Kasdan style," or if he preferred to adapt his style to suit the specific movie. He said, "I'm happy to *apply* it differently. I do think that, both in a good way and a bad way, you're in a box, because I have strong senses, like 'that's okay, and that isn't.'" Such a philosophy is supported by the analyses of his early directorial works in Chapter 3 and Chapter 4, which demonstrated his ability to alter his visual approach to serve different material, his overall style developing via his subjects and themes rather than intrusive camerawork or editing.

Surprisingly, perhaps, for someone who has written six screenplays for other directors, Kasdan is a proponent of the auteur theory, or, more specifically, the director-as-auteur theory. He says that:

> I had totally bought, and still do, the auteur theory, where people [. . .] were so strong in their artistic vision that they became very personal movies. For Hawks and Ford, and these are not necessarily people who can write [. . .], but their style and their interests are so strong, they might as well have been writers, might as well have been writing those movies.

Certainly, Kasdan's world view is consistent throughout his filmography, adding weight to this assertion. However, a belief in the auteur theory is rather undermined in his screenplays for other directors, in which Kasdan's personal concerns emerge repeatedly, suggesting that he, as the writer, has the agency to inflect the work substantially. The search for equilibrium in a hostile, chaotic world is present in both his directorial works and in his scripts, as is the duality that interests Kasdan; for example, Frank in *The Bodyguard*, torn between desire and duty when he finds himself falling in love with his charge; Han Solo in Kasdan's four Star Wars scripts, forever navigating a path between his own wants and a grander cause, constantly pulled in opposite directions; or the identity crisis suffered by Kylo Ren in *The Force Awakens*, drawn to the Dark Side even as he yearns to return to his family. Each faces the push-pull of conflicting wishes and needs as the unfriendly universe impinges upon the characters' lives, forcing them into action. These narratives were all written for other directors, yet their concerns are entirely in keeping with the rest of Lawrence Kasdan's output, suggesting that his belief in the director-as-auteur does not always hold true; the screenwriter, too, has the power to influence the movies' themes.

CREATIVE PARTNERSHIPS

A belief in the auteur theory does not preclude the possibility that the "author" might be assisted substantially, of course. Even while venerating the unique artistic visions of Howard Hawks and John Ford, Kasdan adds that "they also were surrounded by extraordinary writers that they would use again and again." As mentioned above, Kasdan has directed two films from other writers' screenplays, and in interviews he is at pains to make this clear. When he was introduced at the beginning of a podcast with a list of movies that he had written, he was mistakenly credited with the scripts to *I Love You to Death* and *French Kiss*. Kasdan immediately corrected the error, namechecking Kostmayer and Brooks then adding: "they're both great writers. And they were on set every day and it was wonderful."[1]

There is some contradiction, though, between Kasdan's belief in a personal creative vision and his especial tendency toward collaboration. As well as directing two scripts by others, he frequently works with writing partners. Of his sixteen produced scripts, six were written as part of a duo, while another six came after treatments or drafts by other people. The films that appear to represent Kasdan's interests most strongly are those composed alongside an "ampersand"[2] partner: he wrote *The Big Chill* with Barbara Benedek, *Silverado* with his brother Mark, and *Grand Canyon* and *Darling Companion* with his wife Meg; then he wrote his most personal Star Wars contribution, *Solo*, in tandem with his son Jonathan. Other than Benedek, a TV writer who was also an old friend, the other partners in that list are all family, which may have helped Kasdan keep close control over the narratives and their themes. He says of *Grand Canyon*, for instance, that:

> it was very personal, and it was about our life and our sons and Los Angeles, and what was happening to the country. And that was a very satisfying experience, and it went very smoothly, and, of course, [Meg] was deferring, you know. I had more experience, but it was a wonderful experience.

It is notable how closely the screenplay is aligned to Kasdan's solo works. The fact that the story developed out of the mutual concerns of a married couple probably helped the script remain focused and personal. The same is true of his other collaboration with Meg over twenty years later, *Darling Companion*, based upon the shared experience of losing their pet dog. As Kasdan suggests, the process was aided by his having more experience and, we can presume, seniority as the director, allowing him to mold the co-authored screenplay to fit his needs as a filmmaker. However, Kasdan has expressed satisfaction with all of his ampersand partnerships, both with family members and others, and even when working alongside a more "senior" partner in director J. J. Abrams on *The Force Awakens*. Unlike some writing teams, who might outline stories together but write scenes separately, Kasdan prefers to work closely with his co-author:

> Generally, I've written in the room with people and don't swap scenes. We just sit across. I'd sit at the keyboard and sometimes they type. [. . .]

I certainly did it that way with J. J. and *Force Awakens*. We just sat in a room and talked it out, and sometimes we'd write a little bit separately, but basically together. So that's generally a very intimate moment when you're struggling through what is a difficult task, together.

Such a working method contributes to a simpatico relationship between partners, which allows the styles and concerns of Kasdan's screenplays to remain consistent, even as he has participated in five different ampersand teams. It may also partially explain why there is occasional friction, such as when he wrote the screenplay to *Solo* with his son Jonathan. There was initial hesitancy to the arrangement from both parties, and Kasdan says that when they started, "as you would expect working with your son, it was fraught, and we went through a very tough period." However, they eventually overcame these difficulties, and they were entirely "in sync" by the time they finished the script. In fact, they became, according to Kasdan, "comrades" during the troubled production of *Solo*, in which the original directors were fired four months into the shoot. Both Lawrence and Jonathan Kasdan were central to the behind-the-scenes drama as executive producer and co-producer respectively, when Phil Lord and Christopher Miller's vision for the film clashed with the Kasdans' and Lucasfilm's intentions (a situation described more fully in Chapter 12). As well as testament to Lawrence Kasdan's close partnership with a family member, this incident further contradicts the notion of the director-as-auteur, as in this case it was the writing team whose vision was protected and who took part in the decision to hire Ron Howard as a replacement director.

Kasdan's collaborations are not confined solely to the writing process. As a director, he repeatedly employs the same heads of production. After Richard H. Kline shot *Body Heat*, Kasdan worked with director of photography John Bailey on his next three pictures, then Owen Roizman on four after that. Kasdan says:

one of the primary relationships you ever have is with the cinematographer. And you're very dependent on him or her [. . .] to help you. They're gonna make it look the way you want it to look. And if you have a good connection with them, you're not gonna tell them what to do, you're gonna ask them to give you what you want. And they're gonna have to figure out how to do it.[3]

John Bailey is a cinematographer who, like Kasdan, applies his style differently to each picture, but his preference for understated, naturalistic lighting is consistent, especially through *The Big Chill* and *The Accidental Tourist*. Conversely, *Silverado*, as a classic-style Western, provides a wider, lusher canvas, but Bailey captures the epic landscapes of New Mexico without fuss, allowing the beauty of nature to stand for itself—one of the subtexts of the picture.

His low-key approach, in contrast to the deliberately heightened artifice of Richard H. Kline's work for the melodrama of *Body Heat*, helped to create the color palette of Kasdan's early canon. Even in the interiors of *The Big Chill* or *Silverado*, the light feels diegetic, ambient, in keeping with the rural surroundings; while the moody grays of fall in Baltimore pervade every shot of *The Accidental Tourist*, injecting a realism that betrays Bailey's background as a documentary camera operator, and entirely in keeping with Macon's (William Hurt) emotional inertia.

Owen Roizman was a veteran cinematographer who had worked on *The French Connection* (1971) and *Network* (1976) before he first partnered Kasdan on *I Love You to Death*. Like Bailey, Roizman tends toward a naturalistic style, often using available light to create a gritty, down-to-earth atmosphere. This holds true in his films for Kasdan, but, on *Grand Canyon*, *Wyatt Earp*, and *French Kiss*, he appeared to enjoy drinking in the grand expanses of the American and French vistas, adopting a statelier approach than in his more frenetic work of the 1970s and '80s. Kasdan calls their collaboration "deep and mysterious," with Roizman shooting his final films for Kasdan before his retirement. Clearly, these collaborations proved fruitful for Kasdan on a professional level, the skills of his creative partners matching the needs of the films; but Kasdan also expresses a preference for working with people whose company he enjoys. The fact that his family is often on set, with his sons featuring in many of his films, and his wife Meg occasionally taking roles either in front of the camera or behind, proves that Kasdan strives for a convivial, familial environment. He says that "I like to be surrounded by people I trust and that I can spend all that time with, and not be irritated or bored." His frequent collaborations speak to this, suggesting that these people enjoy working with him, too.

After employing different composers on each of his early pictures—including such luminaries as John Barry, John Williams, and James Horner—Kasdan settled upon James Newton Howard to score all of his directorial works from *Grand Canyon* onwards. Howard's lush sound provides a suitably Americana sheen to, for example, *Wyatt Earp* and *Darling Companion*, but, like Kasdan's cinematographers, he is capable of understatement, and his scores rarely overpower the needs of the story. The one misstep occurs in their very first collaboration, with Howard's stirring fanfare at the end of *Grand Canyon* suggesting a more optimistic conclusion than Kasdan intended.[4] In the most part, though, theirs is a happy professional marriage in which the director's versatility and classical tastes appear to match his composer's. Kasdan admits to being put off from watching a movie if he deems that the director is "showing off" with stylistic affectations, and Howard has the same reaction to what he considers bad music choices: "It's impossible for him to get past the music in the first two minutes," Kasdan says. "And if it puts him off, he can't see even a great movie. And I always make fun of him. But the truth is, I'm a lot like that."

Lawrence Kasdan's longest-lasting collaboration is with the film editor Carol Littleton, who has cut all but two of his features as director. Kasdan was looking specifically for a female editor for *Body Heat*, reasoning that "the movie was so sexual, and I didn't want it to be a man's idea of how these things should go."[5] He interviewed several candidates, but was especially impressed with Littleton:

> The first thing she said was, "I was really surprised how funny it is." And I thought, "Oh, no one says that about this script, but I know it is funny, and there are gonna be some really good laughs in this movie. But no one will ever know it or necessarily remember it because they're gonna be thinking about the plot and the sex and the treachery." But she immediately went to that. And I thought, "Oh my god."[6]

Kasdan adds that Littleton has "a great view of the world," and her approach complements his, in particular when wringing humor from tragedy. *The Big Chill*'s montage scenes—over the opening credits, and when the friends try on their new running shoes—are notable examples of her ability to create meaningful moments out of slight vignettes (the coverage provided by her husband John Bailey's camera). However, Kasdan says that Littleton approaches the material thematically rather than narratively,[7] and her skills are applied most effectively in the many ensemble scenes, where she modulates the tone deftly between drama and comedy, and adds emotion and dynamism to physically static sequences. For example, when the group of friends is gathered in the living room, stoned and melancholic as they discuss Alex's death, Littleton chooses to favor Nick (William Hurt), who espouses bitterly: "No one ever had a cushier berth than we did." For much of the scene, she holds longer on the shots of his reactions rather than of the speakers, accentuating the sense of anger, even as, for example, Karen (JoBeth Williams) attempts to strike a more conciliatory note. One might expect the pace of cutting to accelerate in the lighter scenes in order to match the cut-and-thrust of wisecracks and comments between people who have known each other for many years. However, Littleton and Kasdan often choose to stay on wide shots, trusting the writing, and allowing the performances to breathe naturally. This contributes to the apparently freewheeling quality of the dialogue, and it increases the sense that the viewer is among old friends. This aptitude for editing interior scenes with such tenderness and subtlety is presumably what attracted Steven Spielberg to employ Carol Littleton on *E.T.: The Extra-Terrestrial* (1982) between her first two movies for Kasdan.

Kasdan displays loyalty toward his creative partners, and, paradoxically, it may be his willingness to collaborate closely with others that has helped to develop a Kasdan "style," even when he seeks to apply his skills differently depending on the project. For all the contributions of his favored behind-the-scenes creators, Kasdan's desire to work repeatedly with trusted partners is most conspicuous in his lasting relationships with actors. Not only do these relationships exemplify his collaborative tendencies; they also reveal aspects of Kasdan's world view that otherwise may not be apparent.

KASDAN'S REPERTORY

As well as his regard for the films of Akira Kurosawa, Howard Hawks, and Jean Renoir, Lawrence Kasdan has expressed appreciation for the plays of Anton Chekhov, in which, he says, "the tiny things are terribly important."[8] Aside from his scripts for Lucasfilm, Kasdan's are rarely high-concept movies, and in many cases they are balanced upon similarly "tiny things." Kasdan elucidates, equating Chekhov's approach to that in his own pictures:

> Little bits of movement are big. *The Accidental Tourist* [. . .] is about a guy who moves about a quarter of an inch in the course of it, but it makes all the difference. I think that's really been in all my stuff.[9]

Macon is a remarkably static character to lead a movie; therefore, Kasdan was reliant upon the performance of William Hurt to instill pathos and humor into the role. Hurt achieves this with the barely perceptible twitch of a lip, or a flicker of movement in his eyes, while his body remains almost completely still. Hurt's posture is different from that presented in *Body Heat* or *The Big Chill*. In the former, as small-time lawyer Ned Racine, he stands tall, affecting the pose of the local playboy, able to earn a comfortable living and pick up women with well-worked insouciance, until his shortcomings are exposed by a more cunning antagonist. In the latter, there is furtiveness hiding just beneath Nick's anti-establishment defiance. Here, the narrowing of the eyes or the subtle shake of the head betray his sadness and cynicism, the member of the group who has suffered the most since their halcyon college days. He is still confident and athletic, but his hardships are suggested by his gently sloping shoulders.

Akira Kurosawa, Kasdan's "hero," was well-known for working with the same actors repeatedly, directing Takashi Shimura on twenty occasions and, most famously, Toshiro Mifune sixteen times. With the release of *The Accidental Tourist* in 1988, Kasdan had directed Hurt three times in his first four films, and the actor looked to be fulfilling the Mifune function in Kasdan's expanding canon. Just as Mifune is unmistakable in every role while portraying a wide range of characters for Kurosawa, William Hurt consistently plays a man who is holding back: contained, controlled, a hint of danger simmering just out of view. He has a raw alpha-male physicality, which makes the buttoned-up character of Macon all the more pitiable; the audience knows that he is capable of much more, if only he would open up to the possibilities that the world is offering him.

Kasdan says that he thought no more than "a few seconds" about casting Kathleen Turner opposite Hurt in *The Accidental Tourist*, having played the femme fatale to Hurt's stooge in *Body Heat*, a strikingly different kind of picture. The contrast between the two films becomes clear within the opening scene; yet there may be some added value in re-employing the same pair of performers. As noted in earlier chapters, David Bordwell posits that "prototype schemata" can aid the viewer in processing a narrative.[10] The audience uses its prior knowledge of films and storytelling in order to construct its understanding of a movie. These schemata include identifiable types of places, incidents, or people, informing a viewer's expectations for a picture. A further schema is the viewer's meta-knowledge of the filmmakers and actors themselves. Rather than confusing or misleading the audience, the use of the same lead actors as *Body Heat* might at a subconscious level feed into the sense that Macon is not reaching his potential. For all Ned Racine's faults in the earlier film, he does not suppress his feelings in the way that Macon does. Conversely, while Kathleen Turner's Sarah is a much more sympathetic character than Matty in *Body Heat*, she has the same keen insight into the shortcomings of her male counterpart. She acts with more grace (even as they separate), but the choice of Turner helps the viewer understand her level of perception; we trust that she knows Macon, maybe even better than he knows himself.

William Hurt would go on to appear in four of Lawrence Kasdan's films, taking a supporting role in *I Love You to Death* immediately after *The Accidental Tourist*. It is Kevin Kline, though, who would eventually play more major parts for Kasdan than any other actor, featuring in six of his pictures over a thirty-year period.[11] Kasdan suggests that he had not initially seen Kline as an alter ego, but "it turned out that way." He explains:

> I knew the quality he had, which is very much like Cary Grant, which is that he was an athlete, he was graceful, he was hilarious, he was handsome. I didn't think I would ever identify someone with those qualities as being my alter ego, but I obviously liked it. And he worked in so many different things for me, and he always brought those qualities, but one could be emphasized more than another.

His first role for Kasdan was in *The Big Chill*, only his second major movie after more than a decade in New York theater. As discussed in Chapter 4, Kline's character Harold serves as the central protagonist of the ensemble, his importance highlighted by his being the first main character on-screen. While only a minute long, the opening scene of Harold bathing his son is one of the most realistic and affectionate representations of the everyday relationship between a parent and young child, the dialogue naturalistic but conveying genuine connection. The boy is played by a three-year-old Jonathan Kasdan, future co-writer of *Solo: A Star Wars Story*, and the fact that he is the director's son probably contributes to his obvious ease in front of the camera. Carol Littleton's deft editing and Kline's natural warmth create the illusion of a deep bond, even if Kline was actually acting to nothing but an empty tub in some of the close-up shots.

Of the seven old friends, Harold has steered furthest from their former radical values—or, at least, he is the most honest about it. Kasdan says that all of the characters in *The Big Chill* "are me and Barbara [Benedek, the co-writer], and people I knew," but it is Harold with whom Kasdan identifies most strongly, describing him as "that central, sort of steady guy, the most boring character in a way." In his four roles in films written and directed by Kasdan, Kevin Kline plays variations on Harold; however, rather than being "boring," as Kasdan says, these characters often hide darker sides. In *The Big Chill*, Kline is the small-town entrepreneur, who is "dug in" to the local community, but he also clings to the pain of his wife's affair; in *Silverado*, Paden's actions are honorable and self-sacrificing, even though we learn of his criminal past early in the narrative; Mack in *Grand Canyon* is a likable immigration lawyer and family man, who has had an extramarital affair with his secretary; and in *Darling Companion*, Joseph is a self-absorbed doctor whose sense of certainty is eroded by the loss of a dog. All are professional, capable, and respectable, and the fact that Kasdan relates so strongly to these Kline roles tells us something of his deeper concerns, even when some of these movies are ambiguous in their outlooks if taken as a whole. While ostensibly the steadiest members of their respective ensembles, they are also the most layered and the ones that struggle with their competing inner selves. It is easy to imagine a coiled-spring danger lurking beneath the surface of William Hurt's protagonists, but Kevin Kline comes across as so personable and principled that it is all the more fascinating to scratch beneath the façade and discover hidden aspects of his characters' personalities—ones that they are often afraid to address. These conflicting elements within a person fascinate Kasdan, who says that:

> I believe in dualities, period. I think that's what's interesting to me. And we can say "we think this, we think that." We can say, "I always do this, I always do that." The truth is, we're constantly torn, and it shifts around what the two poles are that you're being torn between.

The characters played by Kevin Kline represent this duality, and they are more relatable for their imperfections. They might also reveal some of Lawrence Kasdan's wider interests. He claims that none of his films have any political agenda,[12] but these Kline roles hint toward a specific world view: socially liberal, economically conservative, with a desire to engage with the community and

Figure 8.1 Kevin Kline in *Darling Companion*

help others. Indeed, Kasdan says that his only "agenda" in his movies is "maybe a humanist one, which is that we should treat each other in a decent way, and the world would be a better place for that."[13] Kline embodies that philosophy, from Harold as the de facto "leader" of the *Big Chill* ensemble, the successful businessman who continues to help his friends with gifts of sneakers and even a home; to Joseph in *Darling Companion*, the well-to-do surgeon hosting his daughter's wedding, who eventually puts aside his misgivings to help find his wife's dog. However, if Kline is an alter ego, then his roles also provide clues to Kasdan's politics, with these characters usually rewarded for their hard work and embracing of 1980s conservative values, as opposed to the less conventional roads taken by, say, William Hurt's Nick in *The Big Chill*, or Richard Jenkins's dreamer Russell in *Darling Companion* (who asks Kline's character for financial help). Accusations that Kasdan's pictures are "Reaganite" and "rightist"[14] are disingenuous, ignoring the range of ideas espoused by his various protagonists; however, if one views them from the perspectives of the Kevin Kline characters, then the impression is that centrist values are favored, Kline as the responsible grown-up to his less reliable friends and family.

Two of Kline's roles for Kasdan were in broad comedies that were written by others, and these show an entirely different aspect of his acting talent. As the serially unfaithful husband Joey in *I Love You to Death*, and the diamond thief Luc in *French Kiss*, Kline displays his athleticism and talent for slap-stick in realizing larger-than-life and not wholly trustworthy characters. Kline appears emboldened in these roles, hamming up their irrepressible charm, and reveling in the chance to affect exaggerated European accents. Clearly, he does not bear the weight of representing the writer-director's viewpoint; however, while these two roles stray from the "straight" characters in his other four movies for Kasdan, it is Kline's innate relatability that keep Joey and Luc on just the right side of sleazy. This allows the audience to empathize with them, even as they lie and cheat in order to serve their own needs.

Appearing in more than half of his features, Kevin Kline is an integral part of Lawrence Kasdan's output. In discussing their collaboration, Kline reveals why not only he, but so many actors, choose to work with Kasdan repeatedly:

> He creates an atmosphere that is pleasant, where the actor [. . .] has been cast for a combination of strengths that he has naturally, plus something that will challenge him in a stimulating way [. . .]. He encourages you to bring your thing, and then he just gently edits or makes suggestions.[15]

It is not only what occurs on set, though, that fosters this atmosphere of collaboration and experimentation. The smooth creative process between director and actor is aided by Kasdan's screenwriting and, unusual in Hollywood, his insistence on rehearsal.

WRITING AND DIRECTING FOR ACTORS

Lawrence Kasdan is a filmmaker concerned with relationships, above all else. He says that a person "may act one way in the morning and another way at night and not notice it themselves, but other people do. And then they're interpreting everybody else's actions, so it's all a big mess." His scripts explore this dichotomy repeatedly, between the way that we view ourselves and the way that others see us. This focus on people is probably what makes his movies so attractive to actors. His eclectic output frequently includes scenes in which groups of people simply talk, expressing character through dialogue and behavior, unencumbered by explicit plot or exposition.

Even in his genre screenplays, Kasdan often writes scenes in which the characters interact in ways that allow relationships to develop interestingly. *The Empire Strikes Back*, for example, provides ample opportunity for Han Solo and Princess Leia to engage in an ongoing battle of barbs and asides that develops into something tenderer, leading to the emotional jolt of their final separation; while Luke Skywalker and Yoda are locked into a lengthy philosophical dialogue that takes up much of the middle act. These scenes on the bog planet Dagobah not only reveal mythical aspects of the Force, but also tell the audience so much about Luke's inner turmoil, and his impatience to become a Jedi even as he displays immaturity; for instance, when he declares it impossible to free his spacecraft from the swamp by the power of the Force alone.

In his own work, unencumbered by the need to push the plot toward the next action sequence, Kasdan frequently composes long scenes in which words take precedence over action, an increasingly rare trait in the blockbuster era. He says that actors "tend to like the text. They come to me because they like to say these words."[16] Kasdan often works with actors from theater backgrounds, where the script is generally respected more than on a movie set; and these performers bring with them a desire to interrogate the text, as well as a talent for delivery. He mentions Joan Plowright (who plays the matriarch Nadja in *I Love You to Death*) as an example of someone from a "British tradition of acting," who is "very open to behavioral talk, to psychological talk, and to technique."[17] He places Kevin Kline in the same category, those who borrow from different schools of thought in order to reach the point where they "don't have to worry too much about technique and can concentrate on the character."[18] Such theater-trained actors are accustomed to intense preparation, too, and Kasdan usually favors a long rehearsal process. Ed Begley Jr. says of *The Accidental Tourist* that rehearsals lasted weeks, "and that's quite a luxury; he really likes to take the time."[19]

Kasdan's predilection for rehearsal began with his very first film, *Body Heat*, when he says that William Hurt insisted upon it: "He came out of theater, could not do anything unless he had rehearsed a lot." Kasdan's rehearsals usually consist of discussions with the cast, allowing everyone to get to know each other better, rather than charting their characters' emotional journeys. They discuss tone and style of performance too, of course; for example, during the two weeks of rehearsal for *Silverado*, Kasdan talked with Kevin Kline "about a way of being, a way of moving, a way of delivering these lines" based upon the "clues" in the script.[20] In a tight ensemble such as *The Big Chill*, Kasdan says, the focus is on the actors "getting to know each other intimately, learning to trust each other. [. . .] And we have to believe their intimacy."[21] However, his attitude to the preparation process has changed over time. At first, he had seen rehearsals as a journey, working toward a goal where the cast would be confident and completely ready by the time the cameras rolled; but he later learned to adapt both his methods and expectations. It was on his fourth film as director, *The Accidental Tourist*, when Kasdan was left dissatisfied with the process:

> I felt like at the end of the rehearsal, things were not settled, that we hadn't really achieved what I wanted to achieve in the rehearsal. And yet I felt, "we're going ahead, this is time to shoot." And it worked out fine. And I changed my attitude about rehearsing because I realized that it's not to finish anything, it's just to get everybody going.

On *Grand Canyon*, Kasdan decided to alter his approach to suit the material. While his previous pictures had focused on groups of people who shared numerous scenes, the ensemble of *Grand Canyon* is fractured, some characters remaining complete strangers throughout the film. Kasdan originally chose to follow the advice of his friend Sydney Pollack, who preferred not to rehearse. Instead of extensive preparation time, Kasdan decided to "see what happens if the actors and I come to set each day with many more questions, with less idea about what each other wants."[22] However, after Steve Martin—taking a rare dramatic role—expressed concern, Kasdan "compromised" by allowing for one week in which, rather than focusing on getting to know one another intimately, the emphasis was on discussing the script and relating it to the actors' own experiences, as well as on playing with tone in order to bring out the humor of the piece. This turned out to be a "pleasant, exciting" experience,[23] and Kasdan continued to rehearse before shooting his future projects, even if he was willing to be flexible with the length and approach.

His predilection for rehearsal, and his willingness to compromise, to discuss, and be open to actors' suggestions, appear to have made Lawrence Kasdan a director with whom actors seek to work. Dennis Quaid, who gave a remarkable performance as Doc Holliday in *Wyatt Earp*, concurs: "Every actor I know wants to work with Larry Kasdan, and every actor that has worked with Larry Kasdan wants to work with him again."[24] Mary McDonnell, who has appeared in two of Kasdan's films, says: "He allows people to be very simply who they are as characters, and somehow finds a way to make that beautiful without giving it some kind of Hollywood glaze, and I think that's very unusual."[25] Kasdan says that at one time he actually wanted to be an actor, so this may explain his affinity with the craft. However, that level of comfort was tested by his very first day on the set of *Body Heat*, when, due to scheduling issues, he had to shoot an explicit sex scene before anything else. Kasdan says:

> [H]ere in the first scene, they're naked, and she's leading him around by his part. And that would've been the last thing I would've said to do first. But it was the first day of shooting. And it was great because all the dams were broken. All the protocols were established in that first day. They got comfortable. I got more comfortable talking to them.[26]

His ease in talking with the cast is not common, and Kasdan claims that many "directors are terrified of actors. The last thing they want to do is spend [time] dealing with the actors' questions about the role and the material." He adds that directors are often "afraid they're going to be asked questions that they can't answer."[27] This fear, he suggests, can then be projected onto the actors, leading to insecurity on both sides of the conversation. The fact that he has usually written the screenplay presumably helps Kasdan feel confident about such questions, as no one knows that material better than he does. The rehearsal process helps, too, with most questions already answered by the time they are on set. During rehearsal, Kasdan says that he is open to experimentation by actors, even if he does not necessarily invite improvisation:

> I always used to say the script is innocent until proven guilty. And so I didn't want to encourage [actors] to change the lines or anything, but if they said, "I have a problem with this line," I'd say, "Okay, well, what would you like to say?" [. . .] and then I try to make them comfortable.

Again, his dual role as writer-director allows Kasdan to judge instantly whether a line change is helpful or whether it might have unintended consequences for that character or on the rest of the film.[28] Additionally, the discussions in rehearsal would benefit the actor in understanding the role more fully, preventing any major detours away from the core of the character, or from the needs of the wider story.

Lawrence Kasdan says that "ninety-nine per cent of my experiences with actors have been positive. I love them." His insistence on rehearsal and preparation appeals to many performers too, with Dennis Quaid saying that "he really does spend time on developing the characters [. . .]. You wind up questioning every action about the character that you're playing, and so he makes you look deeper."[29] This interrogation of the material allows for rare intimacy between director and actor, and contributes to the illusion that his films are improvised, even when they usually are not.

Kasdan's collaborations are not only with performers, of course. By working repeatedly with directors of photography, editor, composer, and numerous other crew members, he fosters an atmosphere of familiarity throughout his productions, aided further by his inclusion of family members in the film-making process. While believing in the notion of the auteur, Kasdan is someone who seeks to surround himself with people that he likes; and he clearly appreciates the input of those around him, keen to hear their ideas. The actor Mary McDonnell says that "Larry's the best listener I've ever met [. . .]. He absorbs people."[30] Such an attitude allows for open discussion between cast and crew, and it may be this above everything else that helps create a particular tone that underpins Kasdan's work: an apparently loose, unfussy approach in which character interactions are utterly believable. Their relationships are infused with intimacy and history, born not out of improvisation, but developed through intensive preparation and rehearsal, as well as through Lawrence Kasdan's close relationships with his most important creative partners.

NOTES

1. Lawrence Kasdan, interviewed by John August and Craig Mazin, "Episode 247: The One with Lawrence Kasdan," *Scriptnotes*, audio podcast, April 26, 2016, http://johnaugust.com/2016/the-one-with-lawrence-kasdan (accessed June 29, 2023). It is still quite rare for screenwriters to be on set during the production of Hollywood motion pictures, so the very fact that Kasdan insisted on Kostmayer and Brooks being present is testament to his respect for the writers' work.

2. The use of the ampersand ("&") between names in a film's screenplay credits denotes that the writers were working as a team, rather than as solo contributors within a chain. The Writers Guild of America West guidelines explain: "When writers perform services as a team, even if just for a single project, writing credit to the team must be designated with an ampersand ('&') between the names of the team members." Conversely, "Use of the word 'and' between writers' names in a credit indicates that the writers did their work

separately, one usually rewriting the other." Writers Guild of America West, *Screen Credits Manual* (Los Angeles: WGA, 2018), 4, https://www.wga.org/uploadedfiles/credits/manuals/screenscredits_manual18.pdf (accessed July 4, 2023).

3. Kasdan, quoted in Jim Hemphill, "Lawrence Kasdan," *Academy of Motion Picture Arts and Sciences: Oral History Collection* (Los Angeles: AMPAS, 2022), transcript, 38.
4. Kasdan, interviewed for *The Directors: Lawrence Kasdan*, DVD (American Film Institute), 1997.
5. Kasdan, quoted in Hemphill, "Lawrence Kasdan," 29.
6. Ibid.
7. Kasdan, quoted in Lawrence Kasdan and Jake Kasdan, *Wyatt Earp: The Film and the Filmmakers* (New York: Newmarket Press, 1994), 45.
8. Kasdan, quoted in Scott Siegel and Barbara Siegel, "Mumford's the Word," *Film Journal International*, October 1999, 12.
9. Ibid.
10. David Bordwell, *Narration in the Fiction Film* (Oxon: Routledge, 1985), 49.
11. Lawrence Kasdan's son Jonathan actually appeared in seven of his father's films, but in minor roles.
12. Kasdan, interviewed for *Directors: Lawrence Kasdan*.
13. Ibid.
14. Michael Ryan and Douglas Kellner, *Camera Politica: The Politics and Ideology of Contemporary Hollywood Film* (Indiana University Press, 1988), 277–9.
15. Kevin Kline, interviewed for *Directors: Lawrence Kasdan*.
16. Kasdan, quoted in Carole Zucker, *Figures of Light: Actors and Directors Illuminate the Art of Film Acting* (New York: Plenum Press, 1995), 289.
17. Ibid., 288.
18. Ibid., 289.
19. Ed Begley Jr., interviewed for *Directors: Lawrence Kasdan*.
20. Kasdan, quoted in Zucker, Figures of Light, 287.
21. Ibid., 292.
22. Ibid.
23. Ibid.
24. Dennis Quaid, interviewed for *Directors: Lawrence Kasdan*.
25. Mary McDonnell, interviewed for *Directors: Lawrence Kasdan*.
26. Kasdan, quoted in Hemphill, "Lawrence Kasdan," 28.
27. Kasdan, quoted in Zucker, Figures of Light, 291.
28. As mentioned earlier, even on the two pictures written by other people, *I Love You to Death* and *French Kiss*, Kasdan had the writers on set with him.
29. Quaid, interviewed for *Directors: Lawrence Kasdan*.
30. McDonnell, interviewed for *Directors: Lawrence Kasdan*.

PART V

A Long Time in a Galaxy Far, Far Away

CHAPTER 9

From Star Wars to Saga: Lawrence Kasdan and *The Empire Strikes Back*

For all the discussion of Lawrence Kasdan as the quintessential baby-boomer filmmaker and as a writer-director who pays homage to movies and genres of the past, he is perhaps best known as the writer of four screenplays in the Star Wars saga, with two episodes at the very beginning of his career and his two most recent theatrical releases. However, Kasdan's contributions to the franchise have rarely been examined in academic or popular discourse, with authorial credit usually assigned to series creator George Lucas. On the release of *The Empire Strikes Back*, one critic claimed that "Lucas, like Disney and Selznick, is a true auteur from conception to final cut."[1] Forty years later, when introducing her *BFI Film Classics* volume analyzing the same film, Rebecca Harrison states that her "small act of rebellion [. . .] is to resist oft-repeated claims about George Lucas and auteurism" and to "focus on stories about the collective endeavours of film-makers and viewers."[2] She fulfils this promise, with Lucas barely mentioned when discussing the production and reception of the film; however, Harrison still veers toward the auteur myth, crediting director Irvin Kershner with *Empire*'s representation of ecological dysfunction, due to his being "a staunch advocate of vegetarianism and spiritual harmony between living things and their habitats,"[3] regardless of the fact that much of this was present in early treatments and screenplay drafts. Conversely, Harrison does not mention Kasdan at all, apart from a single credit in the "Notes" section,[4] even while quoting directly from his drafts of the screenplay.

Harrison's work does succeed, though, in analyzing a Star Wars movie's themes and cinematic form rather than viewing it as a cultural phenomenon or solely as a technical undertaking. As Will Brooker states in his *BFI Classics* book on the original film in the series, "Cinema scholarship seems embarrassed by *Star Wars*," and "any discussions of its themes, story and character tend to be either patronising or contemptuous."[5] Similarly, Harrison contends that the series is "neglected in serious critical and scholarly writing."[6] These prevailing attitudes have led to a dearth of academic discourse regarding the series' thematic and storytelling approaches—those elements present in the screenplay—diminishing Kasdan's standing as a major participant in creating the franchise. This section aims to address the issue by comparing prevalent themes and narrative techniques present in Kasdan's Star Wars screenplays with those in drafts or treatments written by others, ascertaining the extent of his creative contribution to the series. Additionally, by placing these scripts within the context of his overall career, it may be possible to establish just how much Lawrence Kasdan was able to impart his own world view through Star Wars.

"STAR WARS II"

Now considered the best film in the Star Wars series,[7] the writing process for *The Empire Strikes Back* was fraught with problems. Even before the release of the first *Star Wars* in May 1977, George Lucas had outlined a wider saga, and in November of that year he hired Leigh Brackett to begin work on the screenplay for "Star Wars II."[8] Separately, Lucas then employed Lawrence Kasdan to write the script for *Raiders of the Lost Ark*, with the story conference for that film (discussed in Chapter 1) taking place in January 1978. Kasdan spent just under half a year writing the initial draft of *Raiders* before delivering it to Lucas in June. During that time, however, Leigh Brackett had passed away from cancer, only weeks after completing her first draft of *Empire*. This left Lucas without a screenwriter for his Star Wars sequel, so, when Kasdan delivered the *Raiders* script to his office, Lucas took him out for lunch. Kasdan explains:

> [Lucas] says, "I'm in big trouble with the second Star Wars. We've got all these people working [to build sets] in England and I don't have a script." He said, "I'm really in a hole here. Will you write this movie?" And I said, "Don't you want to read *Raiders of the Lost Ark*?" And he said, "Well, I'm going to read it tonight and if I don't like it, I'm going to call you up tomorrow, take back this offer." But he did like it, and we started work on that and it went very quickly because they were so far behind.[9]

Unlike with *Raiders*, when Kasdan was creating the screenplay based upon the notes from the story conference with Lucas and Steven Spielberg (as well as a brief phone conversation with Philip Kaufman), three drafts of *Empire* had already been written: the first by Leigh Brackett, and the next two by Lucas that, Kasdan says, "[Lucas] wrote very quickly" and included "terrible" scenes that were intended as placeholders so that the next writer "would know that a scene covering approximately the same kind of material [. . .] belonged at that point."[10] While these existing documents meant that *Empire* was much more fully developed than *Raiders of the Lost Ark* had been when he began work on the screenplay, Kasdan intimated soon afterward that this was not necessarily helpful:

> Working within [Lucas's "grand scheme"], I was not seeing the story's beginning or conclusion. I felt that I had to develop *Empire*'s screenplay based on my perception of the characters in *Star Wars* and what George wanted them to do in its sequel.[11]

Kasdan admitted that after "intense" story conferences with Lucas and director Irvin Kershner, "I had a big influence on *Empire*, but probably the smallest influence that I've ever had on a film that I've written."[12] The fact that soundstages were already under construction would have added further pressure, Kasdan's narrative choices constrained by the sets available to him.

In Chapter 2, I analyzed Kasdan's writing for *Raiders of the Lost* Ark, comparing his final script with earlier drafts as well as the initial story conferences with George Lucas and director Steven Spielberg, establishing which new elements Kasdan brought to the project. Similarly, this section shall examine Leigh Brackett's first draft of *The Empire Strikes Back* and Kasdan's two versions, marked "fourth draft" and "fifth draft"—the official final draft—as well as Kasdan's handwritten notes and script pages.[13] Furthermore, Bouzereau, Rinzler, and Duncan have reproduced and summarized parts of the story conferences and treatments.[14] These data allow us to understand the major changes that occurred after Kasdan was hired, offering insight into how much he was able to influence the story and themes as well as scene-specific elements such as dialogue and stage directions.

Leigh Brackett was a veteran science-fiction author, who had also written for film, most notably five pictures with director Howard Hawks, including *The Big Sleep* (1946), *Rio Bravo* (1959), and *El Dorado* (1966). Her experience working for a powerful "auteur" figure, her penchant for snappy dialogue (Roger Ebert calls *The Big Sleep* "one of the most quotable of screenplays"[15]), and her background creating sci-fi worlds in ten novels and numerous short stories made Brackett an appropriate fit for the task of expanding the Star Wars saga, as Lucas himself attested.[16] She worked with Lucas in a five-day story conference before the latter produced a treatment;[17] then, from this document, Brackett wrote the first draft of the screenplay, including final handwritten notes dated "Feb 17, 1978," before her death on March 18.

Lucas says: "I didn't like the first script [. . .]. During the story conferences I had with Leigh, my thoughts weren't fully formed yet and I felt that her script went in a completely different direction."[18] This seems an unfair criticism of Brackett's screenplay based on what we know of Lucas's first nine-page treatment,[19] as well as the conference itself. According to the official

Lucasfilm history, the fifty-one-page transcript only records Lucas speaking, suggesting that he was even more dominant than in the *Raiders* conference two months later (discussed in Chapter 1).[20] Leigh Brackett's first draft script meets all the story beats as outlined by Lucas, as well as providing spirited banter between Han Solo and Princess Leia. It also introduces the Yoda character (called Minch in this draft), and Brackett captures his combination of childishness and wisdom, often teasing Luke and chastizing him in the same utterance. For example, when Luke practices wielding his lightsaber, Minch says: "Farmboy! That's not an axe to chop your wood with. [. . .] Lightness, Skywalker! Grace. Speed. Skill. That was how the Jedi knights used the sabre."

The script has a more mystical quality than would eventually be seen on screen, and, at one point, Minch/Yoda fences with the shimmering apparition of Obi-Wan Kenobi, their lightsaber duel "a thing of breathtaking skill and beauty" that begins and ends with a formal salute and bow. Both the spiritual and chivalric aspects are present again when Luke meets the ghost form of his father (in this draft, *not* Darth Vader), who inducts Luke into "the brotherhood of knights" with a solemn vow and the ceremonial touching of laser swords. Certainly, Brackett employs a more literary style than one might expect in a Hollywood screenplay, and she betrays her classical science-fiction background (she had co-written a novel with Ray Bradbury) in this scene in particular. However, Lucas's claim that Leigh Brackett's script was "unworkable"[21] is grossly unfair, all the more so as the dialogue in this scene is quite similar to the exchanges between Palpatine and Anakin in Lucas's own screenplay for the third prequel, *Revenge of the Sith* (2005).

The other element that stands out in Leigh Brackett's screenplay is the to-and-fro between Han Solo and Princess Leia. As in later drafts, and the finished film, the pair engage in heated exchanges for much of the story as they evade their Imperial pursuers on Han's ship, the *Millennium Falcon*. In her book on *Empire*, Harrison contends that "their interactions tend to be gentle rather than aggressive" in Brackett's draft, with Han allowing that women have power—an element that Harrison says is "erased" in Kasdan's iterations of the script.[22] Their exchanges are certainly witty and interesting, and the tone bears similarities to the completed movie. For example, around the halfway point, on page sixty-three, Han "has moved in on Leia again":

```
                    HAN
        We're two people, alone in the
        immensity of space...
            (stops, shakes his head)
        No, no, hold it. That's too
        much even for me.
```

```
Leia suddenly doubles up with laughter.

                    LEIA
        It's a great line, Han, and
        well-polished with use.
```

Despite following Lucas's plot faithfully and establishing aspects that would remain present through subsequent drafts, both Lucas and Lawrence Kasdan suggest that Brackett had not, as Kasdan puts it, "quite gotten what it is about George [. . .]. I think she was just in an entirely different mode."[23] Given that Lucas has referred to *The Empire Strikes Back* as "an homage to '40s movies and a space opera,"[24] I would argue that Brackett's contributions do not "belong in another movie," as the official history contends.[25] However, Brackett's death meant that she would never have the opportunity either to rewrite her script or to defend her decisions, and Kasdan says: "I'm sure that had Leigh lived, she could have made the changes George wanted in an excellent way."[26] Lucas says that he gave Brackett a share of the credit only because, "I liked her a lot. She was sick at the time she wrote the script, and she really tried her best."[27] As Lucasfilm was not a signatory to the Writers Guild of America Agreement, there was no arbitration to decide credits (which would usually be mandatory in such a situation, in which the executive producer was also one of the writers). However, based on the WGA Screen Credits Manual, I would argue that Brackett's draft included much of the dramatic construction found in the final picture, as well as significant characterization, especially of new characters such as Yoda and Lando. If it had gone to arbitration, the threshold for Brackett, as the first screenwriter hired, would be thirty-three per cent of the screenplay, which, in my opinion, she passes.[28] Based on the industry standard, then, Brackett deserved her co-writer credit, irrespective of any professed sentimentality from Lucas. Regardless, after Brackett's passing, George Lucas wrote two rough drafts himself, then hired Lawrence Kasdan to complete the work.[29]

THE MIDDLE ACT: FUN AND CHAOS

Before attempting to ascertain Lawrence Kasdan's impact upon *The Empire Strikes Back*, it is worth defining those elements that contribute to creating a "Kasdan film," based upon the evidence from the previous chapters. The task is rendered more difficult by the fact that some traits are also present in the earlier films of George Lucas, such as nostalgia and a proclivity for borrowing from dormant genres, as well as shared admiration for the work of Akira Kurosawa. Furthermore, other aspects associated with Kasdan dovetail with Leigh Brackett's strengths: quotable "battle of the sexes" dialogue, a preference for classical literary structure, and experience writing crime and cowboy pictures—two genres that inflect the screenplay for *Empire*—as Brackett had written three film noirs and four Westerns; and Kasdan would write and direct the neo-noir *Body Heat* and two Westerns. However, where Kasdan delineates from his predecessors is in the more progressive elements of his "baby-boomer" outlook that frequently occur in his other screenplays and films (discussed in Chapters 5 and 6): his characters' questioning of social norms, the tension between altruism and individualism, a desire to include marginalized groups, and the evolution of family (or surrogate family) roles. Furthermore, even as both Lucas and Kasdan lionize the films of Kurosawa, the former leans toward the epic scope and "the formal Japanese sense of composition and texture,"[30] while Kasdan appears more concerned with Kurosawa's abstract themes, such as the protagonists' struggle to assert their identity and the fear of exposure (discussed in Chapter 7). The inclusion of such elements in *Empire* would suggest that Kasdan was able to inform the finished film, even if he states that he had "the smallest influence."[31]

The Empire Strikes Back, as the middle episode of the trilogy, would not necessarily need to conclude any storylines. This probably lent itself to Kasdan's sensibilities, as he frequently ends his stories ambiguously. For example, during the same period of his career, *Continental Divide* and *Body Heat* both finished on a note of uncertainty, the characters' fates not entirely clear; and even the climax of *Raiders of the Lost Ark* left the hero dissatisfied, the Ark hidden away under piles of wooden crates and government bureaucracy. Kasdan says that "*Empire Strikes Back* is the second act. [. . .] When I realized that immediately I thought this is really fun. [. . .] We want it to be chaos at the end of this movie."[32] Similarly, as the second of the trilogy, he could avoid becoming bogged down in the kind of world-building that he says he does not enjoy. Kasdan's drafts certainly eschew some of the more outlandish aspects present in the earlier iterations of the story. For instance, as well as the cosmic connection between Luke and Darth Vader, Brackett's first draft had a planet inhabited by tall, white-skinned warriors who "ride through the sky on creatures that resemble pale giant manta-rays."[33] Much of this was pared back, first by Lucas, then even more so by Kasdan. On the other hand, Kasdan expands upon the Zen-like teachings of Yoda, devoting much more time to Luke's training on the swamp planet of Dagobah. Kasdan's handwritten fourth draft reveals Yoda's identity as a Jedi Master later than in previous versions; later, too, than in the final film. This, he says, is deliberate, a means of implying Luke's lack of patience even before Yoda begins his explicit instruction. Kasdan says he based Yoda on Kambei Shimada, the lead character in Akira Kurosawa's *Seven Samurai* (1954), who, Kasdan states, "always sees the big picture and is slower to react because he's figured it out."[34] The desire to teach Luke to be more patient also contributes

Figure 9.1 Yoda instructs Luke

to Yoda's distinctive speech pattern, in which he reveals the subject and verb only at the end of a clause. While George Lucas played with inverting Yoda's speech in earlier drafts, Kasdan developed the idea and "found that what I liked best was a repetition of words, a light inversion that had a medieval tone to it."[35] Kasdan connects this choice of syntax to Yoda's "meditation teacher" quality, his utterances designed to make the student listen more attentively: "It slows things down. You have to worry through the sentence to understand. And then that way you're paying more attention."[36]

Kasdan states: "My scripts are people scripts. That approach worked on *Empire* because, take away all the science fiction paraphernalia and you have a character-in-conflict story."[37] As mentioned earlier, his facility for writing dialogue and complex relationships was shared with Leigh Brackett, and it manifests itself most clearly in the exchanges between Han Solo and Princess Leia. Harrison contends that these interactions "become more brusque" in Kasdan's drafts compared to Brackett's;[38] this is implied, too, in one of Kasdan's script notes: "Han acts like a jerk because he can't resist, thereby blowing his chance w/ Leia." His initial handwritten screenplay pages also lean in that direction, Han apparently much more knowing than Leia:

```
                    LEIA
          Han. I need you here... The
          Rebellion needs you.

                    HAN
          Oh, so it's the Rebellion?

                    LEIA
          Yes.
```

```
                    HAN
          Not you?

                    LEIA
          Me?

                    HAN
                (smiles)
          My little princess. I'm afraid
          you don't know yourself very
          well.

                    LEIA
          What do you mean?

                    HAN
          When I met you I thought you
          were not only beautiful, but
          brave. Now I see that you're
          only beautiful.
```

This is a quite different dynamic than in Brackett's draft, in which Han makes clear his feelings within their very first exchange, after Leia has asked Han to accept a dangerous mission. In this instance, it is Leia who appears more in control:

```
                    HAN
          Leia... for you... I'd try even
          that.

                    LEIA
          You would? For me?
```

```
     She smiles. His arms go around her. He pulls her
     closer to him and for a moment it seems that she
     is melting in his arms, ready for his kiss. [...]
     At the very last minute, Leia slaps Han's face
     with a resounding crack and he starts back, let-
     ting her go, thoroughly startled. Coldly angry,
     she faces him.
```

```
                    LEIA
          Captain Solo, a great war is
          raging. What you would do for
          me, or I for you, are matters
          of no consequence. The mission
          is vital.
```

In Brackett's draft, the pair's interactions soon become less caustic, but in Kasdan's version their dialogue remains waspish until much later in the story. Harrison writes that this harsher tone is because "Han's admission of women's power [present in Brackett's draft] is erased,"[39] and the examples above tend to support this argument; but it should also be noted that Brackett's characterization of Leia is much softer throughout her screenplay, with Leia's romantic feelings for Han more evident. For example, just past the midway point, the *Millennium Falcon* is under heavy fire as they hide in the cave of a "planetoid," the characters' situation apparently hopeless:

```
Han takes her in his arms.

                    HAN
          Leia...

                    LEIA
          You're trying to make me say
          what I don't want to say. Han,
          if we live through this,
          there'll still be your mission,
          and mine. We may never see each
          other again.

                    HAN
          Will not saying that you love
          me make that any easier?

                    LEIA
               (after a moment)
          I guess not.

                    HAN
          Then why waste what little time
          we have? You do, don't you?

Leia sighs. What's the use of denying it? It
shows, unmistakably. She kisses him.
```

They are interrupted by Han's friend and co-pilot Chewbacca, but later in the scene they kiss again; then:

```
                    LEIA
          O, Han...

She begins to weep, hugging him closer, burying
her face against his.
```

In Kasdan's final draft, though, Leia is less willing to show any romantic feelings, even if their first kiss comes during the same sequence, when hiding aboard the *Millennium Falcon* inside the asteroid. Unlike in Brackett's draft, where Leia is simply a passenger aboard Han's ship, in Kasdan's version she plays a more active role in repairing the damaged craft. She has just finished welding a valve and is now attempting to "reengage the system by pulling a lever attached to the valve." She then rebuffs Han's attempt to help her, offending him:

> HAN
> Easy, your worship. Only trying
> to help.

> LEIA
> (still struggling)
> Would you please stop calling
> me that?

Han hears a new tone in her voice. He watches her pull on the lever.

> HAN
> Sure.

> LEIA
> Oh, you make it so difficult
> sometimes.

> HAN
> I do, I really do. You could be
> a little nicer, though.
> (he watches her reaction)
> Come on, admit it, sometimes
> you think I'm all right.

She lets go of the lever and licks her sore hand...

> LEIA
> (a little smile, haltingly)
> Sometimes, maybe...
> occasionally, when you aren't
> acting like a scoundrel.

```
                        HAN
                      (laughs)
          Scoundrel... I like the sound
          of that...
```

With that, Han takes her hand and starts to mas-
sage it.

```
                        LEIA
          Stop that.


                        HAN
          Stop what?
```

This leads to the moment when, "with an irresistible combination of physical
strength and emotional power, the space pirate begins to draw Leia toward
him . . . very slowly." Finally, "He kisses her now with slow, hot lips. [. . .] She
has never been kissed like this before, and it almost makes her faint." The scene
illustrates Harrison's observation that Han "demonstrates a lack of respect
for [Leia's] autonomy and consent,"[40] but it also reveals a toughness to Leia's
character that is less apparent through similar scenes in Brackett's draft. In
Kasdan's characterization, she does not swoon into Han's arms, nor does she
sit around the *Falcon* weeping or hugging him. Instead, she repairs the damage
onboard, throwing off Han's attempts to help, and insists on going with him to
fight off the giant bat-like "mynocks" attacking the ship. The dynamic is similar to that between Indy and Marion in *Raiders of the Lost Ark*, Ernie and Nell
in *Continental Divide*, and Ned and Matty in the early scenes of *Body Heat*: a
sexual tension generated by two stubborn people eager not to concede to the
other. Certainly, there is a male-centric bias in each of these examples, the
screenplays all revealing the man first, then the woman from his point of view.
As Harrison notes, in the fourth draft of *Empire* (Kasdan's first draft), there is
almost no physical description of Luke or Han on their first appearance, while
Leia's arrival is described from Han and General Rieekan's perspective: "The
two men turn to see PRINCESS LEIA, dressed in a short white combat jacket
and pants. [. . .] Her hair is braided and tied across her head in a '30's' Nordic
fashion." However, there is at least a recognition of equality, with the women
in all of these films in positions of power, both occupationally and sexually. By
delaying the moment when the pair becomes a romantic couple, Kasdan's draft
increases the friction between Han and Leia, giving Leia more opportunity to
deflate Han's ego with her acerbic wit; a contrast to Brackett's version, in which
Leia, after the midway point when she and Han kiss, becomes more stereotypically feminine. She shivers with cold and needs to return indoors while walking

the gardens of Cloud City; she is "close to tears" and requires comforting by Han when the droid C-3PO is found damaged; and she slams the door petulantly when Han disagrees with her doubts about Lando's trustworthiness.

Leia's sarcasm also becomes less traditionally gendered in Kasdan's drafts. For example, when the *Millennium Falcon* struggles to take off, Leia says: "Would it help if I got out and pushed?" It echoes a similar moment in Brackett's draft, in which "Leia, hugging herself with cold and impatience, watches Han and Chewie [work on the ship]," then says: "Aren't you finished yet? I could do better with a needle and thread!" Kasdan abandons this more stereotypically feminine version of Leia in favor of making her the self-possessed leader of the Rebel Alliance, willing to grab a blaster and fight off stormtroopers, and an equal partner in the screwball exchanges with Han Solo. Therefore, while Kasdan had little say in the plot of the film, and the comic tone was already present in Brackett's script, in his iteration Leia has more agency, and her relationship with Han becomes subtly more egalitarian in terms of class and gender; something that Kasdan has attempted in most of his screenplays.

As discussed in Chapter 6, Kasdan repeatedly includes women and people from marginalized groups at the center of his narratives. *Empire* features the saga's first non-white human, Lando Calrissian, at the behest of George Lucas, who, according to his first authorized biography, was "smarting from criticism that *Star Wars* was racist."[41] In both Brackett's and Kasdan's versions, Lando is a complex character, and in the final draft he is a former gambler, now the administrator of a mining facility, who betrays his old friend Han in order to save his workers, before finally aiding Leia's escape at the risk of his own life. It is an improvement over other representations of black people in contemporary Hollywood films, avoiding either the comedy sidekick or "Magical Negro" tropes that prevailed at the time. However, Harrison observes that Lando's "overt sexualisation of [Leia] is in keeping with white stereotypes of black men threatening racial purity," while the audience is guided to accept Han's "far more aggressive" advances toward her, presumably due to his skin color. On the other hand, once Han is abducted, a "progressive new alliance" is forged, with Lando and Leia working together as equals, along with the "other" characters of a wookiee and two droids, and without a white male "authority figure" leading them.[42] As with Kasdan's directorial works, such as *Grand Canyon* and *Dreamcatcher*, there is an attempt to give power to people that are often excluded from active roles in mainstream cinema.

One aspect of the plot that appears to change significantly in Kasdan's script is Han Solo's attitude toward the Rebel cause and to his friends. In Leigh Brackett's draft, Han is about to embark on a dangerous one-man mission for the Rebellion before he is waylaid by Luke Skywalker going missing in the snow then the Empire's arrival. But in Kasdan's version, Han is readying to abandon the Alliance and his friends in order to pay off Jabba the Hutt. This echoes a theme introduced in *Star Wars*, in which Han said he only helped rescue Princess Leia because he wanted a financial reward, before changing his mind in order to help Luke destroy the Death Star. But the decision to leave is more resonant here, coming after shared adventures over a longer period of time within the story world (between the events of these two films). Furthermore, Kasdan's first draft has Han make his decision quite suddenly, Leia and Luke apparently unaware of his intentions until he is already preparing to depart:

> LEIA
> Captain Sol— Han. Why are you
> leaving us now?

> HAN
> That bounty hunter we ran into
> on Ord Mantell reminded me what
> I've got to do.

> LEIA
> Does Luke know?

> HAN
> He'll know when he gets back.

This is a more callous attitude than Han showed in the finale of *Star Wars*, and very different from Brackett's draft of *Empire*, in which there was no question of him abandoning the cause. While Kasdan is merely building upon the "flyboy" character created by George Lucas, this act positions him alongside the flawed protagonists of Kasdan's other works, and very much in the Kurosawa mode of the reluctant hero. In fact, Kasdan later called Han his "favorite character" in Star Wars;[43] and it is during *Empire* that he becomes a more rounded personality, revealing vulnerability beneath the cocky façade, and eventually choosing to risk his life to help others, even while reveling in his own self-centeredness. Han's initial plan to leave connects the character to other Kasdan protagonists, his individual wants at odds with those of the group, a surrogate family that he had not intended to join, but with whom he ends up entwined in spite of himself. It is a condition that Kasdan often revisits— whether through *The Big Chill* ensemble, Macon in *The Accidental Tourist*, the title character in *Mumford*, or Joseph in *Darling Companion*—and one that echoes a theme in Kasdan's more personal works: the tension between the past self and present self, and the difficulties in reconciling our self-perception with the ways that others view us.

A major structural difference between Kasdan's drafts and Leigh Brackett's is in the more frequent cutting between the main storylines. Kasdan says that he was simply continuing the pattern established in the first film; but whereas in *Star Wars* Lucas had two groups split temporarily within the same space station, in *Empire* Luke Skywalker takes an entirely different path than Han and Leia, both physically and emotionally. Kasdan is pragmatic about his use of this intercutting structure: "When you get bored with the scene you just cut to the other storyline and it gives you an enormous burst of energy."[44] The choice to flip between the two storylines so frequently, though, was Kasdan's, and it contributes to a groundedness that further distances his work from Brackett's more exposition-heavy draft. Even Yoda's pseudo-religious teachings feel truer when delivered in shorter chunks, interspersed with Han and Leia's bickering as they are pursued through space; and it contrasts sharply with the ceremonial, almost theatrical quality of Minch/Yoda's instruction in Brackett's draft. The faster cutting also reminds the audience that this is an ensemble picture, the two groups' fates inexorably connected despite landing in different parts of the galaxy. In this way, Kasdan's screenplay bears similarity to the multi-protagonist dramas for which he would gain attention later in his career, such as *The Big Chill* or *Grand Canyon*. Indeed, Kasdan says that he does not make a distinction between writing for Star Wars and writing his more personal films: "within [the reality that you're creating], there has to be some sense of logic [. . .]. You want the audience not to be comfortable, not to be put to sleep, but to say I recognize something true here."[45] The faster pace aids the viewer in suspending disbelief regarding the more outlandish elements of the script, keeping the emphasis on the human aspects, such as Luke's frustration and Han and Leia's burgeoning romance, rather than focusing on the world-building that is more prominent in earlier treatments and drafts.

A useful tool for summarizing Kasdan's contribution to *The Empire Strikes Back* is Bordwell's paradigm of fabula versus syuzhet (discussed in Chapters 3 and 4).[46] Through this prism, it can be argued that Kasdan stays faithful to the original fabula—the events occurring in the story world—as developed through George Lucas and Leigh Brackett's early discussions and drafts. However, Kasdan's major contribution to *The Empire Strikes Back* is in designing the syuzhet—the presentation of the fabula—in a way that allows the audience to accept the sci-fi elements as given rather than explained, and in maintaining the verisimilitude established in the first movie. Through the frequent juxtaposition of the two main storylines, he keeps the rapid pace expected of a fantasy-adventure film, even as it heads toward its remarkably downbeat finale. George Lucas has been criticized for sacrificing character development for speed, with Kasdan concerned that "Lucas glossed over the emotional content of a scene in his hurry to get to the next one."[47] But the syuzhet as defined in Kasdan's screenplay (along with Irvin Kershner's measured direction) ensures that the "middle act" of the Star Wars trilogy manages to achieve both thematic development and fast-paced action. Furthermore, by making Princess Leia and Han Solo equals in their comedic interactions, he increases the sexual tension and sets up a more emotional moment when they are eventually separated, even if their famous final exchange (Leia: "I love you"/Han: "I know") was improvised on set.[48]

Therefore, although Lawrence Kasdan says that he had "much less of a free hand than on anything else I've ever written,"[49] his screenplay still played a vital role in creating the "best" episode in the entire canon, the one in which the "splintering cracks of style and tone that had first emerged in Lucas' drafts finally split open, breaking off and growing into a separate beast that gave birth to the Star Wars saga."[50] At a time when movie franchises were not commonly successful, *The Empire Strikes Back* was the film that transformed Star Wars from a single surprise hit into a series that would change the face of Hollywood moviemaking for decades to come.

NOTES

1. Tim Allen, "What Empire?" *The Village Voice*, May 26, 1980, 50.
2. Rebecca Harrison, *BFI Film Classics: The Empire Strikes Back* (London: Bloomsbury/British Film Institute, 2020), p. 6.
3. Ibid., 32.
4. Ibid., 84.
5. Will Brooker, *BFI Film Classics: Star Wars* (London: Bloomsbury/British Film Institute, 2009), 8.
6. Harrison, *BFI: Empire*, 2.
7. See, for example, Roger Ebert, "*The Empire Strikes Back*," *Roger Ebert*, April 1, 1997, https://www.rogerebert.com/reviews/the-empire-strikes-back-1997-1 (accessed July 5, 2023); Darren Franich, "What Movies Can Still Learn from *The Empire Strikes Back*," *Entertainment Weekly*, May 21, 2015, https://ew.com/article/2015/05/21/empire-strikes-back-35th-anniversary/ (accessed July 5, 2023); Peter Bradshaw, "Every Star Wars Film—ranked!" *The Guardian*, May 24, 2018, https://www.theguardian.com/film/2018/may/24/every-star-wars-film-ranked-solo-skywalker (accessed July 5, 2023).
8. J.W. Rinzler, *The Making of the Empire Strikes Back* (London: Aurum, 2010), 15. This second film in the Star Wars series was initially titled "Star Wars 2" or "Star Wars II" in internal Lucasfilm and Fox memos (see Rinzler, *Making Empire*, 44), as well as in initial press releases. The later unconventional numbering of episodes in the Star Wars saga began only with George Lucas's second draft of the *Empire* screenplay, then the 1980 release of the film, which opens with the title *Star Wars Episode V: The Empire Strikes Back*. When the original movie was re-released a year later, its name was changed from simply *Star Wars* to *Star Wars Episode IV: A New Hope*, realigning these first films as part of a larger saga.
9. Lawrence Kasdan, "On Story 1011: A Conversation with Lawrence Kasdan," June 20, 2020, Austin Film Festival, https://www.youtube.com/watch?v=rhtF8lKoIWg (accessed July 5, 2023).
10. Kasdan, quoted in James H. Burns, "Lawrence Kasdan: Part 2: From Scripting *The Empire Strikes Back* to Writing and Directing *Body Heat*," *Starlog*, October 1981, 56.

11. Ibid.

12. Ibid.

13. Leigh Brackett, *Star Wars Sequel*, screenplay, 1st draft, February 17, 1978; Leigh Brackett and Lawrence Kasdan, *The Empire Strikes Back*, screenplay, 4th draft, 24 October 24, 1978. Brackett and Kasdan, *The Empire Strikes Back*, 5th draft, screenplay, February 20, 1979; Kasdan, *The Empire Strikes Back*, handwritten notes and pages, 1979, https://johnaugust. com/wp-content/uploads/2020/05/empire-handwritten-pages.pdf (accessed July 5, 2023).

14. Laurent Bouzereau, *Star Wars: The Annotated Screenplays* (New York: Ballantine, 1997); Rinzler, *Making Empire*; Paul Duncan, *The Star Wars Archives: Episodes IV–VI: 1977–1983* (Cologne: Taschen, 2020).

15. Ebert, "*The Big Sleep*," *Roger Ebert*, June 22, 1997, http://www.rogerebert.com/reviews/ great-movie-the-big-sleep-1946 (accessed July 5, 2023).

16. Rinzler, *Making Empire*, 15.

17. Bouzereau, *Star Wars: Annotated*, 123.

18. Ibid., 144.

19. Much of the treatment is reproduced in Duncan, *Star Wars Archives*, 190–7.

20. Rinzler, *Making Empire*, 20.

21. Duncan, *Star Wars Archives*, 220.

22. Harrison, *BFI: Empire*, 27.

23. Rinzler, *Making Empire*, 39.

24. Kristin Baver, "Empire at 40: George Lucas on Making 'Something that had Never Been Done Before,' Again," *Star Wars*, May 21, 2020, https://www.starwars.com/news/ empire-at-40-george-lucas-interview (accessed July 5, 2023).

25. Rinzler, *Making Empire*, 39.

26. Burns, "Lawrence Kasdan: Part 2," 56.

27. George Lucas, quoted in Bouzereau, *Star Wars: Annotated*, 144.

28. Writers Guild of America West, *Screen Credits Manual* (Los Angeles: WGA, 2018), 16–17, https://www.wga.org/uploadedfiles/credits/manuals/screenscredits_manual18.pdf (accessed July 5, 2023).

29. Duncan, *Star Wars Archives*, 230.

30. Dale Pollock, *Skywalking: The Life and Films of George Lucas: Updated Edition* (New York: Da Capo, 1983/1999), 46.

31. Burns, "Lawrence Kasdan: Part 2," 56.

32. Kasdan, interviewed by John August and Craig Mazin, "Episode 452: *The Empire Strikes Back* with Lawrence Kasdan," *Scriptnotes*, transcript, May 26, 2020, https://johnaugust. com/2020/scriptnotes-ep-452-the-empire-strikes-back-with-lawrence-kasdan-transcript (accessed July 5, 2023).

33. In the story conference, George Lucas described these as "semi-stoic [. . .] tall, thin, white ethereal aliens" (Rinzler, *Making Empire*, 23). Similar creatures would appear in the second prequel, *Attack of the Clones* (2002), co-written and directed by Lucas, further suggesting that these were his inventions rather than Leigh Brackett's, and undermining the notion that "her script went in a completely different direction," as Lucas claims (Bouzereau, *Star Wars: Annotated*, 144).

34. Kasdan, interviewed by August and Mazin, "Episode 452."

35. Kasdan, quoted in *The Empire Strikes Back Notebook*, edited by Diana Attias and Lindsay Smith (New York: Ballantine, 1980), 70.

36. Kasdan, interviewed by August and Mazin, "Episode 452."

37. Kasdan, quoted in Duncan, *Star Wars Archives*, 230.

38. Harrison, *BFI: Empire*, 27.

39. Ibid., 27.

40. Ibid., 45.
41. Pollock, *Skywalking*, 213.
42. Harrison, *BFI: Empire*, 47–9.
43. Josh Rottenberg, "Q&A: Star Wars Screenwriter Lawrence Kasdan on the Past, Present and Future of Star Wars," *The Los Angeles Times*, December 3, 2015, http://www.latimes.com/entertainment/herocomplex/la-ca-hc-star-wars-lawrence-kasdan-20151206-story.html (accessed July 5, 2023).
44. Kasdan, interviewed by August and Mazin, "Episode 452."
45. Ibid.
46. David Bordwell, *Narration in the Fiction Film* (Oxon: Routledge, 1985), 49–50.
47. Kasdan, quoted in Pollock, *Skywalking*, 211.
48. Bouzereau, *Star Wars: Annotated*, 207–8.
49. Kasdan, quoted in Burns, "Lawrence Kasdan: Part 2," 56.
50. Michael Kaminski, *The Secret History of Star Wars: The Art of Storytelling and the Making of a Modern Epic* (Kingston, Canada: Legacy, 2008), 193.

CHAPTER 10

Revenge of the Monomyth: Reclaiming the Hero's Journey in *Return of the Jedi*

Any textual analysis of the Star Wars saga will invariably cite the work of Joseph Campbell. His theory of the hero's journey, a monomyth universal to all societies, is exemplified by George Lucas's series.[1] Indeed, Lucas himself frequently accentuates the connection, discussing Campbell in numerous interviews, commissioning documentaries that explore associations between Star Wars and the monomyth, and contributing to Campbell's authorized biography.[2] For all of Lucas's claims that Campbell's work directly influenced his writing of *Star Wars* and its sequels, there is some debate over the actual extent to which it affected the saga. In his comprehensive investigation into the making of the series, Michael Kaminski suggests that both Lucas and Campbell exaggerated connections in order to boost their respective credentials: Lucas receiving "scholastic backing" for his "B-movie" pictures, and Campbell's theories gaining international recognition due to their becoming synonymous with the most commercially successful film of all time.[3] In the official history of the original movie, Lucas claims to have read Campbell when working on the third draft of his *Star Wars* script. Only then, on noticing the unconscious similarity, did he try to make his story fit a more "classic mold."[4] However, in other interviews, he appears to imply a more explicit and earlier link to Campbell:

> I studied anthropology in college and took a class in mythology. I read some of [Campbell's] stuff there. When I started *Star Wars*, I did more research before I wrote the screenplay. I reread *A Thousand Faces* and a few other things he did, and that was the influence he had on me.[5]

As Kaminski notes, Campbell's theory is that most adventure stories follow the hero's journey pattern, and that is the very point of the monomyth: not that storytellers should try to follow it, but that they unconsciously do—something that Lucas said he discovered in early drafts of his outline before reading (or rereading) *The Hero With a Thousand Faces*.[6] So, rather than shaping its creation, Campbell's association with Star Wars was perhaps a result of the first film's reception, as a classical fairy story that became extraordinarily popular so soon after Watergate and the US withdrawal from Vietnam; and in contrast to the grittier, grounded mode of cinema that had dominated the decade. This led to newspaper think pieces on the rebirth of the mythic tale,[7] until *Star Wars* and its sequels became conflated inexorably with Campbell's paradigm.

Joseph Campbell separates the hero's journey into three acts: the departure, the initiation, and the return. Within each of these acts he places a total of seventeen stages (five stages in the first act, and six each in the other two); for example, within the departure, there is the call to adventure, the refusal of the call, the supernatural aid, the crossing of the first threshold, then the "belly of the whale," when the hero enters into a completely new sphere and finally shows willingness to transform.[8] Of course, these specific acts do not necessarily appear explicitly in every "quest" story, but they offer an instructive framework from which we can understand the tenets of mythical narration.

The first *Star Wars* movie certainly includes most of Campbell's acts and stages on a micro level (starting with Luke's departure from his home on Tatooine and ending with a return to the Rebel base—his new home—after learning to trust the Force and defeat the foe). Concurrently, the entire trilogy could be seen to follow the same pattern on a macro level. Film scholar Leah Deyneka posits that, in Campbellian terms, following Luke Skywalker's departure in *Star Wars* (his first foray into the wider universe) and initiation in *The Empire Strikes Back* (as he went through trials and faced his father), then the third episode shows his return, when the protagonist finally succeeds in his task and earns the "freedom to live," Campbell's final stage.[9] I would argue that the films do not fit the template quite as neatly as this, with *Empire* ending before Luke's apotheosis after facing his father, the fifth of six stages within the middle act of the hero's journey. However, in broad terms, the first two episodes of the first Star Wars trilogy suggested an alignment, whether deliberate or not, between Campbell's paradigm and Lucas's saga.

During the making of *The Empire Strikes Back*, George Lucas said that he had planned nine episodes in the saga,[10] and he would frequently claim that he had plotted the series in advance. However, it becomes apparent from researching the outlines, conference transcripts, and screenplay drafts for both *Empire* and *Return of the Jedi* that Lucas did not have as clear a vision of Luke Skywalker's overall quest as is often presumed.[11] In fact, in writing early drafts of the third episode, Lucas appeared to be veering away from the hero's journey at the core of the saga just as the trilogy was reaching its climax. Rather than Lucas, it was Lawrence Kasdan, a reluctant returnee to the franchise, who was perhaps more responsible for guiding the story back to its classical, monomythical roots.

GEORGE LUCAS'S "ROUGH DRAFT"

Even though he was completing post-production on *Body Heat* at the time and had decided to no longer write for others, Kasdan agreed to work on the screenplay for Star Wars "Episode VI" when George Lucas approached him at the request of director Richard Marquand. Kasdan felt that he owed Lucas, who had given him his first paid screenwriting work with *Raiders of the Lost Ark* and *The Empire Strikes Back*, then guaranteed *Body Heat* against overages. Unlike on *Empire*, though, when he was a late replacement for the recently deceased Leigh Brackett, on *Return of the Jedi* he was the first writer hired (other than Lucas himself), and this allowed him to play an active role in the story conference, alongside Lucas, director Marquand, and producer Howard Kazanjian.

Lucas had already begun work on the screenplay before the meeting, and the group started by reading his latest version, a "revised rough draft" that he had finished a month prior. From the excerpts and summaries available,[12] we can see that some key aspects of Luke Skywalker's hero's journey set up in *Empire* appear to have been diminished. Most strikingly, the saga's central protagonist is quite passive through the drama: after the initial rescue of Han from Jabba the Hutt (similar to what would occur in the film), Luke is captured by Imperial guards and taken to the Emperor's lair. There, he reaches out telepathically to Yoda and Obi-Wan, and a transcendental battle of wills follows, between them and the Emperor; meanwhile, Darth Vader tries to gain access to his son surreptitiously, against the Emperor's wishes. The response to this draft among the key creative players appears to have been lukewarm. After reading the script, according to a diplomatic Richard Marquand, "We didn't really say very much about it. We said almost in unison, 'Can we watch the other two films, please?'"[13]

A more confident participant now, compared to during the *Raiders* story conference or his previous Star Wars work, Kasdan says of the *Jedi* meetings, "I'd force George to react to things much more volubly than on *Empire*."[14] The dynamic is certainly different from that of the *Raiders* conference, with Kasdan and Lucas doing most of the talking. Marquand, the newcomer here as Kasdan had been on *Raiders*, pitches in occasionally with shorter ideas and comments, while Kazanjian contributes only intermittently, usually with questions.[15] Kasdan appears comfortable arguing with Lucas; for example, when he posits that one of the main characters should die:

> *Kasdan:*   I think you should kill Luke and have Leia take over.
> *Lucas:*   You don't want to kill Luke.
> *Kasdan:*   Okay, then kill Yoda.
> *Lucas:*   I don't want to kill Yoda. You don't have to kill people. You're a product of the 1980s. You don't go around killing people. It's not nice.

Kasdan: No, I'm not. I'm trying to give the story some kind of an edge
            to it.

Lucas: I know you're trying to make it more realistic, which is what I
            tried to do when I killed Ben [. . .] and froze Han. But this is
            the end of the trilogy and we've already established that there
            are real dangers. I don't think we have to kill anyone to prove
            it.

Kasdan: No one has been hurt.

Lucas: Ben and Han, they've both—Luke got his hand cut off.

Kasdan: Ben and Han are fine. Luke got a new hand two cuts later.[16]

While such disagreements suggest more discord than on *Raiders*, it also points to an open exchange of ideas. Unlike on *Empire*, where Kasdan was hired only after Lucas (with Leigh Brackett) had established the overall structure and main story arcs, he was now part of that process, able to influence not only the plotting of sequences but also the wider story. Kasdan was an active participant who was willing to challenge Lucas, particularly in his desire to have a main character killed, as demonstrated above. He later said that he had wanted to see Han Solo sacrificed as "we're closing off the trilogy. And we want to lose somebody important. It would give some stakes to this thing."[17] Kasdan does not mention Han dying in the available sections of the story conference, but he does say that "the movie has more emotional weight if someone you love is lost along the way."[18] While Lucas initially vetoes the idea of killing off a major character, he later agrees to Yoda dying of old age (but later reappearing in spectral form), an idea which remains in subsequent screenplays and the finished film.

Kasdan streamlines many story threads during the conference, replacing the idea of two Death Stars (as proposed in Lucas's draft script) with just one, clarifying the logistics of Luke's meeting with Darth Vader, and giving Lando Calrissian—a virtual bystander in the rough draft—the role of piloting the *Millennium Falcon* and destroying the Death Star.[19] Above all, Kasdan argues for a simplified story that keeps the focus on the hero, in the Campbellian mode:

I am telling you that the key is to stick Luke into the center of this in an effective way, so that in fulfilling his destiny he helps the rebellion to defeat the Empire. [. . .] There has to be some transfer of power from the Emperor to Luke. That would be very poetic in terms of your whole story. That would be the perfect thing if you had a moment when all these Imperial guys see Luke take over. That would be a real Olympian conclusion to this trilogy.[20]

In order to facilitate this, Kasdan suggests erasing the forest-dwelling Ewoks from the middle act. Lucas admits that they "are causing trouble" in narrative terms, but he eventually argues for the inclusion of the teddy-bear-like creatures that he later admitted he had created to please his baby daughter.[21] While their involvement would prove divisive among the makers, as well as critics and audiences, Lucas has since drawn parallels between the Ewoks and real-life examples of "primitive" forces defeating more technologically advanced armies, citing the Viet Cong's victory over the US in the 1970s.[22] Kasdan remained skeptical, but his and Lucas's final script (they would eventually share screenplay credit, although they wrote their drafts separately) integrates the Ewoks effectively into the plot, even if the problem of connecting Luke's vanquishing of the Emperor with the wider Rebel victory is never fully resolved.[23] Aesthetically, the Ewoks provide a stark and narratively relevant juxtaposition: furry brown creatures dressed in leaves and animal pelts, pitched against the shiny whites, blacks and grays of the Imperial armies. For all Kasdan's protests, they continue a theme established in the previous two Star Wars films, the heroes apparently hewn from nature: Luke Skywalker, a child of the desert, in cream and khaki pajamas; then Yoda, living in a swamp, green-skinned and wrapped in a sackcloth robe. The Ewoks, too, are at one with the forest, defending their land with the simple tools available. Against such a rag-tag adversary, the soldiers of the Empire appear even more uniform in action and dress, and emblematic of history's colonial invaders, a notion to which Lucas himself has alluded.[24] In Campbellian terms, it could be argued that the Ewoks act as the "Rescue from without,"[25] the guides that save the cause when all appears lost, if not specifically for Luke, then for the Rebel Alliance.

Even if accepting Lucas's justifications for including the Ewoks in the movie, Kasdan's opposition points to fundamental disagreement at the heart of the creative process.[26] In the *Raiders of the Lost Ark* story conference, the three creators sometimes differed in opinion, but they appeared satisfied with most solutions. Lucas was clearly pleased with the resulting screenplay, which is why he immediately offered Kasdan the job of writing *The Empire Strikes Back*. Kasdan told me that, on *Raiders*, "I felt a lot of ownership with the story and everything that was finally in the screenplay," but that he did not feel as emotionally invested in the Star Wars scripts. Now, Kasdan would have to write a major part of *Jedi* with characters that he would prefer not to include at all. He would also need to create a story arc for Han Solo, a character that, given a choice, he would have killed off at the opening of the film. In addition, Kasdan was no longer writing what he considered the "fun" second act, in which the film could end in "chaos."[27] Instead, *Return of the Jedi* needed to tie up all of the storylines in a way that would satisfy an increasingly invested fanbase as well as George Lucas's preference for stirring, life-affirming heroism.[28] As discussed previously, Kasdan's sensibilities lean toward ambiguity, but Lucas told Kasdan that the Star Wars trilogy is a "fairy tale" with a climax aimed to make the audience "be real uplifted, emotionally and spiritually."[29]

THE LATER DRAFTS

Structurally, the subsequent drafts of the *Return of the Jedi* screenplay build upon its predecessors' pattern of having multiple storylines take place simultaneously for much of the film. In the film's climactic battle, the protagonists are spread especially wide: Luke is alone on the Death Star in his confrontation with Darth Vader and the Emperor, while Han and Leia fight alongside Chewbacca and the droids on the forest moon; concurrently, Lando leads a Rebel spaceship assault on the Death Star. This approach continues the multi-strand structure utilized so effectively in *The Empire Strikes Back*; however, in *Jedi* the story is focused much more strongly on the hero's journey rather than the supporting members of the ensemble. It is a logical choice within the Campbellian structure of the trilogy, with the emotional core of the story about Luke's defeat of the Dark Side—within his father and himself—by overcoming the Emperor's attempts to turn him away from the Light. However, whereas in *Empire* Lawrence Kasdan assigned almost equal screen time to Han and Leia's relationship alongside Luke's trials with Yoda, in *Jedi* these supporting characters are relegated to a more functional role of fighting off stormtroopers with the Ewoks. Lando too, for all that Kasdan gives him a superficially important part in destroying the Death Star, develops very little, his transformation from betrayer to savior in the previous episode left unexplored as he is mostly kept apart from the leads and paired in the *Millennium Falcon* with a new, thinly drawn co-pilot character, whose name is mentioned only in the end credits. So, although Kasdan's screenplay incorporates every member of the ensemble, most of the characters—with the exception of Luke and Darth Vader—barely evolve during the story. Even Princess Leia's discovery that she is Luke's twin sister and possessed of the Force receives little exploration, despite the fact that we now know she is the "other" last hope for the Jedi that Yoda spoke of in *The Empire Strikes Back*. After Luke reveals this, his conversation with Leia ends, and Han, misunderstanding their relationship, shows his jealousy. This could have developed into an interesting emotional storyline, but the need to further the plot appears to have subsumed the human aspect. Leia and Han's next appearance in the script is when they are scouting the shield generator that they must disable, with Leia saying: "The main entrance to the control bunker's on the far side of that landing platform. This isn't gonna be easy." The quotation exemplifies Leia and Han's scenes in the second half of *Jedi*, the characters relegated to proffering exposition and lending support to the more important events occurring on the Death Star. Such moments add credence to Kasdan's argument that Han Solo should have been killed off early in the movie. It would have solved the problem of trying to create engaging moments for a character who, now that he had been humbled by his love for Leia and his rescue by Luke, no longer had much to contribute to the saga. In turn, Han's death would have given Leia a more dramatic character arc, her romantic partner dying just as she learns of her true lineage and her potential in the ways of the Force—a potential hero's journey of her own that was left unexplored.

The much faster pace of *Jedi*, compared to *The Empire Strikes Back*, may have been an unavoidable consequence of telling the final part of a larger saga. *Empire*, according to Roger Ebert, "surrenders more completely to the underlying mystery of the story" and is the episode in which "the entire series takes on a mythic quality."[30] As the second part of the trilogy, *Empire* is able to explore characters more deeply and open up the wider story with further questions, two aspects that dovetail with Kasdan's particular set of skills. Conversely, *Return of the Jedi* is limited by its responsibility to conclude multiple plotlines, to answer those questions posed in *Empire*, and to provide a satisfactory ending in that same mythic tradition that had been developed in the "middle act." The difficulty of this task was surely exacerbated by the need to deal with plot discrepancies from Episodes IV and V. For example, in *Star Wars*, Obi-Wan Kenobi tells Luke that Darth Vader "betrayed and murdered your father," but in *Empire* Luke discovers that Vader actually *is* his father, an element that was not present in George Lucas's early treatments of *Empire*, nor in Leigh Brackett's first screenplay draft. In order to excuse this apparent deception on the part of Obi-Wan, a Jedi Master whom one would not expect to lie, Kasdan and Lucas devised an inelegant solution, having Obi-Wan's "ghost" tell Luke in *Jedi* that:

```
Your father was seduced by
the Dark Side of the Force. He
ceased to be Anakin Skywalker
and became Darth Vader. When
that happened, the good man who
was your father was destroyed.
So what I told you was true...
from a certain point of view.
```

Furthermore, while *Jedi*'s pace and optimistic tone make it more similar to *Star Wars* than *Empire*, the screenplay has to serve the narratives of not only the original ensemble, but also of all those characters added in the middle episode (Lando, Yoda, and the Emperor having first appeared in *Empire*), as well as introducing new characters in Jabba and the Ewoks. There is necessarily less screen time available, then, to spend on any individual among the supporting cast, leading to the need for ever more frenetic, shorter scenes, and less scope for significant character development.

The ensemble is still very much active, as one would expect in a Kasdan script, but in *Jedi* the main hero's journey story takes greater priority over that of the group. It is this aspect of the film that works most successfully:

Luke Skywalker's temptation toward the Dark Side, then his refusal of the Emperor's attempt to seduce him to evil, leading to his father Darth Vader's ultimate redemption. There is hidden complexity beneath this apparently simple battle of good versus evil, with Vader's secret plan to join with Luke and overthrow the Emperor pitched against the Emperor's own plot to have Luke kill Vader and become his new apprentice. At the center is Luke, still not fully prepared for this final trial on his path to becoming a Jedi, but who believes that he can turn his father away from the Dark Side. These conflicting character goals are clearly defined without the need for excessive exposition; and it is this three-way battle that gives *Jedi* its emotional core. It is surprising, then, that George Lucas's initial script draft had reduced Darth Vader's importance within the Empire (and, therefore, the story as a whole), showing him vie for the Emperor's attention with a rival, Grand Moff Jerjerrod, a completely new character who has the Emperor's ear and to whom Vader is subservient. While Darth Vader had a superior, Grand Moff Tarkin, in the first *Star Wars*, by this stage of the saga, the audience had been primed to understand that Luke, Vader, and the Emperor were at the center of the drama. The introduction of a new villain within this dynamic is jarring, especially as he usurps Vader within the hierarchy of the Empire. After the story conference, Grand Moff Jerjerrod would be excised from all following treatments and drafts, and again, it would appear to be Kasdan's influence that kept the fabula more focused on existing characters and the dramatic question that had been established at the end of *Empire*: whether Luke would accept Vader's offer to join him in defeating the Emperor and to "rule the galaxy as father and son."[31]

During the story conference, Lucas also abandoned his idea of having the apparitional forms of Obi-Wan Kenobi and Yoda aid Luke physically in his fight against the Emperor, later conceding that "Luke is finally on his own and

Figure 10.1 The emotional core: Luke, Darth Vader, and the Emperor

has to fight Vader and the Emperor by himself. If you get a sense that Yoda or Ben [Obi-Wan] is there to help him [. . .], it diminishes the power of the scene."[32] Within the context of the classic hero's journey, this is true, and it is only surprising that he did not realize this until comparatively late in the development process. While it is not certain how much agency Kasdan or director Richard Marquand had in this change, such admissions by Lucas are evidence that, for all his declarations that Star Wars is part of a mythological tradition, some of the most classically "mythic" moments, such as Luke facing his final trial alone, were only present after Lucas had discussed ideas with Kasdan and other collaborators.

It is important to note that George Lucas's first pass at the screenplay was labeled a "rough draft," and he would later explain that, at the beginning of the conference, "I have an outline. I'm making pieces but I don't know exactly how this piece is going to fit in there."[33] This draft, then, was perhaps intended merely as an entry point before the real discussion could begin. According to Richard Marquand, Lucas "is a man interested in collaboration. He'll pick everyone's brains. He doesn't pull rank on anybody."[34] The evidence from the *Raiders* and Star Wars story conferences confirms this. However, Lucas still had a clear goal for *Return of the Jedi*, stating early in the conference that the film will:

> have this undercurrent of a fairly serious study of father and son, and good and evil. The whole concept [. . .] is that Luke redeems his father, which is the classic fairy tale: a good father / bad father who the son will turn back into the good father.[35]

This suggests that Lucas was aiming toward a climax very much in the tradition of the Campbellian monomyth. His first draft, though, was weighed down by a surplus of ideas: a rival to Darth Vader that unintentionally sidelined the prime antagonist, an overly complicated story involving two Death Stars and a home planet for the Empire, and a plethora of new characters such as Jabba and the Ewoks.

Kasdan's major contribution to *Return of the Jedi*, then, is in streamlining both the fabula and syuzhet, corralling the complex central intrigues into an understandable narrative, and completing the trilogy in a way that remains true to its mythical undertones. Those elements of the screenplay to which Kasdan voiced opposition, such as the Ewoks' inclusion and Han's usefulness to the story, are less successful dramatically. The uplifting ending that Lucas had wanted for his trilogy remains intact, but Kasdan's writing probably suffers as a result, with one Lucas biographer calling it "a thankless task" for the screenwriter that resulted in "one of Kasdan's least distinguished works."[36] Nonetheless, the choices made by Kasdan in the *Jedi* screenplay were fundamental in completing a trilogy that had begun as a thrilling, swashbuckling romp in the vein of a 1930s serial, but had now evolved into an epic myth that would resonate globally for decades to come. In particular, the choice of returning Darth Vader to the very center of the story—rather than as one of two rival underlings serving the Emperor, in Lucas's original draft—shaped the audience's perception of the saga's antagonist, no longer a one-dimensional villain but a flawed and ultimately redeemed character, an actualization of the "father figure" that makes up part of the universal monomyth.[37] Importantly, this choice strengthened Luke Skywalker's own story and aligned the whole trilogy much more closely with Joseph Campbell's hero's journey than if following the plot as written in Lucas's initial outline.

Return of the Jedi completed the original Star Wars trilogy, its feel-good climax resulting in even greater box-office success than *The Empire Strikes Back*. However, Lawrence Kasdan's directing career was now well underway as he began production on his second film, *The Big Chill*, and he was adamant that *Jedi* would be his final contribution to the series that had earned him his first screen credit. After the release of the film, Kasdan told himself emphatically: "That's the end of Star Wars for me."[38]

NOTES

1. Joseph Campbell, *The Hero with a Thousand Faces* (Bollingen series XVII, 3rd ed.), Reprint (Novato, CA: New World Library, 1949/2008).

2. For example, the feature-length documentary, *Star Wars: The Legacy Revealed*, was produced by Lucasfilm for the History Channel in 2007, and it referred repeatedly to Campbell's work. Lucas discusses Campbell's influence in the posthumous biography: Stephen Larsen and Robin Larsen, *Joseph Campbell: A Fire in the Mind* (Rochester, Vermont: Inner Traditions, 2002), 541–3.

3. Michael Kaminski, *The Secret History of Star Wars: The Art of Storytelling and the Making of a Modern Epic* (Kingston, Canada: Legacy, 2008), 215.

4. George Lucas, quoted in J.W. Rinzler, *The Making of Star Wars: The Definitive Story Behind the Original Film* (London: Aurum, 2007), 40.

5. Lucas, quoted in Kaminski, *Secret History*, 215.

6. Kaminski, *Secret History*, 217.

7. *Time* magazine, among others, described the film as "mythic." See Kaminski, *Secret History*, 214.

8. Campbell, *Hero with a Thousand Faces*, 74.

9. Leah Deyneka, "May the Myth be With You, Always," in *Myth, Media, and Culture in Star Wars: An Anthology*, edited by Douglas Brode and Leah Deyneka (Plymouth: Scarecrow, 2012).

10. Lucas, quoted in Alan Arnold, *Once upon a Galaxy: The Making of The Empire Strikes Back* (New York: Ballantine, 1980), 177.

11. I first undertook this research when examining creative and philosophical differences between Kasdan and Lucas when writing *Return of the Jedi*, and some parts of the essay are incorporated into this chapter. See Brett Davies, "Ewoks Versus Dead Heroes: Creative Conflict in Writing *Return of the Jedi*," *Revista Geminis* 12, no. 1 (2021), https://www.revistageminis.ufscar.br/index.php/geminis/article/view/599/411

12. Most comprehensively in J.W. Rinzler, *The Making of Return of the Jedi* (London: Aurum, 2013), 47–53; Paul Duncan, *The Star Wars Archives: Episodes IV–VI: 1977–1983* (Cologne: Taschen, 2020), 377–9.

13. Richard Marquand, quoted in Rinzler, *Making Jedi*, 59.

14. Ibid., 60.

15. Rinzler, *Making Jedi*, 62–77; and Duncan, *Star Wars Archives*, 381–411.

16. Rinzler, *Making Jedi*, 64.

17. Kasdan, quoted in Dave Itzkoff, "He's Tried to Leave Star Wars Before. Will This Be It?" *The New York Times*, May 31, 2018, https://www.nytimes.com/2018/05/30/movies/star-wars-lawrence-kasdan.html (accessed July 5, 2023).

18. Rinzler, *Making Jedi*, 64.

19. Clearly still intent on "raising the stakes" by killing off a major character, Kasdan later wrote a scene in which Lando dies and the *Millennium Falcon* explodes "in a supernova of glory" after destroying the Death Star. It was even trialed in preview showings, but the scene was cut after negative audience feedback. See John Baxter, *George Lucas: A Biography* (London: HarperCollins, 1999), 327.

20. Duncan, *Star Wars Archives*, 410.

21. Baxter, *George Lucas*, 329.

22. George Lucas, quoted in Duncan, *Star Wars Archives*, 373.

23. Lawrence Kasdan and George Lucas, *Return of the Jedi*, screenplay, 3rd draft, December 1981. [NOTE: The title page of this document is marked as "second draft: December 19, 1982"; however, this appears to have been added after the fact, and the other pages are dated "Dec 81," apart from the final two pages (101A and 102), which are undated. Based on notes by Bouzereau, this is actually the third and final draft. See Laurent Bouzereau, *Star Wars: The Annotated Screenplays* (New York: Ballantine, 1997), 232 and 320.]

24. Lucas, quoted in Rinzler, *Making Jedi*, 11.

25. Campbell, *Hero with a Thousand Faces*, 178–9.

26. I have discussed these disagreements in more detail in Davies, "Ewoks Versus Dead Heroes."

27. Kasdan, interviewed by John August and Craig Mazin, "Episode 452: *The Empire Strikes Back* with Lawrence Kasdan," *Scriptnotes*, Transcript, May 26, 2020, https://johnaugust.com/2020/scriptnotes-ep-452-the-empire-strikes-back-with-lawrence-kasdan-transcript (accessed July 5, 2023).

28. Lucas, quoted in Baxter, 403.

29. Duncan, *Star Wars Archives*, 385–6.

30. Roger Ebert, "*The Empire Strikes Back*," *Roger Ebert*, April 1, 1997, https://www.rogerebert.com/reviews/the-empire-strikes-back-1997-1 (accessed July 5, 2023).

31. Some of the scenes involving Grand Moff Jerjerrod are reproduced in Rinzler, *Making Jedi*, 21–5. In the final screenplay and film, there is a character called Jerjerrod, the "Death Star commander," but his is a relatively minor role, clearly subordinate to Darth Vader: he swallows nervously as Vader's shuttle lands on the incomplete Death Star, then grovels: "Lord Vader, this is an unexpected pleasure. We're honored by your presence."

32. Lucas, quoted in Bouzereau, *Star Wars: Annotated*, 301.

33. Lucas, quoted in Duncan, *Star Wars Archives*, 380.

34. Marquand, quoted in Duncan, *Star Wars Archives*, 381.

35. Duncan, *Star Wars Archives*, 385.

36. Baxter, 327.

37. Campbell, *Hero with a Thousand Faces*, 125.

38. Josh Rottenberg, "Q&A: Star Wars Screenwriter Lawrence Kasdan on the Past, Present and Future of Star Wars," *The Los Angeles Times*, December 3, 2015, http://www.latimes.com/entertainment/herocomplex/la-ca-hc-star-wars-lawrence-kasdan-20151206-story.html (accessed July 5, 2023).

CHAPTER 11

A New Hope in *The Force Awakens*

It was not only Lawrence Kasdan who was ready to step away from Star Wars on the completion of *Return of the Jedi*. In spite of his stated plans for nine episodes, George Lucas appeared exhausted after just three. He was navigating a divorce during production on *Jedi*, and he was now a single parent: "I figured that was the end of it for me. I figured 'Well, I've done it, I've finished my trilogy.'"[1] This claim, made twenty years later, was not entirely accurate, as Lucas soon began work on a Star Wars spin-off "Movie of the Week" for television. *The Ewok Adventure* (known internationally as *Caravan of Courage: An Ewok Adventure*) was aired by ABC in November 1984; then a sequel, *Ewoks: The Battle for Endor*, was broadcast a year later. Lucas executive-produced two animated TV shows, as well, with *Ewoks* and *Star Wars: Droids: The Adventures of R2-D2 and C-3PO* running concurrently from 1985 to 1986. However, as the popularity of Star Wars waned,[2] Lucas began to focus on producing other projects, including the sequels to *Raiders of the Lost Ark*, with *Indiana Jones and the Temple of Doom* (1984) and *Indiana Jones and the Last Crusade* (1989) continuing the financial success of the first film. There were box-office failures in this period, too, such as *Howard the Duck* (1986) and *Tucker: The Man and His Dream* (1988), while the fantasy pictures *Labyrinth* (1986) and *Willow* (1988) made profits without reaching the level of success that Lucas had envisaged.[3]

It was in the 1990s that George Lucas began contemplating a return to Star Wars. The popularity of a new series of novels by Timothy Zahn, published from 1991 to 1993, proved that there was still a market for the stories.[4] At the same time, technological advances made by Lucasfilm's in-house visual effects department, Industrial Light & Magic, on *The Young Indiana Jones Chronicles* TV series (1992–3), then on Steven Spielberg's *Jurassic Park* (1993), persuaded Lucas that he now had the digital capability at his disposal to create worlds and creatures that he had previously felt were unattainable.[5] This led him to develop the digitally enhanced "Special Editions" of the original Star Wars trilogy. Then, in late 1993, Lucas officially announced his plan to make a new trilogy of "prequels," Episodes I to III, which would tell the story of Anakin Skywalker's path toward becoming Darth Vader.[6]

Lucas approached Lawrence Kasdan to work on these prequel scripts, but Kasdan declined.[7] Instead, Lucas would be the only director and writer (excluding a shared "Screenplay by" credit for Jonathan Hales on the second film) for a trilogy that, despite netting large profits, drew mostly negative reactions from critics, especially with regard to the dialogue. Even in a broadly positive review of the third film, Roger Ebert noted that the "characters talk in what sounds like Basic English, without color, wit or verbal delight, as if they were channeling Berlitz."[8] Kasdan was diplomatic when asked later about the prequels compared to the original trilogy: "The ones I worked on were a long time ago, and they had a slightly different feeling than the ones that followed. [. . .] The first three are all sort of more about people than the [prequels]."[9]

Then, in 2012, Lucas was attempting to increase the value of his company, Lucasfilm, before selling it to Disney and retiring. He invited Kasdan to discuss developing a portfolio of concepts for prospective Star Wars films, including a sequel trilogy and further standalone features. This time Kasdan agreed and, after the sale, his role was eventually expanded, from an advisory position with first refusal to write a Han Solo spin-off film, to working as screenwriter on the first episode of a new trilogy. Kathleen Kennedy, the post-Lucas president of Lucasfilm, said that Kasdan "was one of the first people that I picked up the phone and said 'Larry, we need you to come back in and be a part of this.'"[10] She later stated: "There are very few people who fundamentally understand the way a Star Wars story works like Larry, and it is nothing short of incredible to have him even more deeply involved in its return to the big screen."[11]

So, thirty-two years after Episode VI, *Return of the Jedi*, Lawrence Kasdan was co-writing Episode VII—what would eventually be called *The Force Awakens*—with director J. J. Abrams, after Michael Arndt had already outlined a story but failed to complete his first draft of the screenplay.[12] According to Kasdan, with just six months to go before shooting was due to begin, "We didn't have anything. There were a thousand people waiting for answers on things, and you couldn't tell them anything except 'yeah, that guy's in it.' That was about it. That was really all we knew."[13] This was familiar ground for Kasdan, having started work on *The Empire Strikes Back* and *Return of the Jedi* under similar time constraints. He says that he and Abrams "just sat in a room and talked it out," and they completed a first draft in six weeks. They continued rewrites up to, and even after, filming had begun, making Kasdan's third Star Wars experience as fraught with time pressure as his previous two.

MAKING THINGS RIGHT

In one of the first academic essays to be written about Star Wars Episode VII, the film scholar Benjamin J. Robertson stated: "Whatever we gain as critics from analysis of *The Force Awakens* remains limited until we consider it in the context of the franchise from which it was born and for which it provides a new hope."[14] For all that George Lucas's Star Wars has been associated with the classic hero's journey as described by Joseph Campbell, the trilogy in the nine-film "Skywalker Saga" over which Lucas had the most creative control, Episodes I to III, is the one that strays furthest from Campbell's paradigm. While there are myriad reasons for the failure of the prequel trilogy to work as a satisfying narrative, at its core is a kind of cognitive dissonance: Lucas, who had professed to want to tell a "fairy tale" for young people that made the audience "feel absolutely good about life,"[15] had put himself in a position in which the main character, Anakin Skywalker—with whom younger viewers would likely align themselves—was destined to become one of cinema's most infamous villains. Episode I, *The Phantom Menace* (1999), shows Anakin's "departure," as per Campbell's paradigm, in which nine-year-old Anakin (his age further positioning him alongside the youngest audience members) first refuses the call to adventure before eventually leaving home to start a new life; and Episode II, *Attack of the Clones* (2002), has Anakin go through an "initiation" of trials and temptations, as well as a rebellion against the father, or surrogate "fathers" of the Jedi Order, in this case. However, the third film, *Revenge of the Sith* (2005), rather than show the "return" in which the hero gains "the freedom to live," in Campbell's framework,[16] ends with the galaxy overtaken by the evil Empire, and Anakin turning to the Dark Side, responsible for his wife's death and the murder of dozens of children. Not only does this downbeat climax appear to reject George Lucas's previous hopes for the saga, but it makes the child-friendly comedy and overtly cute characters, such as Jar Jar Binks, sit even more uneasily within the narrative.

With the Disney-era "sequel trilogy," though, the creators had the opportunity to begin a new story with characters unencumbered by the necessity to reach any pre-established endpoint. And, with George Lucas no longer directly involved, Episode VII, *The Force Awakens*, made clear its intentions to echo the structure and tone of the original three films, rather than the prequels, with the central character Rey a similar age to Luke Skywalker in the first *Star Wars*. Like Luke, she is first shown eking out a meagre existence on a desert planet before being pulled by circumstance into a wider universe and a journey toward becoming a Jedi; like Luke, Rey is an archetype, the "chosen hero" from humble beginnings who is not yet conscious of her significance, and this episode shows her departure from ordinary life. There are similarities here, too, of course, with Anakin in *The Phantom Menace*; however, whereas Anakin was a child of immaculate conception, Rey appears entirely ordinary, more closely aligning her with Luke than the boy who would become Darth Vader. The scholar Antonio Sanna notes the parallels between Rey's story and Luke Skywalker's, including her initial reluctance to take up the mission, then her "strength, resilience and perseverance against evil, temptation and hardship."[17]

This classic hero's journey is part of an overall pattern of allusion to the original trilogy present throughout *The Force Awakens*. In fact, while the film received broadly favorable reviews on its release, the most common criticism was its over-similarity to the original 1977 *Star Wars*. There are obvious associations, with the black-masked Kylo Ren apparently the "new" Darth Vader, and General Snoke a direct substitute for the Emperor (although, unlike in *Star Wars*, we do see the all-powerful leader here, at least in hologram form). There is a final race to destroy the Starkiller base before it devastates more planets, as with the Death Star in the original.[18] And, perhaps most explicitly, there is the death by lightsaber of the mentor character, just as the orphan Rey thought that she had found a father figure. Such allusions were noted by numerous critics, with Cabral Martins stating that *The Force Awakens* is "mimicking the broad strokes" of the first *Star Wars*, and Mullis calling it "in many ways, identical to the original."[19]

However, in a series that embodies the nostalgia of the baby boomers, there is a meta-logic to such allusions. As discussed in a contemporary article, "the filmmakers get what made George Lucas' original trilogy magical, and they recapture that magic."[20] Another reviewer states that "it hardwires that understanding [of the original film] into its own DNA, making legacy a prevailing theme." The critic Ana Cabral Martins quotes co-writer and director J. J. Abrams saying that *The Force Awakens* is both a "reminder" of the original trilogy and a "bridge" to the new one.[21] Therefore, the film displays nostalgia for the first three instalments, just as they were themselves nostalgic throwbacks to the 1936 *Flash Gordon* serial that was replayed on television during George Lucas's youth.[22] According to the co-writer/director J. J. Abrams, it was a deliberate choice to connect the story so directly to the originals:

> One of the things that was really important, I know, for us in this movie was very purposely going backwards to go forwards, and to embrace, like, literally a structure—finding a character in the desert, ending with a trench run—do something that felt very much a very purposeful step backwards, in order to tell a brand new story with brand new characters.[23]

This is a departure from Lucas's prequel trilogy, which, for all its narrative failings, attempted to expand the series and offer new visual experiences. That Abrams and Kasdan were returning to the spirit of the originals and away from the garish CGI and convoluted plots of Episodes I to III is made clear in the screenplay's very first line of dialogue: "This will begin to make things right." Kasdan himself was seen as part of that; another "reminder" and "bridge" to the original trilogy, with J. J. Abrams saying that "one of the enormous, crazy, surreal enticements [to directing *Force Awakens*] was working with [Kasdan]."[24] He provided a literal link to the early films, then, a connection back to the roots of Star Wars that may have helped convince other key creators to join the project.

Another quality that Lawrence Kasdan brought to the screenplay of *The Force Awakens* was a coherency of storytelling. The prequels had been criticized for their "bewildering" plots,[25] but Kasdan and Abrams consciously strove to achieve simplicity, the latter stating that "clarity of story was really important. There are so many movies [. . .] that have very confusing plotlines, [. . .] but this one I knew couldn't be that."[26] As discussed in the preceding chapters, Kasdan's screenplays for *The Empire Strikes Back* and *Return of the Jedi* managed to present the competing narrative strands with remarkable intelligibility, juggling complex relationships and intrigues, but keeping them understandable throughout. The story conference transcript for *Jedi* suggests that it was Kasdan who was responsible for reeling in Lucas's many ideas, stripping them back to create something lean and comprehensible, despite dealing with multiple characters in a variety of locations. Similarly, in *The Force Awakens*, both new and returning characters are drawn clearly, even though there are numerous secrets, double-crosses, and hidden agendas among the half-dozen major characters.

The prequel trilogy, and *The Phantom Menace* in particular, suffered under the weight of seemingly endless exposition about trade federations, embargos, taxes, government systems, and even the nature of the Force itself, with its "midi-chlorian counts" completely undermining the pseudo-spiritual underpinnings of the Force that had been described in the originals. *The Force Awakens* retains a lighter touch, the screenplay revealing backstory without resorting to lengthy explanation. An interesting example is during the opening sequence, when we first see the masked figure of Kylo Ren as he leaves his landing craft to join the massacre in the village. He immediately comes face-to-face with Lor San Tekka, the man who had uttered that opening line, and who we know is an old friend of Leia's:

```
                    KYLO REN
         Look how old you've become.


                  LOR SAN TEKKA
         Something far worse has
         happened to you.
```

[. . .]

<pre>
            KYLO REN
You know what I've come for.

          LOR SAN TEKKA
I know where you come from.
Before you called yourself Kylo
Ren.
</pre>

In a few lines, the screenplay establishes a past intimacy between these two characters, going back many years. We learn the name of the movie's antagonist, as well as the fact that he has changed it from something else. The mention of "where you come from" hints at a connection to Leia, whom San Tekka had discussed in his prior conversation with Poe, and this will later be confirmed when we discover that Kylo is Leia and Han Solo's son. These lines of dialogue are immediately followed by Kylo Ren's slaying of San Tekka, suggesting that he is beyond redemption, and setting up one of the central dramatic questions of the new trilogy: can he be turned back, away from the Dark Side? Like Kasdan's scripts for *Empire* and *Jedi*, as well as for *Raiders of the Lost Ark*, there is a deftness to this exchange, the audience engrossed in the drama and action, even as it subliminally processes a wealth of information.

The three episodes of the Star Wars "Skywalker Saga" to which Lawrence Kasdan contributed were all written in collaboration with more "senior" creative partners, of course—franchise creator and executive producer George Lucas, and now director-producer J. J. Abrams—so Kasdan's level of influence is not always easy to measure. But it is notable that, in the entire series, these are the three instalments that balance intertwining stories and multiple characters most successfully. While Kasdan's aptitude for writing ensemble pieces has often been praised by critics, it has always been discussed in relation to his own work as writer-director, never to his screenplays for Lucasfilm. However, just as in his more personal films, such as *The Big Chill* and *Grand Canyon*, each player's goals in *The Force Awakens* are developed along the lines of Kristin Thompson's four-act paradigm, featuring a recognizable set-up, complicating action, development, and climax.[27] In communicating motivated, goal-driven narratives for Rey, Finn, Kylo Ren, and Han Solo, and to a lesser extent Leia and Poe Dameron, then the screenplay for *The Force Awakens* is further evidence that Kasdan's skill for writing clear and understandable multi-protagonist stories may be just as important in developing the Star Wars series too.

I noted above the barely-hidden message conveyed by the first words uttered in *The Force Awakens*, reassuring the audience that things will be put right. However, in storytelling terms, viewers are primed to expect a return to the more classical mode of the original trilogy even before that line. In the famous opening title crawl that begins every episode of the Star Wars saga, the first sentence reads: "Luke Skywalker has vanished." It is a terse, simple statement, yet in just four words the link to the original films is made clear, as has the goal of the hero—to find Luke Skywalker—even before that hero has herself been revealed. Within the single clause, too, is something of a twist: most viewers were already aware that the original cast would be returning, with the three lead actors from the original trilogy featuring prominently in the marketing campaign, yet expectations shift immediately as the audience learns that the central figure in the entire saga is missing. It is a bravura piece of storytelling, in marked relief to the title crawl that began the prequel trilogy, when *The Phantom Menace* opened with: "Turmoil has engulfed the Galactic Republic. The taxation of trade routes to outlying star systems is in dispute."

Kasdan and Abrams's script for *The Force Awakens* does not shy from ambiguity, and there are numerous "dangling causes" left unresolved by its end, such as Rey's parentage and her mysterious connection to Luke's old lightsaber, the identity of Snoke, Kylo Ren's inner conflict, and whether Luke Skywalker will accept his saber from Rey and rejoin the fight. But in keeping the central thrust of the story straightforward and recognizable, then I argue that those aspects become tantalizing mysteries rather than points of confusion, in a similar vein to the questions and cliffhangers that made the three films in the original trilogy such a cohesive whole.

GENERATIONS

Just before the release of *The Force Awakens*, a *Los Angeles Times* piece likened Lawrence Kasdan to the Jedi Master portrayed by Alec Guinness in the first three Star Wars films: "the Obi-Wan of the franchise."[28] The implication was clear: here was one of the central creative figures of the original trilogy coming back to lend his expertise and guidance to the resurrection of the Star Wars saga. In his mid-sixties by this time, Kasdan was able to utilize his experience of writing for the main characters, appearing again after their absence from the prequels, to bring an authenticity to their dialogue and characterizations, aging as he had with Carrie Fisher, Harrison Ford, and Mark Hamill. Kasdan says of writing for the original protagonists again:

> We'd all gone through thirty years of life, and what it tells you is, you make the same mistakes again and again. I'd gotten older. But my personality hadn't changed [. . .]. But what do you learn, one way or another? What does life teach you? How does your experience make you a more interesting person? And all the regrets you have, and all the disappointments?[29]

In particular, Kasdan has declared an affinity for Han Solo, and actor Harrison Ford says that "I loved the fact that [in *The Force Awakens* script] he turns out to be a reasonable continuum of character, but acknowledging the reality of the passage of thirty years."[30] Kasdan's association with the original trilogy, then, was not merely symbolic; rather, his presence may have helped attract talent, and he also provided a unique understanding of the returning characters and their concerns as they now became the veterans of the saga. On discussing his Lucasfilm work, Kasdan has argued, "Even if it's a genre movie, you're using the genre as a vessel to talk about the things that concern you."[31] *The Force Awakens* and its sensitive treatment of the hopes and regrets of its older characters echo that sentiment at a time, Kasdan says, when "there's a tinge of mortality [. . .] that comes more naturally into your conversation as your friends get older and you get older, too."[32] Ironically, the very fact that the younger characters in the story revere the older ones adds to this sense of "mortality." When Rey and Finn steal a spacecraft and only later realize its identity, Rey is awed. The screenplay has her saying: "This is the Millennium Falcon? *You're Han Solo?*" Han's response—"I used to be"—is suitably deadpan, very much in keeping with the character established in the original films, but there is melancholy, too, an awareness of the passing of time and the diminishing relevance as one becomes older. In Rey's very veneration of him, too, she is implying that his best years are behind him, a legend more than an active player in the present. Given that Kasdan has repeatedly aligned himself with Harrison Ford's character, then there are echoes in the script of Kasdan's standing within the making of the new films: the reminder of the past who is now passing the torch to a new generation.

In narrative terms, this passing of the torch allowed Kasdan to fulfil a goal that he had first expressed three decades prior: to kill off a beloved character.

Figure 11.1 Han and Rey

In the *Return of the Jedi* story conference, George Lucas had rejected Kasdan's suggestion of having one of the heroes die. On *The Force Awakens*, though, Kasdan was working with a collaborator who appeared more in tune with his sensibilities, and he says of the decision to have Kylo Ren murder his father Han Solo: "there was a lot of discussion about it, and J. J. and I went back and forth and talked about a lot of different things, and this is where we came." Abrams adds that the film is "a generational hand-off [. . .] and you can't have that hand-off without cost. It needed to serve this purpose of giving our new characters a mantle, and that was a big, scary decision."[33] Compared to the deaths of Obi-Wan Kenobi in *Star Wars* or Yoda in *Return of the Jedi*, Han Solo's demise feels more shocking, as Harrison Ford's character is one of the saga's most popular. It is more final too, with Han unable to return as a "Force ghost" like the Jedi Obi-Wan and Yoda.[34] So, three decades after he had been vetoed from doing so in his screenplay for *Return of the Jedi*, Kasdan finally had the opportunity to, as he puts it, "lose somebody important [and] give some stakes to this thing."[35] The decision appeared to set the tone for the entire sequel trilogy, with all three protagonists from the original films dying by the end of the series (even if Kasdan did not contribute to Episodes VIII and IX). This would lead to a greater sense of peril throughout, and a more emotionally fraught hero's journey for Rey before she could finally "return" to the desert planet of Tatooine, where the entire saga had begun, at the end of the final instalment, *The Rise of Skywalker* (2019).

Through the death of Han, too, *The Force Awakens* sets a precedent for the sequel trilogy, allowing a focus on new characters, even as they echo the traits and mistakes of their predecessors: Rey as the new Luke, and Kylo Ren as the new Vader, as noted above; also, Poe as a quasi-Han, and BB-8 taking on the R2-D2/C-3PO role, with the older droids largely sidelined. Only Finn stands out as an entirely unique new character, separated from his parents as a child, and indoctrinated into the First Order army before deserting them during his first battle. His attempts to forge a new identity and cover the secrets of his past are reminiscent of previous Kasdan creations, and his morals are as murky as the doctor's in *Mumford*, if not Matty's in *Body Heat*. Actor John Boyega's performance conveys perfectly Finn's state of anxiety. He is torn between fight and flight, between the truth of his past and a less painful fiction. That it is Kasdan's alter ego in the series, Han Solo, who punctures the faux-cocky façade lends an added layer of discomfort to Finn's situation. Han is the first to see through his lies to Rey about being a "big deal" in the Resistance: "Listen big deal, you've got another problem. Women always figure out the truth." This is not the monk-like moralizing of a Jedi Master, but the advice of some-one we imagine being guilty of the same offense in the past. The sighs and sideways glances at Finn's actions are the results of experience, yet it does not appear that Han has learned a great deal himself. For all his apparent maturity,

Han is a smuggler again, in contrast to his position of authority at the end of the original trilogy; he is back to taking care of himself (and Chewbacca), and no longer with Leia. This is indicative of the cyclical nature of the entire saga, the repetition of mistakes by the same characters and even across generations. We soon learn that this return to type is the direct result of Han and Leia's child turning to the Dark Side, of course. Unlike in the prequels, when cross-generational traumas were retrofitted and intrinsically less upsetting (Ewan McGregor's portrayal of Obi-Wan in *The Phantom Menace* could almost be a different character entirely from Alec Guinness's iteration), *The Force Awakens* is the first time that the Star Wars audience experiences the linear passing of time over a long period. As different as the two films are in execution, there are thematic parallels with Kasdan's previous picture, *Darling Companion*, as older characters express regret at past actions, but struggle to change. That such issues were being discussed in an independent release is rare, but all the more so in a major franchise movie. Like *Darling Companion*, there is extra poignancy in the knowledge that the senior characters have less opportunity to change, especially in the case of Han Solo, who will not survive the end of the film.

While the screenplay for *The Force Awakens* has been criticized by some as derivative, Lawrence Kasdan and J. J. Abrams contribute significantly to shaping the final Star Wars trilogy by establishing a new, clearly defined hero's journey with deliberate allusion to the originals. The film succeeds in its aims to serve as a "bridge" to the past, while also facilitating the "hand-off" from old characters to new. Through Kasdan's skill at writing for ensembles, the central story remains clear, even while allowing multiple characters to pursue individual goals, much as he has achieved with his noted multi-protagonist dramas such as *The Big Chill* or *Grand Canyon*. And, by allowing his own favorite character to be killed, Kasdan (with co-writer Abrams) injects the saga with added emotional weight and a sense of peril absent from previous films. Conversely, through the reveal of Luke Skywalker in the final scene, his old lightsaber offered back to him by his protégé-in-waiting Rey, the hero's journey established in that first line of the opening crawl is fulfilled. It is a satisfying denouement to the movie, while also teasing to future episodes in the new trilogy. Lawrence Kasdan would not participate in these, the passing of the torch on that remote island a metaphor for change.

However, this was not the end of Kasdan's association with Star Wars, nor with his favorite character, despite Han Solo's death. For the first time in his career, Kasdan was ending a Star Wars project in the knowledge that he would be returning. Almost immediately after completing *The Force Awakens*, Lawrence Kasdan began preparing the standalone Star Wars film that had attracted him back to the franchise in the first place: a Han Solo movie.

NOTES

1. George Lucas, interviewed for "Empire of Dreams: The Story of the Star Wars Trilogy," *Star Wars Trilogy*, DVD extras (20th Century Fox), 2004.
2. According to John Baxter, *George Lucas: A Biography* (London: HarperCollins, 1999), 385; and Brian Jay Jones, *George Lucas: A Life* (London: Headline, 2016), 358.
3. Baxter, *George Lucas*, 372.
4. Jones, *George Lucas*, 379.
5. Ibid., 375.
6. Michael Kaminski, *The Secret History of Star Wars: The Art of Storytelling and the Making of a Modern Epic* (Kingston, Canada: Legacy, 2008), 313.
7. James Dyer, "*Star Wars: The Force Awakens*—The Complete History, Part I," *Empire*, December 18, 2015, https://www.empireonline.com/movies/features/star-wars-force-awakens-complete-history-part-i/ (accessed July 5, 2023).
8. Roger Ebert, "Dark Side Shadows Sith," *Roger Ebert*, May 19, 2005, https://www.rogerebert.com/reviews/star-wars-episode-iii-revenge-of-the-sith-2005 (accessed July 5, 2023).
9. Noelene Clark, "Hero Complex: Redrafted for Star Wars; Lawrence Kasdan will be 'Trying to Start Fresh' as He Writes a New Film in the Saga," *The Los Angeles Times*, February 13, 2013, https://www.latimes.com/entertainment/herocomplex/la-ca-hc-star-wars-lawrence-kasdan-20151206-story.html (accessed July 7, 2023).
10. Kathleen Kennedy, interviewed for "Kasdan on Kasdan," *Solo: A Star Wars Story*, Blu-ray extras (Disney), 2018.
11. Kennedy, quoted in Mark Olsen, "Star Wars: Episode VII: Lawrence Kasdan's Big Move," *The Los Angeles Times*, October 24, 2013, https://www.latimes.com/entertainment/movies/moviesnow/la-et-mn-lawrence-kasdan-jj-abrams-star-wars-episode-vii-20131024-story.html (accessed July 10, 2023).
12. "Written by" credit was eventually shared, with Kasdan and Abrams as an "ampersand" writing team. A complete shooting script is available at Lawrence Kasdan, J. J. Abrams, and Michael Arndt, *Star Wars: The Force Awakens*, screenplay, 2015, http://galactic-voyage.com/Star%20Wars-The%20Force%20Awakens-Final%20Script.pdf (accessed July 5, 2023).
13. Lawrence Kasdan, quoted in Kevin Jagernauth, "George Lucas' Original Star Wars Sequel Treatments Focused on Teenage Characters," *IndieWire*, May 8, 2015, https://www.indiewire.com/2015/05/george-lucas-original-star-wars-sequel-treatments-focused-on-teenaged-characters-264251/ (accessed July 5, 2023).
14. Benjamin J. Robertson, "'It's Just Us Now': Nostalgia and *Star Wars Episode VII: The Force Awakens*," *Science Fiction Film and Television* 9, no. 3 (2016), 480.
15. Paul Duncan, *The Star Wars Archives: Episodes IV–VI: 1977–1983* (Cologne: Taschen, 2020), 385–6.
16. Joseph Campbell, *The Hero with a Thousand Faces* (Bollingen series XVII, 3rd ed.), Reprint, (Novato, CA: New World Library, 1949/2008), 205.
17. Antonio Sanna, "The Reawakening of Star Wars: Nostalgia, Machinery, and Epic Grandeur," *Cinematic Codes Review* 1, no. 2 (2016), 92.
18. "Starkiller" was one of George Lucas's potential family names for Luke, as well as for "Annikin," in his early drafts of *Star Wars*, another meta nod to the original film. See J.W. Rinzler, *The Making of Star Wars: The Definitive Story Behind the Original Film* (London: Aurum, 2007), 19–30.

19. Ana Cabral Martins, "A Bridge and a Reminder: *The Force Awakens*, Between Repetition and Expansion," *Kinephanos: Journal of Media Studies and Popular Culture* 8, no. 1 (2018), 30; and Justin Mullis, "Ritual, Repetition, and the Responsibility of Relaying the Myth," in Ken Derry and John C. Lyden (eds.), *The Myth Awakens: Canon, Conservatism, and Fan Reception of Star Wars* (Eugene, OR: Cascade, 2018), 106. It is noteworthy just how many academic articles emerged about the movie in the years immediately after its release, a marked contrast to the dearth of academic writing on the original trilogy until quite recently, and a sign of how the previously condescending treatment of Star Wars in film scholarship has changed.

20. Chris Nashawaty, "*Star Wars The Force Awakens*: EW Review," *Entertainment Weekly*, December 16, 2015, https://ew.com/article/2015/12/16/star-wars-force-awakens-review/ (accessed July 6, 2023).

21. A.A. Dowd, "For Better and Worse, *The Force Awakens* Returns Star Wars to its Roots," *AV Club*, December 16, 2015, https://film.avclub.com/for-better-and-worse-the-force-awakens-returns-star-wa-1798186037 (accessed July 6, 2023); and Cabral Martins, "Bridge and Reminder."

22. Rinzler, *Making Star Wars*, 4–5.

23. J. J. Abrams, "*Star Wars: The Force Awakens* DGA Q&A with J. J. Abrams & Lawrence Kasdan," December 22, 2015, Directors Guild of America, https://www.youtube.com/watch?v=VlrfnT5KNGc (accessed July 6, 2023).

24. Abrams, "Force Awakens DGA Q&A."

25. Robbie Collin, "*Star Wars: The Force Awakens* Review: The Magic is Back," December 14, 2017, *The Daily Telegraph*, https://www.telegraph.co.uk/films/0/star-wars-force-awakens-review-magic-back/ (accessed July 6, 2023).

26. Abrams, "*Force Awakens* DGA Q&A."

27. Kristin Thompson, *Storytelling in the New Hollywood: Understanding Classical Narrative Technique* (Cambridge, MA: Harvard University Press, 1999), 28–9.

28. Josh Rottenberg, "Q&A: Star Wars Screenwriter Lawrence Kasdan on the Past, Present and Future of Star Wars," *The Los Angeles Times*, December 3, 2015, http://www.latimes.com/entertainment/herocomplex/la-ca-hc-star-wars-lawrence-kasdan-20151206-story.html (accessed July 5, 2023).

29. Kasdan, quoted in Dave Itzkoff, "He's Tried to Leave Star Wars Before. Will This Be It?" *The New York Times*, May 31, 2018, https://www.nytimes.com/2018/05/30/movies/star-wars-lawrence-kasdan.html (accessed July 5, 2023).

30. Harrison Ford, quoted in Itzkoff, "He's Tried to Leave."

31. Kasdan, "Lawrence Kasdan on His Career," *The Criterion Collection*, August 6, 2014, https://www.criterion.com/current/posts/3255-lawrence-kasdan-on-his-career (accessed July 6, 2023).

32. Kasdan, quoted in Chuck Wilson, "Lawrence Kasdan Interview," *LA Weekly*, April 19, 2012, https://www.laweekly.com/lawrence-kasdan-interview/ (accessed July 6, 2023).

33. Kasdan and Abrams, interviewed for "The Secrets of *The Force Awakens*: A Cinematic Journey," *The Force Awakens*, Blu-ray extras (Disney), 2016.

34. Abrams would have Harrison Ford reappear briefly as Han Solo in Episode IX, *The Rise of Skywalker* (2019), but only as a "memory" of Kylo Ren's.

35. Kasdan, quoted in Itzkoff, "He's Tried to Leave."

CHAPTER 12

A Changed Man: *Solo* and Beyond

Lawrence Kasdan did not want to write *Solo: A Star Wars Story*. A film about his favorite character had been the enticement for his return to the Star Wars universe in 2012, and he had agreed to become a consultant on the sequel trilogy on the proviso that he would be allowed to create a Han Solo picture. However, Kasdan said in our interview that his feelings changed in the intervening years. Following Michael Arndt's failure to deliver a screenplay for Episode VII on time:

> [I] then got dragged into *Force Awakens*. It was very lucrative, and it was fine because I liked J. J. [Abrams] a lot, but it took up many years I never would have expected, and [then] I didn't want to do *Solo*. And they said, "You've got to do it." I've got a contract.

His son, Jonathan, had done some uncredited writing on *The Force Awakens*, and the elder Kasdan suggested that they work on *Solo* together. In a contemporary interview, he said this arrangement was designed to "give me a shot in the arm" in order to embark immediately on a new Star Wars film.[1] The reality was more nuanced, with both men initially hesitant to write together, given the potentially difficult nature of a father-son working relationship. Kasdan told me five years later that at first it "was the roughest writing period I've ever had," until they finally became "comrades" as the project progressed.

Despite his reputation as "keeper of the Star Wars flame,"[2] Kasdan had, before *Solo*, always shared writing credit with an executive producer or director. The investigations earlier in this section suggest that he was able to influence the screenplays and final movies to a considerable extent, but his decisions were always open to change by more powerful collaborators—George Lucas on the original trilogy, and J. J. Abrams on *The Force Awakens*, each of whom had the authority to veto, alter, or simply not use any of Kasdan's ideas. With his fourth screenplay for the franchise, though, Kasdan finally had the opportunity to write a Star Wars film as the senior partner, and from page one of the first draft. He could shape the fabula and syuzhet precisely as he intended, and on a topic that he had selected personally. He was freed, too, from having to conform to the wider needs of a saga, with the Han Solo film intended, at least initially, to be a standalone story. The subject matter appeared a perfect fit, with Lucasfilm president Kathleen Kennedy saying that Kasdan "knows Han Solo better than anybody."[3] Kasdan could have been talking about Han specifically when he said in a 1983 interview that:

> There are no simple heroes and villains for me. I'm interested in why you act very well one day and very badly the next. This enormous conflict that people have. How do you try to live an honorable life when the attractions of success or material gain are very strong?[4]

Kasdan's affinity with Han Solo may be due to the fact that he shares traits with many of the protagonists from the films of his "hero" Akira Kurosawa. Kasdan has likened Han to the titular *Seven Samurai*, saying: "Even if he's wrong, it's forward motion."[5] Certainly, Han's characterization in Episodes IV to VII (all but one co-written by Kasdan) has him always looking for the next score, a way out of his current predicament, whether by joining the Rebellion to earn a reward, or abandoning it to pay off his debts. Like many of Kurosawa's leads, there is a vulnerability beneath the self-assured façade, his overblown ego quickly deflated by Leia's jibes or his spaceship's misfires, as if uncomfortably cognizant of his shortcomings while unable to admit them. Kasdan asks the question: "How much is a character aware of his own failings and limits? How much is he sort of foolish in an endearing way?"[6] Han Solo probably is aware of his shortcomings, though he would never admit them, which is precisely what propels him to keep that "forward motion;" and that is what makes him occasionally foolish, but also relatable. Original *Solo* co-director Phil Lord observed that Han is someone "who presented as a pirate but had a big heart underneath."[7] This question of presentation—of identity—is common in Kasdan's work, and it plays an important role here, with the lead character an orphan whose "family name" is given to him on the whim of an administrator. The struggle to understand and establish oneself is a theme prevalent in the films of Akira Kurosawa, too, and it is yet another way that *Solo* pays homage, along with a central mentor-apprentice relationship, a rain-sodden battle driving the plot, and a "peasant" uprising when the droids and wookiees rebel against their captors.[8]

Another reason why Kasdan is so attracted to the character of Han Solo may be that he is a modern incarnation of the archetypal gunslinger from classic Westerns, with the confident swagger, maverick attitude, and low-hanging

Figure 12.1 *Solo* as a Western

holster belt. Kasdan says that cowboy pictures played a major role in fostering his love of cinema as a child, and he later made two himself. From its very beginning, of course, Star Wars has been called a "space western,"[9] and the character of Han Solo encapsulates that spirit. After the sleek cityscapes and clean lines seen throughout much of the prequel trilogy, *The Force Awakens* had returned Star Wars to the dusty, lawless frontier, a decision that was partly Kasdan's. It seemed almost inevitable, then, that *Solo*, too, would take place in rugged terrain—rain and mud, snow-covered mountains, dusty plains—with Han presented as the archetypal outlaw. As with Kasdan's Westerns, *Silverado* and *Wyatt Earp*, the environment impinges upon the events of the film, lending it a crunchy, grungy tactility. Indeed, the characters interact with their surroundings more directly than in any Star Wars film since Han rescued Luke Skywalker on the icy tundra of Hoth in *The Empire Strikes Back*.

As noted above, Lawrence Kasdan wrote the screenplay with his son, Jonathan, whose previous two films as writer-director had been dialogue-led comedy-dramas. There is a rat-a-tat quality to many of the comic exchanges in *Solo* that was last seen in the franchise when Han and Leia bickered their way through *Empire*. Thus, in the aspect of dialogue, *Solo* continues the style established in Kasdan's earliest Star Wars work. On the other hand, as a film standing outside the wider Skywalker Saga, the writers could keep the story more focused and personal than in other episodes, the narrative concerned almost wholly with Han's survival rather than with serving any greater cause. This comparative freedom of storytelling means that there are numerous "Kasdanite"[10] elements to *Solo* that are expanded more fully than in his screenplays for the central saga: the moral uncertainty as the lead characters steal, deceive, and double-cross one another; the sympathy for the disenfranchised, whether Han himself, the enslaved wookiees, or the droid L3-37; and a complex female character, Qi'ra, who grapples with ethical dilemmas and makes morally ambiguous decisions, something that is still rare for women in Hollywood narratives.[11] Actor Emilia Clarke concurs:

> The mystery with regards to "Where does she stand? Is she good or not good?" —that classically doesn't always go to the female role [. . .]. The Kasdans were looking back to the film noir world and kind of bringing that to the forefront, and it's just kind of funny to see that these strong women have been around for a really long time.[12]

Solo also features two ensembles, the kind for which Kasdan has become lauded in his work as writer-director, with Han and Chewbacca first joining Beckett's criminal gang in order to escape the army and gain their freedom, and later forming another team with Beckett, Qi'ra, Lando, and L3-37. A major difference, though, compared to Kasdan's previous Star Wars scripts, is that there is little intercutting between parallel storylines. While this allows for more relationship development and the kind of "camaraderie time" that Kasdan felt was missing from *Return of the Jedi*,[13] it means that the film lacks what he calls the "enormous burst of energy" that pushed the story forward in his previous three instalments each time there was a cut between the different plotlines.[14] Instead, the almost constant presence of the eponymous character aligns *Solo* more closely with *Raiders of the Lost Ark* than other Star Wars scripts. The narrative is focused on one man, propelled by the breathless chase for a physical McGuffin, rather than on the grander, nobler goals of self-fulfillment and of good defeating evil that underpinned Luke Skywalker's hero's journey.

Like *The Force Awakens*, a tinge of nostalgia courses through *Solo*, both in its references to the first Star Wars trilogy (the return of Lando Calrissian for the first time since *Return of the Jedi*; and the inclusion of the "Kessel Run" mentioned in *Star Wars*) and in its allusions to the cowboy movie and film noir. The Western similarities are present in *Solo*'s rocky landscapes, its smoky gambling saloons, and in the finger-twitching gun duels; while the noir elements are expressed through Qi'ra's reappearance in Han's life as an archetypal femme fatale. She is in a relationship with a crime boss, seemingly attracted to the protagonist, but with a hidden agenda of her own. There are further echoes of noir in the complex web of ambiguous and constantly shifting loyalties between characters. Kasdan cites more recent crime films as inspirations—*Heat* (1995) and *Gangster No. 1* (2000)— but he could be talking about classic noir when he says of *Solo*:

> No one is reliable. There's always a chance of betrayal. And, I wanted to take what is essentially a street smart, but very innocent, young man, and figure out how could we start him on the journey to being the character who comes into the cantina [in *Star Wars*]?[15]

Similarly, in the same interview, Kasdan adds that he wants *Solo* to answer the question: "How did he become that Bogart character who has to pronounce that he's only in it for himself? We know that's not true. But where did that come in? He wasn't born that way." The film succeeds in marrying noirish elements to Star Wars, as well as continuing the series' pre-established connection to Westerns. And, in spite of the countless double-crosses and plot twists, the Kasdans manage to maintain narrative clarity throughout the screenplay. As with *The Force Awakens*, numerous characters—Han, Qi'ra, Lando, and Beckett—have well-defined motivations and goals, which allow the audience to understand their intentions even if they are not always admirable. Additionally, *Solo*'s themes—the search for identity, the fear of exposure, and the ways that the protagonist's past actions still have consequences even when he tries to leave them behind—are similar to those explored by Kasdan in his own films as writer-director, making it the most personal of the four Star Wars pictures that he has written.

Solo, however, lacks the emotional core of Kasdan's earlier Star Wars screenplays, as there is, unavoidably, a reduced sense of peril for characters who the audience knows will survive (Han, Lando, Chewbacca), and less investment in characters who the audience knows will not remain in Han's life, with his "future" already revealed in earlier films, a problem that the movie shares with George Lucas's prequel trilogy. A more direct connection to the prequels in *Solo* is the surprise cameo of Darth Maul, a character not seen in a Star Wars film since his apparent death in *The Phantom Menace*. It is a jarring moment, and one that would be all the more confusing for the vast majority of viewers unaware of his resurrection in *The Clone Wars* (2008–20) and *Star Wars Rebels* (2014–18) animated TV series. In attempting to connect the movie to the wider saga, too, I contend that in this moment *Solo* falls prey to the same issue that hamstrung much of Episodes I to III, wherein the connections to known characters and places make the universe feel smaller rather than larger. The problem is perhaps more marked in *Solo* due to the film's previous refusal to engage with the more "saga-esque" elements, such as the Jedi, the Sith, and the Force. While there had been numerous references to earlier films, these had felt in keeping with Han Solo's personality—irreverent, worn lightly, and intended solely to delight. The reveal of Darth Maul's hologram, though, is obviously designed to open up the possibilities for a sequel, and in doing so the picture loses the care-free swagger that had differentiated it from every other instalment since the original *Star Wars*. At its denouement, a movie that had hitherto mirrored the independent attitude of its protagonist suddenly becomes another cog in a corporate franchise, the very antithesis of its subject.

"A HORRIBLE SITUATION"

Lawrence Kasdan says of *Solo: A Star Wars Story* that, "I'm very proud of that movie. I love that movie," and the screenplay serves as a satisfying curtain call to his participation in Star Wars. However, the film perhaps has even greater significance in the way that it reflects Kasdan's status in the Hollywood industry. On both *The Empire Strikes Back* and *Return of the Jedi*, Kasdan was employed comparatively late in the development process. Even on *Raiders of the Lost Ark*, when he had much more time to hone the script, he was only offered the job after George Lucas had already worked on the story with Philip Kaufman, and after Steven Spielberg had signed to direct. With the new Star Wars films, however, he was viewed as a vital creative element from the beginning, hired by Lucas before the sale of his company to Disney, then kept on by new president Kathleen Kennedy to supervise the development of new films in the saga. As discussed above, Kasdan's participation may have influenced J. J. Abrams's decision to join the series as co-writer and director, helping to shape the entire sequel trilogy.

Evidence of Kasdan's elevated status is most prominent in press reports about the production issues that occurred on *Solo*, when original directors Phil Lord and Christopher Miller were fired from the project four months into production, due to "creative differences" with the producers.[16] On the sets of most big-budget films, such machinations would have little to do with the screenwriter. Even if they were consulted by the producers or studio, their input would be unlikely to attract comment in news reports. On *Solo*, however, Lawrence Kasdan was repeatedly mentioned as a participant in the decision-making process. The *Hollywood Reporter*, for example, wrote that "the style and vision of Lord and Miller clashed with that of Lawrence Kasdan, the legendary screenwriter behind the classics *Empire Strikes Back* and *Raiders of the Lost Ark*."[17] The same publication reported that Kathleen Kennedy then asked Kasdan to go to the set to help supervise the directors, and that he was "unhappy with the limited shots and displeased that Lord and Miller were calling out lines for the actors to try from behind the monitor rather than sticking with the script."[18] Kasdan, as well as a screenwriter, was an executive producer on *Solo*; however, with such a credit often merely symbolic, it is still unusual for the writer to assert authority over the directors in this way.

News stories on Lord and Miller's dismissal often quoted anonymous "sources,"[19] and tended to suggest that the original directors' focus on improvisation and comedy was not to Kennedy and the Kasdans' tastes. A later, more comprehensive *Variety* article posits that problems were less to do with style than with the mundane demands of working on such a large-scale production. It quotes a crew member (again anonymous) saying that "Lord and Miller drew Kennedy's ire for stretching days out with experimentation," causing delays and frequent necessity for overtime pay.[20] A quote from Kasdan himself implies that the issue was a combination of both style and logistics:

> Tone is everything to me. That's what movies are made of [. . .]. But this
> was a very complicated situation. When you go to work in the morning

on a Star Wars movie, there are thousands of people waiting for you, and you have to be very decisive and very quick about it. When you are making those split-second decisions—and there are a million a day—then you are committing to a certain tone. If the [producers] think that isn't the tone of the movie, you're going to have trouble.[21]

The same article explains that Lawrence and Jonathan Kasdan were present when Kathleen Kennedy first offered Ron Howard the job as replacement director: "Kennedy and the Kasdans confided that there were ongoing difficulties and that, unfortunately, they were going to be making a change."[22] When I spoke to Kasdan nearly five years after *Solo*'s release, his version of events tallied very closely to contemporary news reports. He called it "a horrible situation," in which Lord and Miller "just weren't close to staying on schedule or budget." The crux of the problem was their unwillingness to stick to the screenplay. As Kasdan tells it, the directors had previously agreed to the script, saying "we love this," then kept trying to change it, against the wishes of the producers and the studio.

They should have [. . .] said, "We don't want the script to be anything like you want it to." They didn't. They said, "Oh, this is great," because the head of the studio said that he loved it, and they wanted to keep the gig. But it was a disaster.

Initially, Jonathan Kasdan was on the UK set with the directors, "trying to shape it a little bit with them," but when Lord and Miller did not change their approach, Lawrence Kasdan flew over from Los Angeles. After two years of work on the project, Kasdan says:

I was pissed, you know, and we gave them many, many opportunities to correct the course, but everyone involved, the editor, you know, they were all aghast that these guys just didn't know what they were doing. They're very funny, they're brilliant guys, but they should never have been doing that movie.

Kasdan calls it "the most uncomfortable and unhappy I've ever been on a movie," in which he found himself in "a caricature villainous situation. I had always hated people who did that kind of thing, and here I thought it was absolutely necessary." The very fact that he found himself in that position on a Star Wars film is quite remarkable given his lowly, writer-for-hire standing on the original trilogy, in which he had "the smallest influence;"[23] and it demonstrates his high status within Lucasfilm that he was flown transatlantic to help resolve probably the most serious production crisis in the history of the franchise. The trade and mainstream press, too, viewed Kasdan as part of the hiring-and-firing process, and this speaks of a major shift in the way that he was regarded by industry watchers. Consequently, this suggests that Kasdan's standing in Hollywood had become much greater overall: the co-writer of four of the first ten live-action feature films in the most influential series in the history of cinema, now viewed as a powerful player, and the "keeper of the Star Wars flame."

KASDAN'S STAR WARS LEGACY

Kasdan received comparatively little recognition in contemporary reviews of his first two contributions to Star Wars, as well as in later academic literature. This is indicative not only of Kasdan's lower standing in Hollywood at that time, but also of the perception of screenwriters in general, in both popular and scholarly discourse on American cinema. When Kasdan returned to Star Wars in the 2010s, however, there was a greater appreciation among collaborators for his expertise in writing for the saga, with producer Kathleen Kennedy saying that he was one of the first people she approached to help realize the new sequel trilogy; while J. J. Abrams intimated that Kasdan's presence was a major factor in his agreeing to direct *The Force Awakens*. Furthermore, Kasdan's contributions were noted by critics, his name appearing more frequently in reviews for the movie than it had in those for his earlier Star Wars work. The pattern continued on *Solo: A Star Wars Story*, with Kasdan often namechecked in reviews, as well as in news stories regarding the production difficulties. These shifts in the way that he was discussed suggest a change in Kasdan's status among both filmmakers and critics. Now, rather than simply being someone who gained "shadow prominence writing scripts for George Lucas," as described by Richard Corliss in 1983,[24] there appeared to be a clearer understanding of his wider value. Kasdan was now considered the saga's "greatest screenwriter [who] wrote all your other favorite movies too" as "the voice of 1980s and 1990s cinema."[25]

In these later contributions to the series, Lawrence Kasdan was able to return a clarity of storytelling after the more convoluted plots of the prequel trilogy, as well as injecting a sense of humor born naturally from the characters and relationships. Alongside co-writer J. J. Abrams, he created a new Campbellian hero's journey for Rey, returning the saga to the more universally mythic tone that George Lucas established with the first *Star Wars* nearly forty years prior. Similarly, in *Solo*, Kasdan reconciled the allusive quality of the original trilogy with its theme of youthful yearning. He achieved this while making the film even more of a "Kasdan" story through the noirish double-crossing of its characters, rugged cowboy-movie settings, a complex female protagonist/antagonist, and the exploration of identity that further aligns the series with the films of Akira Kurosawa. Lawrence Kasdan, then, played an important role both in transforming the original Star Wars trilogy from a one-off success into a franchise that shaped modern American cinema; and later by helping return the series to its roots by establishing the "bridge" between the old and new. Therefore, I contend that, aside from George Lucas himself, Lawrence Kasdan has had a more sustained and important impact on the creation of the Star Wars saga than any contributor in its long history.

AN END AND A BEGINNING

Solo: A Star Wars Story was Lawrence Kasdan's final screenplay. Despite occasionally being linked to projects after *Solo*, he told me in 2023:

> I'd say the last six years or so [. . .] I haven't wanted to write anything. I think it came from writing alone for so long and the disappointment that comes when the movie doesn't work and you spent three years getting it there, and you get beat up, you're not sure what you're supposed to do.

If this is indeed the case (and he has changed his mind in the past, especially regarding Star Wars), then *Solo* serves as a fitting climax to a writing career that lasted four decades and yielded sixteen screenplay credits. While Kasdan has not ruled out the possibility of further features as director, this seems unlikely, too, given that the last of his eleven pictures, *Darling Companion*, was released more than ten years ago. However, this does not mark the end of Kasdan's life in film. Soon after *Solo*'s release, he and his wife Meg discovered that their favorite local diner was closing down. On Meg's suggestion, the Kasdans made a short documentary about its final week of trade.[26] Despite the Kasdans having no prior documentary experience, *Last Week at Ed's* is a hugely engaging film, a human story that celebrates family and community while quietly lamenting the passing of small businesses in big cities. Produced entirely independently, its completion just before the Covid-19 outbreak—when so many eateries were forced to close permanently—lends the film added poignancy, even if the pandemic negatively affected its potential for festival release. Kasdan says that through the creation of the film he discovered the appeal of making documentaries:

> You didn't know the story; you didn't know what was going to happen. You were only operating in an area of interest, and within that area of interest, as you cut the movie, you really got to create, rewrite your ideas, and you found out what movie you were making you didn't realize.

This positive experience led Lawrence Kasdan to want to learn more, and he became something of a student of the form. He met with the documentary team at Imagine Entertainment, *Solo* director Ron Howard's company, and he discussed the possibility of making a film about the history of visual effects. At this time, he was resisting the idea of focusing on Industrial Light & Magic, Lucasfilm's effects house, perhaps wary of continuing his Star Wars association. However, he soon realized that it was an "obvious" direction to take, and with Kathleen Kennedy and Disney enthusiastic, he set to work on a six-part series "about the people [of ILM], not so much about the technology."[27] Released on the Disney+ streaming platform in 2022, *Light & Magic* is a remarkably affecting piece of work that makes good on its promise to focus on the human aspect. Kasdan equates the story to two of his favorite movies, *Seven Samurai* and *The Magnificent Seven*, as he shows the molding of disparate individuals into a team: "What can he give us, and what can he? And he'll be the explosives guy, and he'll be the sharpshooter, he'll be the morphing guy." Kasdan had written screenplays for three early Lucasfilm productions that established ILM as the preeminent effects house in the world; then he had employed the company himself to create the "shit weasels" of *Dreamcatcher*, before he became central to the new Star Wars movies in which ILM's work was present in nearly every shot. For all this, Kasdan confessed to knowing very little about visual effects. And, despite his long acquaintance with the company's founder, Kasdan "did not go into it wanting to do a George Lucas thing." Kasdan had known Lucas for nearly forty-five years, from the *Raiders of the Lost Ark* story conference, when he was stunned to be in the same room as the creator of *Star Wars*, to the co-writer of *Return of the Jedi* who was so willing to argue with him, then through to his return to Star Wars just before Lucas's retirement. "We had been friends and not been friends," Kasdan says, more recently viewing Lucas as a kind of "Citizen Kane, and harder and harder to relate to." However, after conducting hundreds of hours of interviews, including six hours with Lucas himself, Kasdan realized the extent of his former mentor's vision in bringing together so many "geniuses" and understanding what might be possible through the development of visual effects and digital cinema. Kasdan's opinion of Lucas changed drastically: "I was like, 'Fuck! This guy's amazing.'"

Both *Last Week at Ed's* and *Light & Magic* share qualities with Kasdan's more celebrated features as writer-director, like *The Big Chill*, *The Accidental Tourist*, or *Grand Canyon*. Loose networks are formed through circumstance, creating new, and sometimes unexpected, familial units. The truths of the characters are conveyed not through declamatory speeches but in the subtext of apparently casual utterances. Kasdan says of documentaries that his subjects "had whole lives that they could communicate to you in a sentence. Without meaning to, you could get volumes about what they had lived through."[28] In the final episode of *Light & Magic*, Steve "Spaz" Williams, the computer graphics animator who was fundamental to the creation of *Jurassic Park*'s digital dinosaurs, talks about ILM as a school from which he will never graduate. Until this point in the documentary, Williams had presented himself as a rebel, knowingly cocky and utterly self-assured. In his closing statement, though, there is melancholy, a brief glimpse of pain in his eyes when he says of his time at the company:

"It made the way that I thought okay."

Kasdan's writing has been called "casually platitudinous,"[29] and this comment of Williams's is in precisely that vein, conveying the joy of his ILM experience while hinting at a past that may not have been entirely happy, a vulnerability beneath the frat-boy swagger. Just as Kasdan layers story and character into apparently inconsequential exchanges in his ensemble dramas, he manages to tease such insights from his interviewees, imbuing these factual films with surprising and emotive revelations. While his career in features may have come to an end, then, Lawrence Kasdan continues to develop documentary projects, and he still has more stories to tell.

Before this study, Lawrence Kasdan's career as writer and director had been mostly overlooked by scholars and critics. On those occasions when his work is discussed, his screenplays and films tend to be viewed in isolation. Kasdan himself says that "style is not something that drives my pictures,"[30] and this self-effacing attitude, in an age when the auteur myth still pervades,[31] may have contributed to the lack of serious analysis of his filmography. Yet very early in his career, his work was being described as "Kasdanite," suggesting a unique aspect to his output, while recently his elevated status within the Star Wars creative hierarchy has gained wider attention. Furthermore, his inclusion in documentaries such as *Five Came Back* (2017), and in retrospective discussions on his films, suggests a growing appreciation for Kasdan's work.[32] However, until now, there has not been a single in-depth analysis of his canon. It is my hope that this volume rectifies this oversight, and that it acts as an invitation to future scholars to undertake further research into Kasdan's pictures.

In a profile of his output during the 1980s, the film critic and historian Stephen Prince praised Lawrence Kasdan's ability to create "an intelligent body of work that showed the importance of a solid script, and the written and spoken word, for a distinguished film."[33] While accepting that Kasdan's pictures as director have been less critically and commercially successful later in his career, I conclude that Prince's observation remains valid. Even if the kind of dialogue-driven films for which he is best known are less *en vogue* in the twenty-first century than in the 1980s and 1990s, Kasdan's movies have had a profound influence upon adult-oriented ensemble drama in recent decades, both in cinema and on television. His focus on middle-class baby boomers over a thirty-year period contributed to America's perception of its largest generation, and his films have included examinations of race and class that are unusual among his cohort, and far more daring than he is given credit for. Finally, his scripts for Star Wars and Indiana Jones employed elements of pastiche that exemplified the era, helped to reconfigure audiences' expectations for popular film series, and changed the ways that studios would approach future franchises. Kasdan's screenplays and motion pictures, then, have had a lasting impact, as either exemplars or disruptors, on industry modes, filmmaking styles, and the wider cultural landscape. For these reasons, Lawrence Kasdan's filmography stands as a significant contribution to modern American cinema.

NOTES

1. Anthony Breznican, "How *Treasure Island*, *The Big Lebowski*, and *Heat* inspired *Solo: A Star Wars Story*," *Entertainment Weekly*, February 12, 2018, https://ew.com/movies/2018/02/12/solo-a-star-wars-story-influences/ (accessed July 6, 2023).
2. Kim Masters, "Star Wars Firing Reveals a Disturbance in the Franchise," *The Hollywood Reporter*, June 26, 2017, https://www.hollywoodreporter.com/heat-vision/star-wars-han-solo-movie-firing-new-details-behind-phil-lord-chris-miller-exit-1016619 (accessed July 6, 2023).
3. Kathleen Kennedy, interviewed for "Kasdan on Kasdan," *Solo: A Star Wars Story*, Blu-ray extras (Disney), 2018.
4. Lawrence Kasdan, 1983 interview quoted in "Kasdan on Kasdan," *Solo: A Star Wars Story*, Blu-ray extras (Disney), 2018.
5. Kasdan, quoted in Dave Itzkoff, "He's Tried to Leave Star Wars Before. Will This Be It?" *The New York Times*, May 31, 2018, https://www.nytimes.com/2018/05/30/movies/star-wars-lawrence-kasdan.html (accessed July 5, 2023).
6. Kasdan, interviewed for "Kasdan on Kasdan."
7. Phil Lord, quoted in Alex Pappademas, "Alden Ehrenreich is Ready to Prove He's Worthy of Han Solo," *Esquire*, April 24, 2018, https://www.esquire.com/entertainment/movies/a19834126/alden-ehrenreich-star-wars-han-solo-interview/ (accessed July 6, 2023).
8. This scene has obvious echoes of the peasant uprising at the mine in *The Hidden Fortress* (1958). I discussed this, too, in Chapter 7, and even more fully in a separate article. See Brett Davies, "Droids and Peasants: Akira Kurosawa's Thematic Influence on the Star Wars Saga," *The Kyoto Conference on Arts, Media & Culture 2021: Official Conference Proceedings* (January 2022), 57, http://papers.iafor.org/wp-content/uploads/conference-proceedings/KAMC/KAMC2021_proceedings.pdf (accessed July 4, 2023).
9. For example, Charles Champlin's contemporary *LA Times* review was titled: "*Star Wars* Hails the Once and Future Space Western," *The Los Angeles Times*, May 22, 1977, https://www.latimes.com/entertainment/movies/la-et-mn-star-wars-hails-the-once-and-future-space-western-20151202-story.html (accessed July 6, 2023).
10. Harlan Jacobsen, "Surviving," *Film Comment* 19, no. 5 (1983), 21.
11. Discussed by John August and Craig Mazin, "Episode 483: Philosophy for Screenwriters, Transcript," *Scriptnotes*, January 28, 2021, https://johnaugust.com/2021/scriptnotes-episode-483-philosophy-for-screenwriters-transcript (accessed July 6, 2023).
12. Emilia Clarke, quoted in Kristopher Tapley, "Inside *Solo: A Star Wars Story*'s Bumpy Ride to the Big Screen," *Variety*, May 22, 2018, https://variety.com/2018/film/features/solo-a-star-wars-story-directors-reshoots-ron-howard-1202817841/ (accessed July 6, 2023).
13. Kasdan, quoted in Paul Duncan, *The Star Wars Archives: Episodes IV–VI: 1977–1983* (Cologne: Taschen, 2020), 391–2.
14. Kasdan, interviewed by John August and Craig Mazin, "Episode 452: *The Empire Strikes Back* with Lawrence Kasdan," *Scriptnotes*, transcript, May 26, 2020, https://johnaugust.com/2020/scriptnotes-ep-452-the-empire-strikes-back-with-lawrence-kasdan-transcript (accessed July 5, 2023).

15. Breznican, "How *Treasure Island* inspired *Solo*."
16. Borys Kit, "Star Wars: Why the Han Solo Film Directors were Fired," *The Hollywood Reporter*, June 20, 2017, https://www.hollywoodreporter.com/heat-vision/star-wars-why-han-solo-movie-directors-were-fired-1015474 (accessed July 6, 2023).
17. Ibid.
18. Masters, "Star Wars Firing."
19. For example, Kit, "Why *Solo* Directors Fired."
20. Tapley, "Inside *Solo*."
21. Ibid. Original parentheses.
22. Ibid. The breakfast meeting between Ron Howard, Kathleen Kennedy, and the Kasdans was confirmed by Kasdan four years later in an interview with Jim Hemphill, "Lawrence Kasdan," *Academy of Motion Picture Arts and Sciences: Oral History Collection* (Los Angeles: AMPAS, 2022), transcript, 51.
23. Kasdan, quoted in James H. Burns, "Lawrence Kasdan: Part 2: From Scripting *The Empire Strikes Back* to Writing and Directing *Body Heat*," *Starlog*, October 1981, 56.
24. Richard Corliss, "Cinema: You Get What You Need," *Time*, September 12, 1983, http://content.time.com/time/subscriber/article/0,33009,926203,00.html (accessed July 6, 2023).
25. Adam Rogers, "Star Wars' Greatest Screenwriter Wrote All Your Other Favorite Movies Too," *Wired*, November 18, 2015, https://www.wired.com/2015/11/lawrence-kasdan-qa/ (accessed July 6, 2023).
26. Kasdan, quoted in Hemphill, "Lawrence Kasdan," 55.
27. Ibid., 57.
28. Ibid., 56.
29. Eric Hynes, "The Other America: Revisiting Lawrence Kasdan's *Grand Canyon*," *The Village Voice*, April 18, 2012, http://www.villagevoice.com/film/the-other-america-revisiting-lawrence-kasdans-grand-canyon-6434596 (accessed July 6, 2023).
30. Kasdan, quoted in Graham Fuller, "Lawrence Kasdan," in *Back Story 4: Interviews with Screenwriters of the 1970s and 1980s*, edited by Patrick McGilligan (Berkeley: University of California Press, 2006), 170.
31. As noted in Chapter 8, Kasdan himself subscribes to the auteur theory: "I had totally bought, and still do, the auteur theory, where people [. . .] were so strong in their artistic vision that they became very personal movies."
32. Most notably, Kasdan was interviewed extensively by Jim Hemphill in 2022; see Hemphill, "Lawrence Kasdan." Kasdan and his work have been the subject of other interviews and retrospectives in recent years, too; for example, John August and Craig Mazin, "Episode 73: *Raiders of the Lost Ark*," *Scriptnotes*, audio podcast, January 22, 2013, https://johnaugust.com/2013/raiders-of-the-lost-ark (accessed July 6, 2023); August and Mazin, "Episode 452: *The Empire Strikes Back* with Lawrence Kasdan," *Scriptnotes*, transcript, May 26, 2020, https://johnaugust.com/2020/scriptnotes-ep-452-the-empire-strikes-back-with-lawrence-kasdan-transcript (accessed July 6, 2023); Phil Maciak, "We're Not Leaving. We're Never Leaving: *The Big Chill* and the Enduring Power of Quarter-life Crisis Movies," *Slate*, July 29, 2014, https://slate.com/culture/2014/07/the-big-chill-and-the-quarter-life-crisis-film.html (accessed July 6, 2023).
33. Stephen Prince, *A New Pot of Gold: Hollywood under the Electronic Rainbow, 1980–1989* (New York: Charles Scribner's Sons, 2000), 256.

PART VI

An Interview with Lawrence Kasdan

In early 2023, Lawrence Kasdan agreed to talk with me about his life and career. Excerpts from our discussion, lasting over two hours, feature throughout this volume and account for all of the unattributed quotations in the text. Below are further excerpts that provide insights into his filmmaking processes and rationales.

The interview was conducted over Zoom on February 1 (PST)/February 2 (JST), 2023. Lawrence Kasdan was at his home in Los Angeles, and I was on the Nakano campus of Meiji University in Tokyo.

EARLY FRUSTRATION

BD: How frustrated did you feel in those years between college and selling your first screenplay?

LK: Yeah, very frustrated. But in retrospect, it actually happened very quickly. But when you're living it—and I didn't start it from when I graduated; it started from when I started writing screenplays, which was my junior year. [. . .] So that's, you know, around '68, and I sold something seven years later. *The Bodyguard* was optioned and then immediately *Continental Divide* was bought for a lot of money, which was just beyond my—I just wanted to do *anything*. So, the first one was very small money and turned out to be very big money over the years, they had to keep optioning it. But *Continental Divide* was this immediate thing that I had always dreamed of, which is more than one person wanted it, and Steven Spielberg got it. So, I'd been writing screenplays for about seven years, right through the end of college and into five years of working in advertising. I was terribly frustrated. And when I see that I was twenty-seven or twenty-eight when I sold my first screenplay, that doesn't seem too old now; at the time, I felt like I was just not getting there, I kept writing these things, so I was terribly frustrated. I had moved from Detroit, where I was working in advertising, to LA, just to be closer to it. I took an advertising job in LA, too, but I needed to be closer. I had to come out here to do commercials, and I thought, I've got to be there. That's where the studios are, that's where the mixing is. Everything is here. [. . .] I got an agent, finally, in '75. That's why we moved. And I worked in advertising for two years, and the agent was relentless about *The Bodyguard*, even though he was just about to give up on me at the end; and he did get it sold. So that took two years, so now it's 1977, and I sell it in the summer, in July or something. . . and by the end of the year, I'm working with Steven and George on *Raiders of the Lost Ark*, so that's a big turnaround. In fact, I used to keep a journal all through college, and it was all about these things which eventually came to happen, but seemed very distant at the time.

And I came upon the journal several years later, because I stopped writing [it], of course, immediately, and it goes up to the point where *The Bodyguard* is not selling, it's going around to every place in town, and I'm thinking, like, *Can this happen?* I had no alternative plan, I always feel that saved me, but I was very doubtful . . . And then the journal ends, and then it picks up again, and I'm directing *Body Heat*. Like, there was nothing to write about in the three years after I sold. It was like everything was happening so fast, I had no time to write a journal. I was writing movies. [LAUGHS.]

STARTING OUT

BD: When you worked on *Raiders*, how did that feel at that time when you're that new, that young? And I know Spielberg and Lucas aren't that different in age, but of course, they had just made *Jaws* and *Star Wars*.

LK: Yeah, I'd just seen *Close Encounters*, like, right before I met Steven, and *Star Wars* had already happened, and *Jaws*, and I mean, it was beyond belief. But I think I mentioned in the history[1] that I went in very intimidated and within a day I felt like, oh, I get where I fit in here. I can do this part they can't do; and them setting it up and us working out the story together, but them saying "And I want one of these, and I want one of those." That was incredible for me, because I'd always worked alone, completely alone. And all they were asking me to do is, "Can you make this work great?" And I was able to. I could see very early on that that was possible, even though these guys were at the absolute peak of the business. I got over it very quickly because I understood why they had hired me, even though it was shocking that that was my first job. But you get it, and you see that with athletes all the time, which is that they find themselves in the Super Bowl in the first year, and they think that's what their career is going to be. Of course, as they're told again and again by experienced people, you may never get back there. So, you can misinterpret the ease with which something happened. And I think it was great for me, because it just built my confidence so much, and then I felt like, oh, not only am I achieving what I wanted to do in record time, but it's exactly what I thought it was. It was great.

BD: Was it a fear, though, at that time when you did *Raiders* and *Empire*, and not long after, *Jedi* . . . Did you worry that you might end up stuck?

LK: No, because I had always had a scheme which was, I'm going to become such a successful writer, that—because that had happened with Coppola and happened with Schrader, and they had all gotten to direct, and I thought that was my best chance of getting to direct. I had no idea that it would happen times ten in the shortest amount of time possible. And so I had achieved this thing of becoming "hot." First of all, you don't think you can sell anything—it took me seven years to sell anything—and yet the goal is not to sell anything; it's to become such a hot writer that they're going to make you a director. And yet it did happen like *that*, after seven years, so there was no fear. It was like, oh my god, my dream has come true. Here's what I'm going to do with it. And what I was going to do with it was *Body Heat* and *Big Chill* and *Silverado*, and there was no fear there. And that's one of the gifts of youth: no fear.

BD: Then with *Body Heat*, of course, a very stylish film, visually, I think. Did you feel like you had lots and lots of ideas because it was your first movie?

LK: I did, and I also chose film noir because it opened those doors so wide. As I had come to know noir in college, I was blown away by it. Not only was this right in my interest, it was right in everything I found sexy, which is an overwhelming thing when you're that age. And it was funny, you know, these movies I was seeing, funny and violent, and they had the mix of everything I wanted. So, when I first was exposed to noir, I was like, oh my god. And then I dove deeply in that. I was thinking, what could I direct first when my technical skills are not developed at all? Well, there's this genre which gives you enormous license to do anything you want because these movies had been radically stylized, and the lighting, and the action, the dialogue, all so stylized, and it gave you enormous freedom. And I thought, I'm going to do one of those.

THE BIG CHILL AND THE BABY BOOM

BD: You got talked about as the baby-boomer filmmaker. Is that something that bothers you or irritates you as time goes on, or are you happy with that title?

LK: It was not that big a thing at the time. I mean, it wasn't like now where everybody knows what that means and it's an insult. But it wasn't an insult then. It was a huge chunk of the population that had an undue influence on the culture and had a lot of inflated, delusory ideas about our impact and our importance. That was all within the time, you know, and I wrote [*The Big Chill*] partially recognizing that, you know, that we had thought we were so important, and then I wanted to see what happens fifteen years later, what *really* happened. [. . .] And I thought, whoa, this is funny, because we all thought we were changing everything, but a lot of things never change. And things we thought we wanted, and ideals we thought we had, become questionable—not wrong, just you question them. And I thought there's a lot of humor in that, and I find it funny in my own life and among my friends. [. . .] There are parts of the movie that I cringe at because I just didn't write them well enough, because they were too on the nose, or everything slows when it should be happening in the action, like what you were talking about, it should just be moving along, with the draft notice²—that's the ideal. But there are times when the movie just sort of stops to talk about these things, and it shouldn't. Then there are other very static, long conversations that I'm very proud of; they're interesting and they're funny and they're very true to my life. So, there was no bad thing about being a boomer at that moment. Now it's "Okay, Boomer." One of the things that I talk about—*we* talk about, people my age—is that the only acceptable "ism" is ageism. Anything else, you're canceled, but if you are an ageist, you've impunity. And that wasn't always the case in history, but it's certainly the case now. And I turned seventy-four the last week or two, and that's so far past. Ageism starts when you're fifty. You feel, "Oh, so they don't like boomers." Tell me something else I don't know. They don't like anything. Basically, they're free to say, "We don't like old people. Get out of our way." I relate to that, I understand it.

BD: But, certainly, with no judgment at all on the term "baby-boomer," do you feel some satisfaction that a lot of people, a lot of critics talk about you as that?

LK: Yeah, that's what I was going to say, is that after I did *Body Heat* and it was a success. It did all right financially, but it was a huge success for me, and that meant that I was going to get to do more movies. Every movie felt that way: you were just hoping it would open the door for you to have a longer career. I'd had the success, a sort of dream come true, and I'm thinking, what am I going to do next? And I knew I wanted it to be out of my life and about my friends. But the main thing was I felt like no one had captured the sound of our generation, the way they talked to each other, the kind of jokes that were funny to each other . . . It had not been on screen. And I thought, that's what I'm missing, I want to see a movie like that, where they talk like that. In that sense, it's very specific to the generation. I wanted to hear my generation, which I thought I was not hearing in the movies.

BD: Yeah. Certainly, from my research, it's really the first kind of Hollywood movie that does that, I think.

LK: I didn't expect to be identified that way, but I was very proud of . . . You know, the night it opened, it was limited, there were many theaters, but not *wide* wide. And when you get the box office report, it was like "I did okay." And we were having dinner, and the producer came in and said, "Have you seen the Avco [Theater]? [. . .] It's around the block." Well, the Friday night performance had not prepared us for that. And Saturday was a smash, and the movie, because it wasn't in that many theaters, never made huge amounts on any weekend, but it lasted forever. But much more important than that was that it absolutely penetrated the culture in a way that very rarely happens. This is before social media, this is before the internet, and it just was every newspaper wrote something about it, every magazine, and it was kind of shocking for me.

DUALITY AND UNCERTAINTY

BD: You said that you felt some uncertainty when you were growing up. Of course, there was a lot of movement with your family. Do you feel that's come through in your pictures since?

LK: Yeah. You get to be in your seventies, and you're looking back, [. . .] and you think, well, why do I behave this way, and what patterns do I see? And am I interpreting them correctly, or is it a fantasy that I've constructed? Same way with memories. And we have these stories we tell again and again. Sometimes, on closer examination, it turns out it wasn't exactly that way, you may never know if it was that way, and maybe the important thing is what you have chosen to construct it as [. . .]. Why did I choose to interpret it that way? Have I used it as an excuse to behave certain ways? And so on. So, I find all that interesting. I find that in writing characters I like that. I like the audience to think, "Well, is that really the truth, what he's saying about himself?" and let other characters give you a different perspective on it. That's often very illuminating, and it's very funny, you know, that we've constructed these stories about ourselves, but the people who know us well will often say, "Well, not exactly." Or I'll say something to my wife or my friends, say, "I've always been such and such;" and they'll go like, "Nah, I don't think so" [LAUGHS]. I'm amused by all that.

BD: Actually, you talked once about two characters, and a character giving shade to another character, so is there a sense of that: one character thinks this, and then the other character shines a light?

LK: Yes, that's always been inherent in everything I've written, and certainly when I got to make my own movies, and *Body Heat* is really just all about that: how people see it, how they interpret other people's actions, how you can be blind to things because of obsessions which rule our lives. The Ted Danson character has a very jaundiced view of Ned, and so does the cop, and it turns out Matty has an even clearer view and has chosen him for the very reason that he's so blind to so many things, that he's simply manipulated; and she's picked up on that, and that just makes him perfect for her. And I think it goes right into *The Big Chill* and onward, which is: What is the story we're telling ourselves about our life? What is the story other people are seeing with a different view? They may not be correct either, but everything we do is a kind of mix, a soup of these fantasies that people have about themselves, about other people, interpreting their actions, being impacted emotionally by what they've done. Now, you're feeling this and they're feeling that. [. . .] And in a movie, you get this chance to see drama, that people are not always aware of what impact they're having and yet are operating from their own volatile sense of themselves. [. . .] The truth is, we're constantly torn, and it shifts around what the two poles are that you're being torn between, and I've always found that interesting to write about because people are never one thing, and very often they're feeling this frisson between what they think—this—and then they're feeling—that. And there's another underlying thing for me, which is that so much human action is driven by fear, and it's a fear of reality, of life, of recognizing how brutal the world can be. Once they start to invest in other people, partners, children, the fear increases because you're worried about the welfare of the people you love. And people deal with that fear many different ways: some run five miles a day, and some drink a bottle of liquor every day, and some work all the time and ignore their family [. . .]. We try to control that underlying fear and anxiety. I always felt that, and now it seems more relevant than ever.

THEME, STORY, AND CHANGING ATTITUDES

BD: Do you tend to start with some theme, "I really want to explore this," and then begin developing from there? Or does it tend to be some plot point that gets you inspired originally, then the theme emerges?

LK: I wish it was. Did I tell that story at the Academy about Alvin Sargent where he and I were talking? "Finally, a plot."[3] He and I both were agreeing about it. It's always about character. It starts with character. But for me, it also had to do with these ideas, the kind of things that we've just been talking about, and what character embodies those issues, and what character can they meet who embodies the contradictory attitudes? So, it always started with character, and then I had to find a story. What brings this out, what dramatizes it, what gives it action? And it's hard, and it's always been hard. As the world changes, it becomes harder. Certainly, for me, right now I don't think I could write a movie. When you look at old movies now and you think these are just as great as I remember them. But in a modern audience, there would be objections to this, this, this, and this. They would be spurious in my mind, they would be irrelevant to art in my mind, but they would be the end of the thing in today's world. It's scary, fearful that we're going the opposite way. The idea was always to have art expand the world, and now art and universities . . . Watch your step.

BD: I think you mentioned in the Academy interview that *Grand Canyon* is a film that maybe you couldn't make now. At the time, did it feel controversial, did you feel you had to be very careful to discuss race and class?

LK: There were still obviously issues, but not where you can't do this and you can't do that, and that a white director can't have black characters. And then if you dare to have black characters, you're appropriating something, or you're misinterpreting it, or you're falling into the old mythologies, which have naturally been irritants to a lot of people over the years and which privileged white people never thought much about. But the pendulum swings so widely that for old-fashioned ideas of art and literature, you're sort of lost. [. . .] The other end of the scale is more extreme, more oppressive, so you're not really anywhere. You don't want to be over here, and you don't want to be over there. And when I say I don't know if I could write a movie now, that middle ground was where I lived, and it didn't seem to me to be equivocating; it seemed to me to take in the confusion of life. That's really what [my] movies are about. But even when I was in my heyday, there was a school of criticism that Pauline Kael led to some extent, but was part of a trend, which is, "Well, if it's not wildly extreme, I'm not going to notice it."

ACTORS AND CASTING

BD: You've been called an actor's director. When it comes to casting in the first place, people like Mark Duplass or Zooey Deschanel, and these—at the time—young, up-and-coming actors, you seem to have a good eye. How do you find them? Is it through the usual casting agents channels?

LK: I did have one casting agent through the first period that was just great, this woman named Wally Nicita, and she brought me Kathleen [Turner]. And I was slightly, barely aware of Mickey Rourke, but she brought him in, and she was really good. After her, I had Jennifer Shull, who was a legendary casting director. [. . .] But, also, I had been thinking about acting since I was very young because I wanted to act, and I reacted very strongly to seeing people. Sometimes they were old stars, and sometimes they were brand new and I was seeing them for the first time. I remember seeing a Joan Silver movie called *Between the Lines*, and it's about an underground paper in Boston, and in it is Jeff Goldblum, who just explodes out of it, but everybody in it is good: John Heard, Jill Eikenberry, people I love, Lindsay Crouse. It's loaded with great people. And I would see something like that that and I'd say, "Oh my god, that's where I want to be." And a couple of years later, I was making *The Big Chill* with that just that kind of crowd, and it was very much influenced by *Between* *the Lines*, which is very funny. And there was this wave of New York actors who were getting to Hollywood, but they were mainly theater actors, and that was Kevin Kline and Bill Hurt and JoBeth [Williams] and all these people, Glenn [Close], who had come out of New York. Kathleen was unknown, she had been in a soap. But Bill had just appeared in *Altered States*, and when I met him, he was making his second movie [*Eyewitness*], and I went to New York to meet him while he was shooting that. He had a very difficult reputation, even though he was young and just happening, but we got together and talked for hours, and then he was drinking a lot, and it went on forever. My producer, who had been one of the ADs on *The Godfather*, a very tough New York guy, we were in the hotel in a suite, and it's going on and on, and Hurt's drinking more and more. My producer left, he went next door to his suite, and he called me and he said, "Should I kick him out? I'll throw him out." I said, "No, give me a little more time." And it ended well. Next day, his agent called and said, "Bill really wants to do this movie, but he doesn't think there should be a murder in it." Okay, well, then, nice meeting you; we have nothing to talk about . . . And then they called back an hour later and said, "No, he really wants to do it." But I didn't give it to him; I tested him [. . .]. But he was exploding in New York theater. He was in a particular theater company, and he had already won a Tony, and he was a kid. And then when I met Kline, he had also won a Tony already, and he had just done *Sophie's Choice*, he was a huge star on Broadway, and we're talking about thirty years old, maybe. I just love these New York actors, and I love the Hollywood actors. [. . .] There are so many good actors and so few good parts for them to be in. I admire them like athletes. I don't understand how they do it, I love watching them do it.

DIRECTING FOR OTHER WRITERS; WRITING FOR OTHER DIRECTORS

BD: If you're directing someone else's script, do you approach that differently at all? For example, *French Kiss* or *I Love You to Death*?

LK: In both cases, the writer was there every day because I believed in that, I wanted them there, I liked having them around. I had heard people say, well, I don't want the writer; a lot of directors don't want the writer around, it scares the hell out of them. But I never was worried about that. I had never wanted to be on a movie that I had written, I didn't want to stand around and watch them do it; but these two writers were wonderful guys, and they were there the whole time, and that changes your experience. You're talking to them all the time, they're sometimes saying to you, "I don't think this is working." So, I found it fun to have a collaborator. But there was something missing for me in terms of feeling that it was *my* movie, and not because anyone was challenging me. When I was coming up, you would hear these stories about all these directors, people that I knew and liked, Sydney Pollack and so on, who would just work over screenwriters like crazy. They'd say, "Oh, I love the script," and then they'd say, "Let's start on page one and change it." And I knew writers who had worked for them, and I thought that was stupid. But I realized finally that they had to take possession and ownership of the movie. The fact that they had not written it was worrisome to them, and they wanted to do this rewriting because then they could own every second of it. And I understood that finally, but I didn't feel that way about the two that I did from other people's scripts. I felt like, "Oh, they're here. We'll talk about it." [. . .]

BD: And then vice versa. When you've written scripts that other people have directed, how painful is it? Or can you be philosophical about it?

LK: I'm very philosophical about it [LAUGHS]. When I first saw *Raiders*, it was in a tiny little screening, and the heads of the studio were there, and George and Steven. [. . .] I felt a lot of ownership with the story and everything that was finally in the screenplay. And I was sitting there squirming, and it was my wife and I, and everybody's loving it, you know; and I'm there, like, *That's not right, and why did they do that?* I didn't express that to Steven. They probably knew that I was uncomfortable with some of it. Now it's forty years later, and. . . I think it's pretty damn good [LAUGHS].

BD: It holds up [LAUGHS].

LK: I started to really love it twenty-five years ago, and I got over all that. It was just a new experience for me to see it, and it's not easy for me. I had written *The Bodyguard*, the first thing I ever sold, and at one point I was going to direct it, then I didn't. Meg and I were making *Grand Canyon*, then we hired a very good British director [Mick Jackson], who'd done a wonderful miniseries in England. And the movie just, I thought, missed in every way it could, and Kevin [Costner] didn't like it, and we recut it, which is, again, the other time, I was the villain, you're doing what you don't want anyone to do to you.[4] And we made it better, but it would never be the right tone for me, and I didn't like the guy's taste. It should have been like *Bullitt*, which is why I wrote it, and it wasn't at all. And yet it was right in so many ways, and it was a gigantic hit, and so all my carping about it, and even Kevin's, went out the window [. . .]. I've seen it a couple of times, but it's hard for me because it's just like everything's off by twenty-five per cent, in my mind. That movie I really made in my head a hundred times, you know, because I worked a long time on that script. And I should have directed it, but I'm not sure if I wanted to, you know? And when I got an excuse to not do it, I took the excuse. The only thing I regret is I think it could have been a better movie. I don't regret not doing it, but I thought it should have been better. And part of that is the writer hearing something completely different, and if you're not exactly the same sensibility as that director, [. . .] then you're lost, because it's not what you want, and that's why I stuck to mainly directing my own stuff. That hasn't necessarily been the most productive approach, I would certainly not do it that way again. I was offered many, many movies, and I didn't do them because I hadn't written them [. . .]. Just like Sydney Pollack wanted to make his [films] all his, I had that same problem. I'd be offered stuff, and I was offered a lot of stuff, and now, looking back, I'd say I should have done four more movies. I wanted to, I liked doing it, and by sticking only to my own stuff and then having that stuff not work, you were fucked. And you can't then go back to being sort of a director-for-hire, which I probably would have liked more than I thought I would. It's about getting over these early ideas that you have, and we were talking about that before [regarding duality and uncertainty].

NOTES

1. Jim Hemphill, "Lawrence Kasdan," *Academy of Motion Picture Arts and Sciences: Oral History Collection* (Los Angeles: AMPAS, 2022).
2. Kasdan is referring to our previous discussion regarding the final scene of *The Big Chill*, when Alex's draft notice is mentioned for the first time. See Chapter 4.
3. According to Kasdan, Alvin Sargent said: "Here's what it will say on my tombstone— 'Finally, a plot!'" Kasdan did not mention this in his Academy interview with Jim Hemphill; however, he relayed the story in his Hopwood Lecture at the University of Michigan: Lawrence Kasdan, "POV," *Michigan Quarterly Review* 38, no. 4 (1999).
4. Kasdan is referring to the situation on *Solo: A Star Wars Story*, when he took part in the decision to fire the directors. See Chapter 12.

Lawrence Kasdan: Writing and Directing Credits

Lawrence Kasdan's films and television series as screenwriter and/or director, in order of US release.

The Empire Strikes Back (a.k.a. *Star Wars Episode V: The Empire Strikes Back*)
Directed by Irvin Kershner
Screenplay by Leigh Brackett and **Lawrence Kasdan**; Story by George Lucas
Produced by Gary Kurtz
Main cast: Mark Hamill, Harrison Ford, Carrie Fisher, Billy Dee Williams, Anthony Daniels
Production company/studio: Lucasfilm; 20th Century Fox
Release date: May 17, 1980

Raiders of the Lost Ark (a.k.a. *Indiana Jones and the Raiders of the Lost Ark*)
Directed by Steven Spielberg
Screenplay by **Lawrence Kasdan**; Story by George Lucas and Philip Kaufman
Produced by Frank Marshall
Main cast: Harrison Ford, Karen Allen, Paul Freeman, Ronald Lacey, John Rhys-Davies
Production company/studio: Lucasfilm; Paramount
Release date: June 12, 1981

Body Heat
Written and Directed by **Lawrence Kasdan**
Produced by Fred T. Gallo
Main cast: William Hurt, Kathleen Turner, Richard Crenna, Ted Danson
Production company/studio: The Ladd Company; Warner Bros.
Release date: August 28, 1981

Continental Divide
Directed by Michael Apted
Written by **Lawrence Kasdan**
Produced by Bob Larson
Main cast: John Belushi, Blair Brown
Production company/studio: Amblin Entertainment; Universal
Release date: September 18, 1981

Return of the Jedi (a.k.a. *Star Wars Episode VI: Return of the Jedi*)
Directed by Richard Marquand
Screenplay by **Lawrence Kasdan** and George Lucas; Story by George Lucas
Produced by Howard Kazanjian
Main cast: Mark Hamill, Harrison Ford, Carrie Fisher, Billy Dee Williams, Anthony Daniels
Production company/studio: Lucasfilm; 20th Century Fox
Release date: May 25, 1983

The Big Chill
Directed by **Lawrence Kasdan**
Written by **Lawrence Kasdan** & Barbara Benedek
Produced by Michael Shamberg
Main cast: Tom Berenger, Glenn Close, Jeff Goldblum, William Hurt, Kevin Kline, Mary Kay Place, Meg Tilly, JoBeth Williams
Production company/studio: Carson Productions; Columbia
Release date: September 30, 1983

Silverado
Directed by **Lawrence Kasdan**
Written by **Lawrence Kasdan** & Mark Kasdan
Produced by **Lawrence Kasdan**
Main cast: Kevin Kline, Scott Glenn, Kevin Costner, Danny Glover, Jeff Goldblum, Linda Hunt
Production company/studio: Columbia
Release date: July 10, 1985

The Accidental Tourist
Directed by **Lawrence Kasdan**
Screenplay by Frank Galati and **Lawrence Kasdan**; based upon the novel by Anne Tyler
Produced by Michael Grillo, **Lawrence Kasdan**, Charles Okun
Main cast: William Hurt, Kathleen Turner, Geena Davis
Production company/studio: Warner Bros.
Release date: December 23, 1988

I Love You to Death
Directed by **Lawrence Kasdan**
Written by John Kostmayer
Produced by Jeffrey Lurie, Ron Moler
Main cast: Kevin Kline, Tracey Ullman, Joan Plowright, River Phoenix, William Hurt, Keanu Reeves
Production company/studio: Chestnut Hill Productions, Tri-Star
Release date: April 6, 1990

Grand Canyon
Directed by **Lawrence Kasdan**
Written by **Lawrence Kasdan** & Meg Kasdan
Produced by **Lawrence Kasdan,** Charles Okun, Michael Grillo
Main cast: Danny Glover, Kevin Kline, Steve Martin, Mary McDonnell, Mary-Louise Parker, Alfre Woodard
Production company/studio: 20th Century Fox
Release date: December 25, 1991

The Bodyguard
Directed by Mick Jackson
Written by **Lawrence Kasdan**
Produced by Kevin Costner, **Lawrence Kasdan**, Jim Wilson
Main cast: Kevin Costner, Whitney Houston, Gary Kemp
Production company/studio: Kasdan Pictures; Warner Bros.
Release date: November 25, 1992

Wyatt Earp
Directed by **Lawrence Kasdan**
Written by Dan Gordon and **Lawrence Kasdan**
Produced by Kevin Costner, **Lawrence Kasdan**, Jim Wilson
Main cast: Kevin Costner, Dennis Quaid, Gene Hackman
Production company/studio: Warner Bros.
Release date: June 24, 1994

French Kiss
Directed by **Lawrence Kasdan**
Written by Adam Brooks
Produced by Tim Bevan, Eric Fellner, Meg Ryan, Kathryn F. Galan
Main cast: Meg Ryan, Kevin Kline, Timothy Hutton
Production company/studio: Polygram Filmed Entertainment, 20th Century Fox
Release date: May 5, 1995

Mumford
Written and Directed by **Lawrence Kasdan**
Produced by **Lawrence Kasdan**, Charles Okun
Main cast: Hope Davis, Loren Dean, Jason Lee, Mary McDonnell, David Paymer, Martin Short, Pruitt Taylor Vince, Alfre Woodard, Zooey Deschanel
Production company/studio: Kasdan Pictures; Touchstone
Release date: September 24, 1999

Dreamcatcher
Directed by **Lawrence Kasdan**
Screenplay by William Goldman and **Lawrence Kasdan**; based upon the novel by Stephen King
Produced by **Lawrence Kasdan**, Charles Okun
Main cast: Morgan Freeman, Thomas Jane, Jason Lee, Damian Lewis, Timothy Olyphant, Tom Sizemore, Donnie Wahlberg
Production company/studio: Castle Rock Entertainment; Kasdan Pictures; Warner Bros.
Release date: March 21, 2003

Darling Companion
Directed by **Lawrence Kasdan**
Written by Meg Kasdan & **Lawrence Kasdan**
Produced by **Lawrence Kasdan**, Anthony Bregman, Elizabeth Redleaf
Main cast: Diane Keaton, Kevin Kline, Dianne Wiest, Richard Jenkins, Elizabeth Moss, Mark Duplass, Ayelet Zurer, Sam Shephard
Production company/studio: Werc Werc Works; Sony Pictures Classics
Release date: April 20, 2012

The Force Awakens (a.k.a. *Star Wars Episode VII: The Force Awakens*)
Directed by J. J. Abrams
Written by **Lawrence Kasdan** & J. J. Abrams and Michael Arndt
Produced by Kathleen Kennedy, J. J. Abrams, Brian Burk
Main cast: Harrison Ford, Mark Hamill, Carrie Fisher, Adam Driver, Daisy Ridley, John Boyega, Oscar Isaac
Production company/studio: Lucasfilm; Bad Robot; Disney
Release date: December 18, 2015

Solo: A Star Wars Story
Directed by Ron Howard
Written by Jonathan Kasdan & **Lawrence Kasdan**
Produced by Kathleen Kennedy, Allison Shearmur, Simon Emanuel
Main cast: Alden Ehrenreich, Woody Harrelson, Emilia Clarke, Donald Glover, Thandiwe Newton, Phoebe Waller-Bridge, Joonas Suotamo, Paul Bettany

Production company/studio: Lucasfilm; Disney
Release date: May 25, 2018

Last Week at Ed's (documentary short)
Directed by **Lawrence Kasdan** & Meg Kasdan
Produced by **Lawrence Kasdan**, Meg Kasdan
Production company/studio: Kasdan Pictures; The Film Sales Company
Release date: October 26, 2019

Light & Magic (6-part documentary TV series)
Directed by **Lawrence Kasdan**
Executive Producers: Marc Gilbar, Brian Grazer, **Lawrence Kasdan**, Meredith
Kaulfers, Kathleen Kennedy, Michelle Rejwan, Justin Wilkes
Production company/studio: Lucasfilm; Imagine; Kasdan Pictures; Disney
Release date: July 27, 2022

Filmography

This is an alphabetical list of all feature films, serials, and TV series mentioned in the text, excluding those written or directed by Lawrence Kasdan (which are listed separately above). The filmography also excludes 'Making of' documentaries and Blu-ray/DVD extras, which are listed in the bibliography.

A.I. Artificial Intelligence (2001), Wrs: Steven Spielberg, Ian Watson (based upon the short story *Supertoys Last All Summer Long* by Brian Aldiss), Dir: Steven Spielberg, USA: Warner Bros./Dreamworks.

Altered States (1980), Wr: Paddy Chayefsky, Dir: Ken Russell, USA: Warner Bros.

American Graffiti (1973), Wrs: George Lucas, Gloria Katz, Willard Huyck, Dir: George Lucas, USA: Universal.

Attack of the Clones (a.k.a. *Star Wars Episode II: Attack of the Clones*) (2002), Wrs: George Lucas, Jonathan Hales, Dir: George Lucas, USA: Lucasfilm/20th Century Fox.

Back to the Future (1985), Wrs: Robert Zemeckis, Bob Gale, Dir: Robert Zemeckis, USA: Universal.

Back to the Future Part II (1989), Wrs: Robert Zemeckis, Bob Gale, Dir: Robert Zemeckis, USA: Universal.

Back to the Future Part III (1990), Wrs: Robert Zemeckis, Bob Gale, Dir: Robert Zemeckis, USA: Universal.

*The Bad Sleep Well/Warui yatsu hodo yoku nemuru/*悪い奴ほどよく眠る (1960), Wrs: Hideo Oguni, Eijiro Hisaita, Akira Kurosawa, Ryuzo Kikushima and Shinobu Hashimoto, Dir: Akira Kurosawa, Japan: Toho.

Between the Lines (1977), Wrs: Fred Barron, David M. Helpern Jr., Dir: Joan Micklin Silver, USA: Midwest Films.

The Big Sleep (1946), Wrs: William Faulkner, Leigh Brackett, Jules Furthman (based upon the novel by Raymond Chandler), Dir: Howard Hawks, USA: Warner Bros.

Bonnie and Clyde (1967), Wrs: David Newman and Robert Benton, Dir: Arthur Penn, USA: Warner Bros.

Boyz n the Hood (1991), Wr/Dir: John Singleton, USA: Columbia.

Bringing Up Baby (1938), Wrs: Dudley Nichols, Hagar Wilde (based upon the short story by Hagar Wilde), Dir: Howard Hawks, USA: RKO.

Bullitt (1968), Wrs: Alan R. Trustman, Harry Kleiner (based upon the novel *Mute Witness* by Robert L. Fish), Dir: Peter Yates, USA: Warner Bros.-Seven Arts.

The Clone Wars (2008–20), Creator: George Lucas, USA: Lucasfilm.

Close Encounters of the Third Kind (1977), Wr/Dir: Steven Spielberg, USA: Columbia.

Diner (1982), Wr/Dir: Barry Levinson, USA: MGM/UA.

Double Indemnity (1944), Wrs: Billy Wilder and Raymond Chandler (based upon the novel by James M. Cain), Dir: Billy Wilder, USA: Paramount.

*Drunken Angel/Yoidore tenshi/*酔いどれ天使 (1948), Wrs: Akira Kurosawa and Keinosuke Uegusa, Dir: Akira Kurosawa, Japan: Toho.

Easy Rider (1969), Wrs: Peter Fonda, Dennis Hopper, Terry Southern, Dir: Dennis Hopper, USA: Columbia.

El Dorado (1966), Wr: Leigh Brackett (based upon the novel *The Stars in Their Courses* by Harry Brown), Dir: Howard Hawks, USA: Paramount.

E.T.: The Extra-Terrestrial (1982), Wr: Melissa Mathison, Dir: Steven Spielberg, USA: Universal.

The Ewok Adventure (a.k.a. *Caravan of Courage: An Ewok Adventure*) (1984), Wrs: Bob Carrau, George Lucas, Dir: John Korty, USA: Lucasfilm/20th Century Fox/ABC Television.

Ewoks (1985–6), Created by Paul Dini, Bob Carrau, George Lucas, USA/Canada/Taiwan: Nelvana/Lucasfilm/Wang/ABC Television.

Ewoks: The Battle for Endor (1985), Wrs: Ken and Jim Wheats, George Lucas, Dir: Ken and Jim Wheats, USA: Lucasfilm/20th Century Fox/ABC Television.

Eyewitness (1981), Wr: Steve Tesich, Dir: Peter Yates, USA: 20th Century Fox.

The Fabelmans (2022), Wrs: Steven Spielberg, Tony Kushner, Dir: Steven Spielberg, USA: Universal.

Five Came Back (2017), Wr: Mark Harris (based upon the book by Mark Harris), Dir: Laurent Bouzereau, USA: Netflix.

Five Easy Pieces (1970), Wr: Adrien Joyce, Dir: Bob Rafaelson, USA: Columbia.

Flash Gordon (1936), Wrs: Frederick Stephani, Ella O'Neill, George Plympton, Basil Dickey (based upon the comic by Alex Raymond), Dir: Frederick Stephani, USA: Universal.

Four Weddings and a Funeral (1994), Wr: Richard Curtis, Dir: Mike Newell, UK: Polygram/Working Title/Channel Four.

The French Connection (1971), Wr: Ernest Tidyman (based upon the novel by Robin Moore), Dir: William Friedkin, USA: 20th Century Fox.

Gangster No. 1 (2000), Wrs: Johnny Ferguson, Louis Mellis, David Scinto, Dir: Paul McGuigan, UK: Film Four.

Girls (2012–17), Creator: Lena Dunham, USA: Warner Bros./HBO.

The Godfather (1972), Wrs: Mario Puzo, Francis Ford Coppola (based upon the novel by Mario Puzo), Dir: Francis Ford Coppola, USA: Paramount.

The Good, the Bad and the Ugly/Il buono, il brutto, il cattivo (1966), Wrs: Age & Scarpelli, Luciano Vincenzoni, Sergio Leone, Dir: Sergio Leone, Italy: Produzioni Europee Associate/United Artists.

Hannah and Her Sisters (1986), Wr/Dir: Woody Allen, USA: Orion.

Heat (1995), Wr/Dir: Michael Mann, USA: Warner Bros.

*The Hidden Fortress/Kakushi toride no san akunin/*隠し砦の三悪人 (1958), Wrs: Ryuzo Kikushima, Hideo Oguni, Shinobu Hashimoto and Akira Kurosawa, Dir: Akira Kurosawa, Japan: Toho.

High and Low (a.k.a. *Heaven and Hell*)/*Tengoku to jigoku/*天国と地獄 (1963), Wrs: Ryuzo Kikushima, Hideo Oguni, Eijiro Hisaita and Akira Kurosawa (based upon the novel *King's Ransom* by Ed McBain), Dir: Akira Kurosawa, Japan: Toho.

Hook (1991), Wrs: Jim V. Hart, Malia Scotch Marmo, Dir: Steven Spielberg, USA: Tri-Star

House Party (1990), Wr/Dir: Reginald Hudlin, USA: New Line.

Howard the Duck (1986), Wrs: Willard Huyck, Gloria Katz (based upon the comic by Steve Gerber), Dir: Willard Huyck, USA: Universal.

Ikiru (a.k.a. *To Live*)/生きる (1952), Wrs: Akira Kurosawa, Shinobu Hashimoto and Hideo Oguni, Dir: Akira Kurosawa, Japan: Toho.

Indiana Jones and the Last Crusade (1989), Wrs: Jeffrey Boam, George Lucas, Menno Meyjes, Dir: Steven Spielberg, USA: Lucasfilm/Paramount.

Indiana Jones and the Temple of Doom (1984), Wrs: Willard Huyck, Gloria Katz, George Lucas, Dir: Steven Spielberg, USA: Lucasfilm/Paramount.

It Happened One Night (1934), Wr: Robert Riskin (based upon the short story *The Night Bus* by Samuel Hopkins Adams), Dir: Frank Capra, USA: Columbia.

I Wanna Hold Your Hand (1978), Wrs: Robert Zemeckis, Bob Gale, Dir: Robert Zemeckis, USA: Universal.

Jaws (1975), Wrs: Peter Benchley, Carl Gottlieb (based upon the novel by Peter Benchley), Dir: Steven Spielberg, USA: Universal.

Jurassic Park (1993), Wrs: Michael Crichton, David Koepp (based upon the novel by Michael Crichton), Dir: Steven Spielberg, USA: Universal.

Labyrinth (1986), Wrs: Terry Jones (uncredited: Jim Henson, Laura Phillips, Elaine May, George Lucas), Dir: Jim Henson, UK/USA: Tri-Star.

Lawrence of Arabia (1962), Wrs: Robert Bolt, Michael Wilson, Dir: David Lean, UK: Columbia.

Leave it to Beaver (1957–63), Creators: Joe Connelly, Bob Mosher, USA: CBS Television/ABC Television.

The Magnificent Seven (1960), Wr: William Roberts (uncredited: Walter Bernstein and Walter Newman), Dir: John Sturges, USA: United Artists.

Midnight Cowboy (1969), Wr: Walso Salt (based upon the novel by James Leo Herlihy), Dir: John Schlesinger, USA: United Artists.

The Most Beautiful/Ichiban utsukushiku/一番美しく (1944), Wr/Dir: Akira Kurosawa, Japan: Toho.

Murder, My Sweet (a.k.a. *Farewell, My Lovely*) (1944), Wr: John Paxton (based upon the novel *Farewell, My Lovely* by Raymond Chandler), Dir: Edward Dmytryk, USA: RKO.

My So-Called Life (1994–5), Creator: Winnie Holzman, USA: ABC Television.

Network (1976), Wr: Paddy Chayefsky, Dir. Sidney Lumet, USA: MGM/UA.

1941 (1979), Wrs: Robert Zemeckis, Bob Gale, John Milius, Dir. Steven Spielberg, USA: Universal/Columbia.

Out of the Past (a.k.a. *Build My Gallows High*) (1947), Wr: Daniel Mainwaring (based upon the novel *Build My Gallows High* by Daniel Mainwaring), Dir: Jacques Tourneur, USA: RKO.

The Phantom Menace (a.k.a. *Star Wars Episode I: The Phantom Menace*) (1999), Wr/Dir: George Lucas, USA: Lucasfilm/20th Century Fox.

Poltergeist (1982), Wrs: Steven Spielberg, Michael Grais, Mark Victor, Dir: Tobe Hooper, USA: MGM/UA.

Rashomon/羅生門 (1950), Wrs: Akira Kurosawa and Shinobu Hashimoto (based upon the short story *In a Grove* by Ryunosuke Akutagawa), Dir: Akira Kurosawa, Japan: Daiei.

Rear Window (1954), Wr: John Michael Hayes (based upon the short story *It Had to Be Murder* by Cornell Woolrich), Dir: Alfred Hitchcock, USA: Universal.

La Règle du jeu/The Rules of the Game (1939), Wrs: Jean Renoir, Carl Koch, Dir: Jean Renoir, France: Gaumont.

Return of the Secaucus 7 (1980), Wr/Dir: John Sayles USA: Libra Films.

Revenge of the Sith (a.k.a. *Star Wars Episode III: Revenge of the Sith*) (2005), Wr/Dir: George Lucas, USA: Lucasfilm/20th Century Fox.

Rio Bravo (1959), Wrs: Jules Furthman, Leigh Brackett (based upon the short story by B. H. McCampbell), Dir: Howard Hawks, USA: Warner Bros.

The Rise of Skywalker (2019), Wrs: J. J. Abrams, Chris Terrio, Derek Connolly, Colin Trevorrow, Dir: J. J. Abrams, USA: Lucasfilm/Disney.

Romancing the Stone (1984), Wr: Diane Thomas, Dir: Robert Zemeckis, USA: 20th Century Fox.

The Royal Tenenbaums (2001), Wrs: Wes Anderson, Owen Wilson, Dir: Wes Anderson, USA: Buena Vista.

*Seven Samurai/Shichinin no samurai/*七人の侍 (1954), Wrs: Akira Kurosawa, Shinobu Hashimoto and Hideo Oguni, Dir: Akira Kurosawa, Japan: Toho.

Sophie's Choice (1982), Wr/Dir: Alan J. Pakula (based upon the novel by William Styron), USA: Universal.

Star Wars (a.k.a. *Star Wars Episode IV: A New Hope*) (1977), Wr/Dir: George Lucas, USA: Lucasfilm/20th Century Fox.

Star Wars: Droids: The Adventures of R2-D2 and C-3PO (1985–6), Creators: Peter Sauder, Ben Burtt, George Lucas, USA/Canada: Nelvana/Lucasfilm/20th Century Fox/ABC Television.

Star Wars Rebels (2014–18), Creator: Simon Kinberg, Dave Filoni, Carrie Beck, USA: Lucasfilm/Disney.

Star Wars: The Legacy Revealed (2007), Dir: Kevin Burns, USA: Lucasfilm/The History Channel.

*Stray Dog/Nora inu/*野良犬 (1949), Wrs: Akira Kurosawa and Ryuzo Kikushima, Dir: Akira Kurosawa, Japan: Toho.

Taxi Driver (1976), Wr: Paul Schrader, Dir: Martin Scorsese, USA: Columbia.

Thirtysomething (1987–91), Creators: Edward Zwick, Marshall Herskovitz, USA: MGM/UA/ABC Television.

Tombstone (1993), Wr: Kevin Jarre, Dir: George P. Cosmatos, USA: Buena Vista.

The Treasure of the Sierra Madre (1948), Wr/Dir: John Huston (based upon the novel by B. Traven), USA: Warner Bros.

Tucker: The Man and His Dream (1988), Wrs: Arnold Schulman, David Seidler, Dir: Francis Ford Coppola, USA: Paramount.

Used Cars (1980), Wrs: Robert Zemeckis, Bob Gale, Dir: Robert Zemeckis, USA: Columbia.

Who Framed Roger Rabbit (1988), Wrs: Jeffrey Price, Peter S. Seaman (based upon the novel *Who Censored Roger Rabbit?* by Gary K. Wolf), Dir. Robert Zemeckis, USA: Buena Vista.

The Wild Bunch (1969), Wrs: Walon Green, Sam Peckinpah, Roy N. Sickner, Dir: Sam Peckinpah, USA: Warner Bros.

Willow (1988), Wrs: Bob Dolman, George Lucas, Dir: Ron Howard, USA: MGM.

*Yojimbo/*用心棒 (1961), Wrs: Ryuzo Kikushima, Akira Kurosawa and Hideo Oguni, Dir: Akira Kurosawa, Japan: Toho.

The Young Indiana Jones Chronicles (1992–3), Creator: George Lucas, USA: Amblin/Lucasfilm/Paramount/Family Channel/ABC Television.

Bibliography

Abrams, J. J. "*Star Wars: The Force Awakens* DGA Q&A with J. J. Abrams & Lawrence Kasdan." Directors Guild of America, YouTube, December 23, 2015. https://www.youtube.com/watch?v=VlrfnT5KNGc (accessed July 6, 2023).

Abrams, J. J. "The Secrets of *The Force Awakens*: A Cinematic Journey." *The Force Awakens*, Blu-ray extras, USA: Disney, 2016.

Allen, Tim. "What Empire?" *The Village Voice*, May 26, 1980.

Anderson, Melissa. "*Darling Companion*." *The Village Voice*, April 18, 2012. http://www.villagevoice.com/film/darling-companion-6434614 (accessed July 4, 2023).

Arnold, Alan. *Once upon a Galaxy: The Making of The Empire Strikes Back*. New York: Ballantine, 1980.

August, John and Craig Mazin. "Episode 73: *Raiders of the Lost Ark* [Audio podcast]." *Scriptnotes*, January 22, 2013. https://johnaugust.com/2013/raiders-of-the-lost-ark (accessed July 6, 2023).

August, John and Craig Mazin. "Episode 247: The One with Lawrence Kasdan [Audio podcast]." *Scriptnotes*, April 26, 2016. http://johnaugust.com/2016/the-one-with-lawrence-kasdan (accessed June 29, 2023).

August, John and Craig Mazin. "Episode 452: *The Empire Strikes Back* with Lawrence Kasdan, transcript." *Scriptnotes*, May 26, 2020. https://johnaugust.com/2020/scriptnotes-ep-452-the-empire-strikes-back-with-lawrence-kasdan-transcript (accessed July 6, 2023).

August, John and Craig Mazin. "Episode 483: Philosophy for Screenwriters, Transcript." *Scriptnotes*, January 28, 2021 https://johnaugust.com/2021/scriptnotes-episode-483-philosophy-for-screenwriters-transcript (accessed July 6, 2023).

Attias, Diana and Lindsay Smith. *The Empire Strikes Back Notebook*. New York: Ballantine, 1980.

Bailey, John. "*The Big Chill*: A Reunion." *The Big Chill*, DVD extras, USA: Columbia TriStar, 1998.

Balingit, JoAnn. "Review of *Grand Canyon*." In *Magill's Cinema Annual: 1992: A Survey of the Films of 1991*, edited by Frank Magill. Englewood Cliffs, NJ: Salem, 1992.

Baver, Kristin. "*Empire* at 40: George Lucas on Making 'Something That Had Never Been Done Before,' Again." *Star Wars*, May 21, 2020. https://www.starwars.com/news/empire-at-40-george-lucas-interview (accessed July 5, 2023).

Baxter, John. *George Lucas: A Biography*. London: HarperCollins, 1999.

Bilbow, Marjorie. "Marjorie Bilbow's Reviews: *The Big Chill*." *Screen International (Archive: 1976–2000)*, January 21, 1984. https://search-proquest-com.proxy.library.dmu.ac.uk/docview/963327638?accountid=10472 (accessed July 7, 2023).

Borde, Raymond and Etienne Chaumeton. *Panorama du film noir américain 1941–1953 (A Panorama of American Film Noir 1941–1953)*. Translated by P. Hammond. San Francisco: City Lights Books, 1955 (Reprint, 2002).

Bordwell, David. *Narration in the Fiction Film*. Oxon, UK: Routledge, 1985.

Bordwell, David. *Making Meaning: Inference and Rhetoric in the Interpretation of Cinema*. Cambridge, MA: Harvard University Press, 1989.

Bordwell, David. *The Way Hollywood Tells It*. Berkeley, CA: University of California Press, 2006.

Bordwell, David and Kristin Thompson. *Film Art: An Introduction*, 6th ed. New York: McGraw Hill, 2001.

Bouzereau, Laurent. *Star Wars: The Annotated Screenplays*. New York: Ballantine, 1997.

Bradshaw, Peter. "Every Star Wars Film—Ranked!" *The Guardian*, May 24, 2018. https://www.theguardian.com/film/2018/may/24/every-star-wars-film-ranked-solo-skywalker (accessed July 5, 2023).

Breznican, Anthony. "How *Treasure Island*, *The Big Lebowski*, and *Heat* inspired *Solo: A Star Wars Story*." *Entertainment Weekly*, February 12, 2018. https://ew.com/movies/2018/02/12/solo-a-star-wars-story-influences/ (accessed July 6, 2023).

Brik, Osip. "From the Theory and Practice of the Screenwriter." Translated by D. Matias. *Screen: The Journal of the Society for Education in Film and Television* 15, no. 3. (1974 [original article, 1936]).

Broeske, Pat H. "*Chill* Director-Writer Lawrence Kasdan: 'I Make the Kind of Pictures I Like to See.'" *Hollywood Drama Logue* 45 (November 10–16, 1983).

Brooker, Will. *BFI Film Classics: Star Wars*. London: Bloomsbury/British Film Institute, 2009.

Brown, Joe. "*Grand Canyon*." *The Washington Post*, January 10, 1992. http://www.washingtonpost.com/wp-srv/style/longterm/movies/videos/grandcanyonrbrown_a0add9.htm (accessed July 3, 2023).

Browning, Mark. *Stephen King on the Big Screen*. Bristol, UK: Intellect, 2009.

Buckland, Warren. "A Close Encounter with *Raiders of the Lost Ark*: Notes on Narrative Aspects of the New Hollywood Blockbuster." In *Contemporary Hollywood Cinema*, edited by Steve Neale and Murray Smith. New York: Routledge, 1998.

Buckland, Warren. *Directed by Steven Spielberg: Poetics of the Contemporary Hollywood Blockbuster*. New York: Continuum, 2006.

Bunch, Sonny. "In Film, '*It*' Tosses out the Most Powerful Part of Stephen King's Novel." *The Washington Post*, September 8, 2017. https://www.washingtonpost.com/news/act-four/wp/2017/09/07/in-film-it-tosses-out-the-most-powerful-part-of-stephen-kings-novel/ (accessed July 4, 2023).

Burns, James H. "Lawrence Kasdan: Part 2: From Scripting *The Empire Strikes Back* to Writing and Directing *Body Heat*." *Starlog* 51 (October 1981).

Cabral Martins, Ana. "A Bridge and a Reminder: *The Force Awakens*, Between Repetition and Expansion." *Kinephanos: Journal of Media Studies and Popular Culture* 8, no. 1 (2018).

Campbell, Joseph. *The Hero with a Thousand Faces*. Bollingen series XVII, 3rd ed. Novato, CA: New World Library, 1949 (Reprint, 2008).

Canby, Vincent. "Screen: *The Big Chill*, Reunion of 60's Activists." *The New York Times*, September 23, 1983. https://www.nytimes.com/1983/09/23/movies/screen-the-big-chill-reunion-of-60-s-activists.html (accessed July 3, 2023).

Champlin, Charles. "*Star Wars* Hails the Once and Future Space Western." *The Los Angeles Times*, May 22, 1977. https://www.latimes.com/entertainment/movies/la-et-mn-star-wars-hails-the-once-and-future-space-western-20151202-story.html (accessed July 6, 2023).

Chute, David. "Tropic of Kasdan." *Film Comment* 17, no. 5 (1981).

"Cinemetrics Database." *Cinemetrics*, 2019. http://www.cinemetrics.lv/database.php

Clark, Noelene. "Hero Complex: Redrafted for Star Wars; Lawrence Kasdan will be 'Trying to Start Fresh' as He Writes a New Film in the Saga." *The Los Angeles Times*, February 13, 2013. https://www.latimes.com/entertainment/herocomplex/la-ca-hc-star-wars-lawrence-kasdan-20151206-story.html (accessed July 7, 2023).

Cogan, Brian and Thom Gencarelli. *Baby Boomers and Popular Culture: An Inquiry into America's Most Powerful Generation*. Santa Barbara, CA: Praeger, 2015.

Collin, Robbie. "*Star Wars: The Force Awakens* Review: The Magic is Back." *The Daily Telegraph*, December 14, 2017. https://www.telegraph.co.uk/films/0/star-wars-force-awakens-review-magic-back/ (accessed July 6, 2023).

Collins, Scott. "Eightiessomething." *The Los Angeles Times*, August 23, 2009. https://www.latimes.com/archives/la-xpm-2009-aug-23-ca-thirtysomethingmain23-story.html (accessed July 4, 2023).

Corliss, Richard. "Cinema: You Get What You Need." *Time*, September 12, 1983. http://content.time.com/time/subscriber/article/0,33009,926203,00.html (accessed July 6, 2023).

Davies, Brett. "*Seven Samurai* in *Silverado*: Kurosawa's Influence on Lawrence Kasdan's Revival Western." *Global Japanese Studies Review* 9, no. 1 (2017).

Davies, Brett. "Ewoks Versus Dead Heroes: Creative Conflict in Writing *Return of the Jedi*." *Revista Geminis* 12, no. 1 (2021). https://www.revistageminis.ufscar.br/ index.php/geminis/article/view/599/411

Davies, Brett. "Droids and Peasants: Akira Kurosawa's Thematic Influence on the Star Wars Saga." *The Kyoto Conference on Arts, Media & Culture 2021: Official Conference Proceedings* (January 2022). http://papers.iafor.org/wp-content/uploads/ conference-proceedings/KAMC/KAMC2021_proceedings.pdf (accessed July 4, 2023).

Davies, Brett. "Characterization, Dialogue and Performance in Lawrence Kasdan's Screenplay for *Raiders of the Lost Ark*." In *Bloomsbury Handbook of Global Screenplay Theory*, edited by Ann Igelstrom and Andrew Gay. London: Bloomsbury, forthcoming.

Denzin, Norman K. *Reading Race: Hollywood and the Cinema of Racial Violence*. London: Sage, 2002.

Deyneka, Leah. "May the Myth be with You, Always." In *Myth, Media, and Culture in Star Wars: An Anthology*, edited by Douglas Brode and Leah Deyneka. Plymouth: Scarecrow, 2012.

Dowd, A. A. "For Better and Worse, *The Force Awakens* Returns Star Wars to its Roots." *AV Club*, December 16, 2015. https://film.avclub.com/for-better-and-worse-the-force-awakens-returns-star-wa-1798186037 (accessed July 6, 2023).

Duncan, Paul. *The Star Wars Archives: Episodes IV–VI: 1977–1983*. Cologne: Taschen, 2020.

Dunham, Lena. "*The Big Chill*: These Are Your Parents." *The Criterion Collection*. July 29, 2014. https://www.criterion.com/current/posts/3250-the-big-chill-these-are-your-parents (accessed July 4, 2023).

Dutka, Elaine. "Lawrence Kasdan's Grand Balancing Act." *The Los Angeles Times*, December 24, 1991. http://articles.latimes.com/1991-12-24/entertainment/ca-947_1_grand-canyon/3 (accessed June 29, 2023).

Dyer, James. "*Star Wars: The Force Awakens*—The Complete History, Part I." *Empire*. December 18, 2015. https://www.empireonline.com/movies/features/star-wars-force-awakens-complete-history-part-i/ (accessed July 5, 2023).

Ebert, Roger. "*Wyatt Earp*." *Roger Ebert*, June 24, 1994. https://www.rogerebert.com/reviews/wyatt-earp-1994 (accessed July 4, 2023).

Ebert, Roger. "*The Empire Strikes Back*." *Roger Ebert*, April 1, 1997. https://www.rogerebert.com/reviews/the-empire-strikes-back-1997-1 (accessed July 5, 2023).

Ebert, Roger. "*The Big Sleep*." *Roger Ebert*, June 22, 1997. http://www.rogerebert.com/reviews/great-movie-the-big-sleep-1946 (accessed July 5, 2023).

Ebert, Roger. "*Body Heat*." *Roger Ebert*, July 20, 1997. http://www.rogerebert.com/reviews/great-movie-body-heat-1981 (accessed June 30, 2023).

Ebert, Roger. "*Dreamcatcher*." *Roger Ebert*, March 22, 2003. https://www.rogerebert.com/reviews/dreamcatcher-2003 (accessed July 4, 2023).

Ebert, Roger. "Dark Side Shadows Sith." *Roger Ebert*, May 19, 2005. https://www.rogerebert.com/reviews/star-wars-episode-iii-revenge-of-the-sith-2005 (accessed July 5, 2023).

Edelman, Rob. "*The Big Chill*." *Cineaste* 13, no. 2 (1984).

Eichenbaum, Rose. *The Director Within: Storytellers of Stage and Screen*. Middletown, CT: Wesleyan University Press, 2014.

Elsaesser, Thomas. "The Pathos of Failure: American Films in the 70s—Notes on the Unmotivated Hero." *Monogram*, 6 (1975).

Emery, Robert J. *The Directors: Take One*. Read by John Bell. New York: Allworth Press, 2002. Audiobook.

Fawell, John. *Hitchcock's Rear Window: The Well-Made Film*. Carbondale and Edwardsville, IL: Southern Illinois University Press, 2001.

Field, Sid. *Screenplay: The Foundations of Screenwriting*, 3rd ed. New York: Dell, 1979 (Reprint, 1994).

Franich, Darren. "What Movies can Still Learn from *The Empire Strikes Back*." *Entertainment Weekly*, May 21, 2015. https://ew.com/article/2015/05/21/empire-strikes-back-35th-anniversary/ (accessed July 5, 2023).

Fuller, Graham. "Lawrence Kasdan." In *Back Story 4: Interviews with Screenwriters of the 1970s and 1980s*, edited by Patrick McGilligan. Berkeley: University of California Press, 2006.

Giroux, Henry A. *Disturbing Pleasures*. New York: Routledge, 1994.

Gleiberman, Owen. "Mumford." *Entertainment Weekly*, September 24, 1999. https://ew.com/article/1999/09/24/mumford-2/ (accessed July 4, 2023).

Goldman, William. *Adventures in the Screen Trade: A Personal View of Hollywood*. London: Macdonald, 1984.

Goodsell, Luke. "Five Favorite Films with Lawrence Kasdan." *Rotten Tomatoes*, April 20, 2012. https://editorial.rottentomatoes.com/article/five-favorite-films-with-lawrence-kasdan/ (accessed July 4, 2023).

Greene, Andy. "Stephen King: The Rolling Stone Interview." *Rolling Stone*, October 31, 2014. https://www.rollingstone.com/culture/culture-features/stephen-king-the-rolling-stone-interview-191529/ (accessed July 4, 2023).

Greiving, Tim. "It Happened that Way." *Wyatt Earp Original Motion Picture Soundtrack*. Burbank, CA: La-La Land Records, 2013.

Grice, H. Paul. "Logic and Conversation." In *Syntax and Semantics*, Vol. 3, edited by Peter Cole and Jerry L. Morgan. New York: Academic Press, 1975.

Grigsby Bates, Karen. "They've Gotta Have Us." *The New York Times Magazine*, July 14, 1991. https://www.nytimes.com/1991/07/14/magazine/theyve-gotta-have-us.html (accessed July 3, 2023).

Hansen, Regina. "Stephen King's *IT* and *Dreamcatcher* on Screen: Hegemonic White Masculinity and Nostalgia for Underdog Boyhood." *Science Fiction Film and Television* 10, no. 2 (2017).

Harmetz, Aljean. "How He Became Hollywood's Hot Writer." *The New York Times*, November 1, 1981. http://www.nytimes.com/1981/11/01/movies/how-he-became-hollywood-s-hot-writer.html?pagewanted=all (accessed June 29, 2023).

Harrison, Rebecca. *BFI Film Classics: The Empire Strikes Back*. London: Bloomsbury/British Film Institute, 2020.

Hemphill, Jim. "Lawrence Kasdan." *Academy of Motion Picture Arts and Sciences: Oral History Collection*, Los Angeles: AMPAS, Transcript (2022).

Heung, Marina. "The Big Score: Work and Survival in the Films of Lawrence Kasdan." *Michigan Quarterly Review* 24, no. 4 (1985). https://quod.lib.umich.edu/m/mqrarchive/act2080.0024.004/49:3?page=root;rgn=full+text;size=100;view=image (accessed June 29, 2023).

Holden, Stephen. "Sure, the Doctor is in: In Demand and in Trouble." *The New York Times*, September 24, 1999. https://www.nytimes.com/1999/09/24/movies/film-review-sure-the-doctor-is-in-in-demand-and-in-trouble.html (accessed July 4, 2023).

Hornaday, Ann. "The Misfits of *Mumford*; Review: A Psychologist Administers to a Small Town's Many Eccentrics in Lawrence Kasdan's New Ensemble Comedy." *The Baltimore Sun*, September 24, 1999. https://www.baltimoresun.com/news/bs-xpm-1999-09-24-9909240361-story.html/ (accessed July 4, 2023).

Hoyt, Eric, Kevin Ponto, and Carrie Roy. "Visualizing and Analyzing the Hollywood Screenplay with ScripThreads." *Digital Humanities Quarterly* 8, no. 4 (2014). http://www.digitalhumanities.org/dhq/vol/8/4/000190/000190.html (accessed July 3, 2023).

Hynes, Eric. "The Other America: Revisiting Lawrence Kasdan's *Grand Canyon*." *The Village Voice*, April 18, 2012. http://www.villagevoice.com/film/the-other-america-revisiting-lawrence-kasdans-grand-canyon-6434596 (accessed July 6, 2023).

Illing, Sean. "How the Baby Boomers—not Millennials—Screwed America." *Vox*, October 26, 2019. https://www.vox.com/2017/12/20/16772670/baby-boomers-millennials-congress-debt (accessed July 4, 2023).

Itzkoff, Dave. "He's Tried to Leave Star Wars Before. Will This Be It?" *The New York Times*, May 31, 2018. https://www.nytimes.com/2018/05/30/movies/star-wars-lawrence-kasdan.html (accessed July 5, 2023).

Jacobsen, Harlan. "Surviving." *Film Comment* 19, no. 5 (1983).

Jagernauth, Kevin. "George Lucas' Original Star Wars Sequel Treatments Focused on Teenage Characters." *IndieWire*, May 8, 2015. https://www.indiewire.com/2015/05/george-lucas-original-star-wars-sequel-treatments-focused-on-teenaged-characters-264251/ (accessed July 5, 2023).

James, Caryn. "Review/Film: *Wyatt Earp*; Into the Heart and Soul of Darkness." *The New York Times*, June 24, 1994. http://www.nytimes.com/1994/06/24/movies/review-film-wyatt-earp-into-the-heart-and-soul-of-darkness.html (accessed July 4, 2023).

Jameson, Fredric. *Postmodernism, or, The Cultural Logic of Multinational Capitalism*. Durham, NC: Duke University Press, 1991.

Jermyn, Deborah. *Nancy Meyers*. London: Bloomsbury, 2017.

Johnson, Brian D. "City of Catastrophe." *Maclean's*, January 13, 1992.

Jones, Brian Jay. *George Lucas: A Life*. London: Headline, 2016.

Kagan, Norman. *The Cinema of Robert Zemeckis*. Lanham, MD: Taylor, 2003.

Kaminski, Michael. *The Secret History of Star Wars: The Art of Storytelling and the Making of a Modern Epic*. Kingston, Canada: Legacy, 2008.

Kasdan, Lawrence. "*Grand Canyon*: Featurette." *Grand Canyon*, DVD extras, USA: 20th Century Fox, 1992.

Kasdan, Lawrence. *The Directors: Lawrence Kasdan*, DVD, USA: American Film Institute, 1997.

Kasdan, Lawrence. "*The Big Chill*: A Reunion." *The Big Chill*, DVD extras, USA: Columbia TriStar, 1998.

Kasdan, Lawrence. "POV." *Michigan Quarterly Review* 38, no. 4 (1999).

Kasdan, Lawrence. "DreamMakers—A Journey Through Production." *Dreamcatcher*, DVD extras, USA: Warner Bros. 2003.

Kasdan, Lawrence. "*DreamWeavers*—The Visual Effects of *Dreamcatcher*." *Dreamcatcher*, DVD extras, USA: Warner Bros. 2003.

Kasdan, Lawrence. "It's Like Life." *The Accidental Tourist*, DVD extras, USA: Warner Bros. 2003.

Kasdan, Lawrence. "Reflections of *The Accidental Tourist*." *The Accidental Tourist*, DVD extras, USA: Warner Bros. 2003.

Kasdan, Lawrence. "*Darling Companion*: Behind the Scenes." *Darling Companion*, DVD extras, USA: Metrodome, 2013.

Kasdan, Lawrence. "Lawrence Kasdan on his Career." *The Criterion Collection*, August 6, 2014. https://www.criterion.com/current/posts/3255-lawrence-kasdan-on-his-career (accessed July 6, 2023).

Kasdan, Lawrence. "The Secrets of *The Force Awakens*: A Cinematic Journey." *The Force Awakens*, Blu-ray extras, USA: Disney, 2016.

Kasdan, Lawrence. "Kasdan on Kasdan." *Solo: A Star Wars Story*, Blu-ray extras, USA: Disney, 2018.

Kasdan, Lawrence. "Lawrence Kasdan for *The Big Chill* 1983—Bobbie Wygant Archive." The Bobbie Wygant Archive, YouTube, 2 June, 2020. https://www.youtube.com/watch?v=iT1WnT3uA-Q (accessed July 4, 2023).

Kasdan, Lawrence. "On Story 1011: A Conversation with Lawrence Kasdan." Austin Film Festival, YouTube, 20 June, 2020. https://www.youtube.com/watch?v=rhtF8lK0IWg (accessed July 5, 2023).

Kasdan, Lawrence, and Jake Kasdan. *Wyatt Earp: The Film and the Filmmakers*. New York: Newmarket Press, 1994.

Kasdan, Meg. "*Darling Companion*: Behind the Scenes." *Darling Companion*, DVD extras, USA: Metrodome, 2013.

Keller, Bill. "The Entitled Generation." *The New York Times*, July 29, 2012. https://www.nytimes.com/2012/07/30/opinion/keller-the-entitled-generation.html (accessed July 4, 2023).

Kennedy, Kathleen. "Kasdan on Kasdan." *Solo: A Star Wars Story*, Blu-ray extras, USA: Disney, 2018.

King, Stephen. "Stephen King on the Laziness of the Baby Boomers." *Entertainment Weekly*, February 1, 2007. https://ew.com/article/2007/02/01/stephen-king-laziness-baby-boomers/ (accessed July 4, 2023).

Kit, Borys. "Star Wars: Why the Han Solo Film Directors were Fired." *The Hollywood Reporter*, June 20, 2017. https://www.hollywoodreporter.com/heat-vision/star-wars-why-han-solo-movie-directors-were-fired-1015474 (accessed July 6, 2023).

Kline, Karen. "*The Accidental Tourist* on Page and on Screen: Interrogating Narrative Theories about Film Adaptation." *Literature/Film Quarterly* 24, no. 1 (1996).

Knight, Arthur. "*The Big Chill*: THR's 1983 review." *The Hollywood Reporter*, September 30, 2018. https://www.hollywoodreporter.com/review/big-chill-review-1983-movie-1147771 (accessed July 3, 2023).

Kurosawa, Akira. *Something Like an Autobiography*. Translated by A.E. Bock. New York: Vintage, 1983.

Langford, Barry. *Post-Classical Hollywood: Film Industry, Style and Ideology Since 1945*. Edinburgh University Press, 2010.

Larsen, Stephen and Robin Larsen. *Joseph Campbell: A Fire in the Mind*. Rochester, VT: Inner Traditions, 2002.

Lauzen, Martha M. "It's a Man's (Celluloid) World, even in a Pandemic Year: Portrayals of Female Characters in the Top U.S. Films of 2021." *Center for the Study of Women in Television and Film*, 2022, https://womenintvfilm.sdsu.edu/wp-content/uploads/2022/03/2021-Its-a-Mans-Celluloid-World-Report.pdf (accessed July 10, 2023).

"Lawrence Kasdan," *Rotten Tomatoes*, 2020. https://www.rottentomatoes.com/celebrity/lawrence_kasdan (accessed July 3, 2023).

Lee, Nora. "*The Accidental Tourist* is No Accident: Novel to Film Translation Challenges All." *American Cinematographer* 69, no.11 (1988).

Lucas, George. "Empire of Dreams: The Story of the Star Wars Trilogy." *Star Wars Trilogy*, DVD extras, USA: 20th Century Fox, 2004.

Maciak, Phil. "We're Not Leaving. We're Never Leaving: *The Big Chill* and the Enduring Power of Quarter-life Crisis Movies." *Slate*, July 29, 2014. https://slate.com/culture/2014/07/the-big-chill-and-the-quarter-life-crisis-film.html (accessed July 4, 2023).

Maslin, Janet. "A Tourist Lost En Route to the Screen." *The New York Times*, January 15, 1989. https://www.nytimes.com/1989/01/15/movies/film-view-a-tourist-lost-en-route-to-the-screen.html (accessed July 3, 2023).

Maslin, Janet. "The Accidents and Miracles in Everyday Life." *The New York Times*, December 25, 1991. https://www.nytimes.com/1991/12/25/movies/review-film-the-accidents-and-miracles-in-everyday-life.html (accessed July 4, 2023).

Masters, Kim. "Star Wars Firing Reveals a Disturbance in the Franchise." *The Hollywood Reporter*, June 26, 2017. https://www.hollywoodreporter.com/heat-vision/star-wars-han-solo-movie-firing-new-details-behind-phil-lord-chris-miller-exit-1016619 (accessed July 6, 2023).

McAleer, Patrick. "I Have the Whole World in my Hands . . . Now What?: Power, Control, Responsibility and the Baby Boomers in Stephen King's Fiction." *The Journal of Popular Culture* 44, no. 6 (2011).

McBride, Joseph. *Steven Spielberg: A Biography*, 2nd ed. Jackson: University Press of Mississippi, 2010.

McCarthy, Todd. "Review: *Wyatt Earp*." *Variety*, 1994. http://variety.com/1994/film/reviews/wyatt-earp-1200437510/ (accessed July 4, 2023).

McKee, Robert. *Story: Substance, Structure, Style, and the Principles of Screenwriting*. New York: Regan, 1999.

Mikulec, Sven. "*Raiders of the Lost Ark*: Lucas and Spielberg's Epitome of Action-Adventure Films Still Waiting to be Surpassed." *Cinephilia and Beyond*, no date. Accessed April 17, 2023. https://cinephiliabeyond.org/raiders-lost-ark-lucas-spielbergs- epitome-action-adventure-films-still-waiting-surpassed/ (accessed June 30, 2023).

Morton, Ray. "Darling Companions: A Conversation with Lawrence and Meg Kasdan." *Script*, April 26, 2012. https://scriptmag.com/features/darling-companions-a-conversation-with-lawrence-and-meg-kasdan (accessed July 4, 2023).

Mullis, Justin. "Ritual, Repetition, and the Responsibility of Relaying the Myth." In *The Myth Awakens: Canon, Conservatism, and Fan Reception of Star Wars*, edited by Ken Derry and John C. Lyden. Eugene, OR: Cascade, 2018.

Nadel, Alan. "1983: Movies and Reaganism." In *American Cinema of the 1980s: Themes and Variations*, edited by S. Prince. New Brunswick, NJ: Rutgers University Press, 2007.

Nashawaty, Chris. "*Star Wars The Force Awakens*: EW review." *Entertainment Weekly*, December 16, 2015. https://ew.com/article/2015/12/16/star-wars-force-awakens-review/ (accessed July 6, 2023).

Neale, Steve. *Genre and Hollywood*. New York: Routledge, 2000.

Newman, Kim. "*The Big Chill*." *Monthly Film Bulletin* 51, no. 600 (1984).

O'Hehir, Andrew. "*Darling Companion*: A Death Knell for the Baby Boom?" *Salon*, April 18, 2012. http://www.salon.com/2012/04/18/darling_companion_a_death_knell_for_the_baby_boom/ (accessed July 4, 2023).

Olsen, Mark. "*Star Wars: Episode VII*: Lawrence Kasdan's Big Move." *The Los Angeles Times*, October 24, 2013. https://www.latimes.com/entertainment/movies/moviesnow/la-et-mn-lawrence-kasdan-jj-abrams-star-wars-episode-vii-20131024-story.html (accessed July 10, 2023).

Orr, Christopher. "Cain, Naturalism and Noir." *Film Criticism* 25, no. 1 (2000).

Pappademas, Alex. "Alden Ehrenreich is Ready to Prove He's Worthy of Han Solo." *Esquire*, April 24, 2018. https://www.esquire.com/entertainment/movies /a19834126/alden-ehrenreich-star-wars-han-solo-interview/ (accessed July 6, 2023).

Pollock, Dale. "Kasdan: A 'Chill' of His Very Own." *The Los Angeles Times*, September 18, 1983.

Pollock, Dale. *Skywalking: The Life and Films of George Lucas: Updated Edition*. New York: Da Capo, 1983/1999.

Price, Steven. *The Screenplay: Authorship, Theory and Criticism*. Hampshire, UK: Palgrave Macmillan, 2010.

Prince, Stephen. *A New Pot of Gold: Hollywood under the Electronic Rainbow, 1980–1989*, New York: Charles Scribner's Sons, 2000.

Propp, Vladimir. *Morphology of the Folk Tale*, 2nd ed. Translated by L. Scott. Austin: University of Texas Press, 2009.

Pulver, Andrew. "Star Wars Director JJ Abrams: We Always Wanted Women at the Centre of *The Force Awakens*." *The Guardian*, December 17, 2015. https://www.theguardian.com/film/2015/dec/17/star-wars-director-jj-abrams-women-the-force-awakens-daisy-ridley-lupita-nyongo-carrie-fisher (accessed July 4, 2023).

Rinzler, J. W. *The Making of Star Wars: The Definitive Story Behind the Original Film*. London: Aurum, 2007.

Rinzler, J. W. *The Complete Making of Indiana Jones*. London: Ebury, 2008.

Rinzler, J. W. *The Making of The Empire Strikes Back*. London: Aurum, 2010.

Rinzler, J. W. *The Making of Return of the Jedi*. London: Aurum, 2013.

Roberts, Soraya. "The Big Thaw: Togetherness and What *Thirty-something* Means Now." *Los Angeles Review of Books*, March 8, 2015. https://lareviewofbooks.org/article/big-thaw-togetherness-thirtysomething-means-now/ (accessed July 4, 2023).

Robertson, Benjamin J. "'It's Just Us Now': Nostalgia and *Star Wars Episode VII: The Force Awakens*." *Science Fiction Film and Television* 9, no. 3 (2016).

Rogers, Adam. "Star Wars' Greatest Screenwriter Wrote All Your Other Favorite Movies Too." *Wired*, November 18, 2015. https://www.wired.com/2015/11/lawrence-kasdan-qa/ (accessed July 6, 2023).

Rottenberg, Josh. "Diane Keaton and Kevin Kline Sign on for the Baby Boomer-centric *Darling Companion*." *Entertainment Weekly*, September 22, 2010. http://ew.com/article/2010/09/22/diane-keaton-and-kevin-kline-sign-on-for-the-baby-boomer-centric-darling-companion/ (accessed July 3, 2023).

Rottenberg, Josh. "Q&A: Star Wars Screenwriter Lawrence Kasdan on the Past, Present and Future of Star Wars." *The Los Angeles Times*, December 3, 2015. http://www.latimes.com/entertainment/herocomplex/la-ca-hc-star-wars-lawrence-kasdan-20151206-story.html (accessed July 5, 2023).

Russell, Catherine. *Classical Japanese Cinema Revisited*. London: Continuum, 2011.

Russell, James and Jim Whalley. *Hollywood and the Baby Boom: A Social History*. London: Bloomsbury, 2018.

Ryan, Michael and Douglas Kellner. *Camera Politica: The Politics and Ideology of Contemporary Hollywood Film*. Indiana University Press, 1988.

Sanna, Antonio. "The Reawakening of Star Wars: Nostalgia, Machinery, and Epic Grandeur." *Cinematic Codes Review* 1, no. 2 (2016).

Schiffrin, Deborah. *Approaches to Discourse*. Oxford, UK: Blackwell, 1994.

Schwartz, Ronald. *Noir, Now and Then: Film Noir Originals and Remakes (1944–1999)*. Westport, CT: Greenwood, 2001.

Scorsese, Martin. "Anaheim University Akira Kurosawa 100th anniversary memorial tribute." Anaheim University, YouTube, June 13, 2013. https://www.youtube.com/watch?v=ErelcWcNelQ (accessed July 4, 2023).

Shimizu, Fred. "Directors: Akira Kurosawa." In *Japan: Directory of World Cinema*, edited by John Berra. Bristol, UK: Intellect, 2010.

Shumway, David R. "Rock 'n' Roll Soundtracks and the Production of Nostalgia." *Cinema Journal* 38, no. 2 (1999).

Shumway, David R. *John Sayles*. Chicago: University of Illinois Press, 2012.

Siegel, Scott and Barbara Siegel. "Mumford's the Word." *Film Journal International*, October 1999.

Simon, Alex. "Chillin' Big with Lawrence Kasdan." *The Hollywood Interview*, December 3, 2012. http://thehollywoodinterview.blogspot.com/2008/03/lawrence-kasdan-hollywood-interview.html (accessed June 30, 2023).

Sragow, Michael. "High-end Horror? Keep Dreaming." *The Baltimore Sun*, March 21, 2003. https://www.baltimoresun.com/news/bs-xpm-2003-03-21-0303210131-story.html (accessed July 4, 2023).

Sternberg, Claudia. *Written for the Screen: The American Motion-Picture Screenplay as Text*. Tübingen, Germany: Stauffenberg, 1997.

Summers, Jimmy. "Reviews: *Silverado*." *Box Office (Archive: 1920–2000)* 121, no. 9 (1985).

Tannen, Deborah. "Discourse Analysis—What Speakers do in Conversations." *Linguistic Society of America*, 2019. https://www.linguisticsociety.org/resource/discourse-analysis-what-speakers-do-conversation (accessed June 29, 2023).

Tapley, Kristopher. "Inside *Solo: A Star Wars Story*'s Bumpy Ride to the Big Screen." *Variety*, May 22, 2018. https://variety.com/2018/film/features/solo-a-star-wars-story-directors-reshoots-ron-howard-1202817841/ (accessed July 6, 2023).

"The Whys and Hows of Generation Research." *Pew Research Center*, September 3, 2015, https://www.people-press.org/2015/09/03/the-whys-and-hows-of-generations-research/ (accessed July 4, 2023).

Thompson, David. *Levinson on Levinson*. London: Faber & Faber, 1993.

Thompson, Kristin. *Storytelling in the New Hollywood: Understanding Classical Narrative Technique*. Cambridge, MA: Harvard University Press, 1999.

Tomasulo, Frank. "Mr. Jones Goes to Washington: *Raiders of the Lost Ark*." *Quarterly Review of Film Studies* 7, no. 4 (1982).

Travers, Peter. "Movies—*Grand Canyon* Directed by Lawrence Kasdan." *Rolling Stone*, January 23, 1992.

Tyler, Anne. *The Accidental Tourist*. New York: Random House, 1985.

Weinraub, Bernard. "Director Criticizes *Grand Canyon* Critics." *The New York Times*, January 16, 1992. https://www.nytimes.com/1992/01/16/movies/director-criticizes-grand-canyon-critics.html?searchResultPosition=1 (accessed July 3, 2023).

Whitley, John. "Filmmakers on Film: Lawrence Kasdan." *The Daily Telegraph*, April 27, 2002. http://www.telegraph.co.uk/culture/film/3576515/Filmmakers-on-film-Lawrence-Kasdan.html (accessed July 4, 2023).

Williams, JoBeth. "*The Big Chill*: A Reunion." *The Big Chill*, DVD extras, USA: Columbia TriStar, 1998.

Wilmington, Michael. "*Big Chill* Still a bit Chilly at 15." *Chicago Tribune*, November 6, 1998. https://www.chicagotribune.com/news/ct-xpm-1998-11-06-9811060485-story.html (accessed July 3, 2023).

Wilson, Chuck. "Lawrence Kasdan Interview." *LA Weekly*, April 19, 2012. https://www.laweekly.com/lawrence-kasdan-interview/ (accessed July 3, 2023).

Windolf, Jim. "Q&A: Steven Spielberg." *Vanity Fair*, January 2, 2008. https://www.vanityfair.com/news/2008/02/spielberg_qanda200802?currentPage=4 (accessed June 29, 2023).

Wodak, Ruth. *Aspects of Critical Discourse Analysis*. London: Sage, 2009.

Writers Guild of America West (2018), *Screen Credits Manual*, Los Angeles: WGA. https://www.wga.org/uploadedfiles/credits/manuals/screenscredits_manual18.pdf (accessed July 5, 2023).

Wyatt, Justin. *High Concept: Movies and Marketing in Hollywood*. Austin: University of Texas Press, 1994.

Yakir, Dan. "Lawrence Kasdan Interviewed." *Film Comment* 17, no. 5 (1981).

Zucker, Carole. *Figures of Light: Actors and Directors Illuminate the Art of Film Acting*. New York: Plenum Press, 1995.

Index